HIS COUNTRY WAS
THE WORLD

By the same Author

Philosophy

THE GARDEN OF THE GOLDEN FLOWER

Fiction

LION ROCK

AWAY COME AWAY

HIS COUNTRY
WAS THE WORLD

A Study of Gordon of Khartoum

CHARLES BEATTY

1954

CHATTO & WINDUS

LONDON

PUBLISHED BY
Chatto and Windus Ltd.
42 William IV Street
LONDON, W.C.2

*

Clarke, Irwin & Co. Ltd.
TORONTO

Everything that man esteems
Endures a moment or a day,
Love's pleasure drives his love away,
The painter's brush consumes his dreams;
The herald's cry, the soldier's tread
Exhaust his glory and his might:
Whatever flames upon the night
Man's own resinous heart has fed.

W. B. YEATS

Author's Note

My object is to allow Gordon to emerge as a lively person, and so the relevance of material has been considered chiefly from that point of view rather than in terms of history or of analysis. Some variation in the spelling of foreign words has been unavoidable.

Contents

✷

Contents

List of Maps

✳

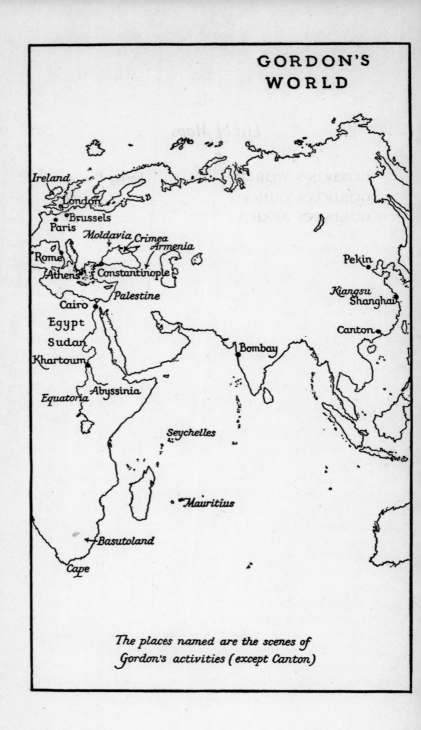

GORDON'S
WORLD

The places named are the scenes of
Gordon's activities (except Canton)

ROUND BRIGHT GARDEN

CHARLES GEORGE GORDON was born on the 28th
day of January in the year 1833, at No. 1 Kemp Terrace,
Woolwich Common; near the Arsenal on the Thames Estuary
where his father was the officer in charge of the (gun) Carriage Department. The rented brick house was at the end of a
row, and presented nine windows to the road, three of them
in a semicircular bow on the left of the front door. The family
was by tradition military. The father of Charles George
became a Lieutenant-General. His grandfather under Wolfe
stormed the Heights of Abraham in 1759. His great-grand-
father was a close friend of the germanic Duke of Cumber-
land, 'Butcher of Culloden', whom he served abroad against
the French and at home against his own clan, who took him
prisoner at Prestonpans in 1745. Perhaps to his astonishment,
he was well treated, but on his release took no further part in
the war, and, emigrating to America, died at Halifax, Nova
Scotia, in 1752.

The family of eleven, of which Charles was the ninth child
and fourth boy, was typical of a period when of wives as of the
Light Brigade it might have been said, 'Theirs not to reason
why . . .' His mother was born Elizabeth Enderby, whose
father sent whalers round the Horn to pioneer that most
difficult passage for commerce. His ships assisted in the early
development of Australia, New Zealand and South America,
and it was tea shipped by Enderby which was thrown into the
harbour at the famous 'Boston Tea-party'. His position was
such that he could secure a private interview with the Prime
Minister, William Pitt the Younger, for guidance upon the
instructions for ships' captains in Spanish territorial waters;
and after him was named Enderby Land in the Antarctic.

The earliest influences on the new baby were of a kind today sometimes regarded as peculiarly subtle and far-reaching.
He adored his mother to the extent of becoming her favourite
child, and feared his father, who never seems to have had any

3

understanding of the boy's intense feelings. Not that the father was cruel, but he must have been an example of the stern if jocular despot which in that generation was elevated to a Jehovah-like ideal. The eldest girl, Augusta, ten years older than Charles, regarded him as her spiritual protégé to such an extent that she eventually excluded all other women from his life and substituted her own arid creed, a dismal doctrine of salvation through suffering, derived from the simple piety of the mother, who though she came of Puritan stock was by no means puritanical.

Young Charles was brought up to believe that every word of the Bible is literally true, but in early life he did not conform to the pattern set, and recalled the family's religious exercises only as boring. He was a normal little boy who lived in a kind, strict, comfortable home among brothers and sisters whose chief characteristic seems to have been a healthy exuberance. Though neither physically strong nor noticeably bright, he shared enthusiastically in the rough games of his elder brothers, some of which must have proved embarrassing to Papa. They had friends among the workmen in the Arsenal and so became possessed of singularly effective weapons such as water-pistols, 'capital articles', he said, 'which wet you through in a moment', and cross-bows. The bows were designed to fire iron bolts, with which many windows were broken (the record was twenty-three—on a Sunday) and at least one officer nearly slain. It was probably with relief that Papa found himself posted, first to Pigeon House Fort in Dublin Bay, then to Leith, and finally to Corfu—at that time a British Protectorate.

The following year the family were back in England and Charles was sent to a boarding-school at Taunton, run by a brother of the family governess. In 1848—though not without twelve months at a crammer's—he passed the stiff entrance examination to the Royal Military Academy, 'The Shop' at Woolwich, destined to be a Gunner like his father. He was then rising sixteen, but his combativeness still survived from the boisterous years, or else it was the Irish blood which is said to have been part of his heredity. He so much resented discipline that he was continually in trouble with the authorities and came near to being expelled. One critical incident was an assault on an under-officer when on duty. Gordon butted him down a flight of steps. When told that with so little respect for authority he was unlikely to make an efficient officer, he tore off his epaulettes and threw them on the ground. On another occasion he is said to have broken the handle of a broom upon the head of a fellow Gentleman Cadet. Possibly owing to his father's position, he was not sent down but ordered to 'drop a term', meaning that he had to stay at The Shop, no matter what his proficiency, for another six months, making nearly three years in all. The penalty was intended to be severe since it would tend to deprive a young officer of seniority, which would handicap him all through his career.

Gordon tried to avoid the full effect of the penalty by choosing the Engineers rather than the Artillery. From The Shop he had no other choice, since Cavalry, Guards and Line Regiments drew their officers from Sandhurst. He may even have been grateful for the dropped term because he was weak in mathematics and otherwise might have failed to pass out. The Sappers were the best-paid branch of the Army, a matter of some importance to him since his father was not in a position to supplement his pay on the scale which was usual in order to allow young subalterns to live the social life of officers and gentlemen. Already Gordon cared nothing for social life. He would be happier among the seriously professional Sappers than among those who sought to climb the Service ladder through the indirect influence of riches and relations, even though, unlike the rest of the Army, both specialist Corps had already abandoned the pernicious system of purchasing commissions and promotion. Above and beyond all practical considerations he had already become aware of the working of the great leaven of his life, in comparison with which all the kingdoms of the world were as dust. He probably went through a spiritual ecstasy of some kind, but there appears to be no record of it, perhaps because, for fear of ridicule, he dared not tell even Augusta, who might have regarded it as suspect if not sinful. At all events his combative exuberance was curbed. He became a very serious Gentleman Cadet.

That the new trend did not prove morbid was due largely to the local parson, Capel Molyneux of Trinity Church, in whom Gordon confided his spiritual problems and whose services he must have attended, less out of a preference for the Church of England than as a reaction against the dullness of the family's Sunday, focussed on an hour-long sermon, which the young man, in spite of his solemnity, regarded as an ordeal. No doubt the Reverend Capel Molyneux wished to have Gordon confirmed, but in this he was to be disappointed. Gordon remained anti-episcopal to the extent of referring, later on, to the rite of the laying-on of hands as 'a useless sin'. The position which he adopted is the more peculiar in that he became an ardent communicant; though he must have been aware that the usual requirement for Church membership is confirmation, without which it is not proper to attend what he called 'the eating'.

He passed out of The Shop in June 1852, when he was nineteen, and was posted to the regimental depôt at Chatham. This establishment served the whole Corps and consequently had a very big Mess in which Gordon and his preoccupations were promptly submerged. It has often been remarked that the immediate product of the Military College or Academy is less like an officer than an automaton whose chief skill lies in brisk obedience, and an ability to polish wood, leather and metal to perfection. Even so, newly joined officers, suspected of having swelled heads just because they had a star upon each shoulder, were immediately put back 'on the square' to learn again the drill in which they had already achieved a wonderful dexterity. In view of Gordon's tendency to resent authority, the system seems to have had its justification. There is no suggestion that he ever again challenged his military superiors, and gradually he himself became a martinet, not only in barracks but at home.

Released from 'the square', he was posted to a new naval base at Pembroke, on the southern tip of Wales. After Chatham it must have seemed a very quiet spot where official duties seldom extended into the afternoon. There for the first time, young Gordon had opportunity to indulge in solitude; for all earlier years had been crowded, at first by the family, thereafter by schoolfellows of one kind or another. Save for an occasional day's shooting, he had no interests outside his religion and his profession, so he took to reading politics, economics and world affairs. Thereby he gained a wide-based knowledge which later stood him in good stead. He claimed that he read every paper that was available, but he still had time to worry whether his parents thought sufficiently 'of eternal things' and he wrote to Augusta frequently and at length. The local vicar was too 'worldly' to please him, but he found a kindred spirit in a Captain Drew, whom he describes as 'very religious', and with him went for long drives in a gig: 'It is a great blessing for me that in my profession I can be intimate with whom I like, and have not the same trials among my brother officers as those in a Line regiment have. I ought not to say this, for "where sin aboundeth, grace aboundeth more fully", but I am such a miserable wretch, that I should be sure to be led away. Dearest Augusta, pray for me.'

Captain Drew was not in a Line regiment, nor was he either a Sapper or a Gunner. He belonged to the Eleventh Hussars, just the kind of sociable set for which Gordon would normally have had least use. It may be that Drew had undergone some kind of conversion through his wife, who, like Augusta, was a devotee of Capel Molyneux. But even to Gordon's unsusceptible eye she was also a 'stylish person', as indeed she must have been to have married into such a smart regiment, even though Pembroke was far away from the waters in which the most fashionable fishes swam. This was an era in which exquisite fops could buy commands over the heads of officers with twenty years' distinguished service. From the Drews Gordon must have heard much gossip of a kind new to him, the irksome luxury of the ceremonial life, the ostentation, the petty tyrannies and jealousies. A man like Gordon might have been forgiven for imagining that the Devil was at work, especially in such a context as Lord Cardigan's order for a flogging on Easter Morning, when two consecutive parades were held in the riding-school, the first by the padre, the second to 'witness punishment'.

On purely professional grounds Drew and Gordon had good reason to shake their heads over inefficiency in the High Command, which, by supporting the purchase-system, was rendering the Army unfit for war. Who could make a new Lieutenant-Colonel work at the study of realities, when for his gilded place on parade he had paid perhaps £40,000?

Drew could hardly have been dependent on his pay, but Gordon was, and the prospect of his dedicated efficiency being handicapped throughout his career by snobs at the Horse Guards must have aggravated the boredom which soon became his chief complaint. Interests were all very well, but it was action not education that he now required, and when in the following year, 1853, England with France took Turkey's part against Russia, the war must have been the best news he had had since leaving The Shop.

The two older Gordon boys soon went out to the Crimea, but Charles was left behind. Why had he been passed over? He could only think that his mother had influenced his father to have him kept back, but he could do nothing. With October came the glorious charge of the Light Brigade which fired him with a dual ambition, to share the other-worldly glory of such a death, and to be an officer incapable of such stupidity. Still he could do nothing but wait. Then came his orders. He must have opened them with the certainty that they were what he wanted—action. But they relegated him to garrison duty in Corfu. So he *had* been the victim of a plot! Nothing less could account for such an appointment, which should have gone to an officer unqualified for battle. It would handicap him all through his service. For the first and almost the last time in his life Gordon demanded that his father's influence should be used on his behalf. Within a week the orders were changed, and with them Gordon's destiny.

Apologising for his enthusiasm, Gordon assured Augusta that he sincerely hoped he would be killed. By this time they seem to have been trying to convince themselves that the body is of so vile a nature that the only proper attitude towards it is complete rejection—a suicidal view in spite of which Gordon appeared at this time to be a cheerful character, an ordinary type of British officer. He was good-looking, hair dark and curly. He wore it rather long and with it a much lighter moustache. In his dress he was neat, even dapper. He was urgent of movement, quick to change expression, and had a schoolboy sense of humour. He does not seem to have given anyone the impression of being a gloomy character, though his intense pale eyes hinted at the tormented depths from which they looked out. He must have tried hard not to appear 'different' to the critical eyes of his contemporaries, who had been through the same tough school with its insistence upon uniformity. In later years he developed an aggressive stance, hunched forward with head tucked in, so that although to his tailor he was five foot nine, he appeared 'under middle height'.

There was nothing heroic about the beginning of Gordon's active military career. He was sent to Portsmouth, there to supervise the loading of huts destined for winter quarters in the Crimea, and so already 'too late': that phrase which would be his requiem. He left Pembroke the same day and, after collecting winter kit in London, reached Portsmouth within forty-eight hours. There he found that the hut-sections were being stowed in colliers, presumably coasters which, if they had any steam at all, would hardly be powered for a long voyage. They may even have been sail, for this was the period of transition before the age of the propeller. The thought of having to go all the way to Russia in one of them made Gordon again seek a change of orders, and again his request was approved—that he might travel independently.

He went by rail to Paris from the coast, and from Paris to Lyons, where, the southern line not being complete, he took a boat down the Rhône to Valence, and so came to Marseilles where he embarked on a French packet-boat. After calls at Messina and the Piraeus—from which he visited Athens and was not impressed—he reached Constantinople on Boxing Day and had time to visit Miss Nightingale's hospital at Scutari, reporting home that the wounded now had all the comforts they needed. Then he shipped to the British base at Balaklava, arriving on New Year's Day 1855, one of the many major events of his life which took place at the nadir of the year. His impressions, even allowing that he may have softened them for home consumption, were at variance with those usually cited in connection with the infamous 'Black Winter'. He noted that even 'swell English cavalry' were to be observed, in a muddle of winter clothing, hunting for food like quite ordinary people, but he complained seriously that the Press exaggerated the horrors, telling 'atrocious fibs about the conditions at the front'. He admits that the men had a hard time, but blames them for not being better able to look

B

after themselves '. . . They are like children, thinking everything is to be done for them'.

He might have added that, quite apart from the loss of
transports owing to bad weather, the planning Staff had some
excuse for being unprepared for a real Russian winter, the
worst for over a century, since the climate of the southern
coast of the Crimea is regarded as sub-tropical, permitting
vineyards, olive groves, figs and the type of flora characteristic of the Mediterranean. As for the medical services,
they were of their time; but had they been ahead of it the
cholera epidemic, once started, would have overwhelmed
even an efficient system. Such issues were outside Gordon's
immediate and narrow field. His huts arrived and were
promptly erected. Eagerly Gordon left the rear area for the
trenches before the great fortress of Sebastopol, protected by
elaborate works heavily armed with cannon, some of which
fired explosive shells though the majority still discharged the
traditional roundshot.

On the first of more than thirty tours of twenty-four hours
in the foremost defended locality, Gordon carried out a
solitary personal reconnaissance between the lines and nearly
found himself cut off by the enemy. He was soon 'blooded',
by stones thrown up into his face by a projectile, and, on receiving first aid, raised a laugh from the men standing by
when he pretended to light a cigar from the doctor's red hair.
But in spite of a zest for action which amounted to irre-
sponsibility, at least as regards his own safety, he rapidly
achieved a reputation as a conscientious officer with more
than average ability. This, added to his calm courage, which
was not the less effective for being founded upon a secret
death-wish, soon brought him to the notice of men who would
become masters in his world, among them Captain Wolseley,
a future Commander-in-Chief, who would lead the Gordon
Relief Expedition, as it was popularly called, to Khartoum.
Another appreciative senior officer was Sir Charles Staveley,
under whom Gordon would serve in China.

When death whizzed past him Gordon would hardly look
up. He said he knew that the time to go to his long home was
not yet; and when a brother officer fell he accepted the fact
with the same nostalgic fatalism, 'I am glad to say he was a

serious man. The shell burst above him and, by what is called chance, struck him in the back, killing him at once.' He seems to have been unwrung by wider tragedies, 'During the night I heard terrible explosions, and, going down to the trenches at four a.m. I saw a splendid sight, the whole town in flames'. In almost anyone else such comments might have represented a Neronic callousness, but Gordon's attitude was due rather to the need to defend an over-sensitive heart, as a compassionate doctor has to seal off the emotional importunity of certain patients. Gordon's first line of defence became constant activity and preoccupation with duty, which developed into a selective response such that he only reacted to 'safe' stimuli. For instance, religious aspiration was still safe, but apart from that, the stimulus usually had to be either so trivial as to make control of the response easy, or so large as to be impersonal. Only in this way could he keep apart the two incompatible worlds of his experience, the military and the spiritual. He never learned to live in both at once, and spent much of his time in the lonely no-man's-land between them, cut off by theological entanglements from the soldiers, and by the line of duty from the saints. In terms of ambition, he longed at the same time to be a leader of men in war and an ascetic hermit, 'a nail in Christ's footstool'.

So it is hardly surprising to find him writing of himself in a double sense as 'the dead man', meaning dead to that world the symbol for which is often woman, and wishing for death to take him 'home'. Even his adulatory biographer Boulger comments, 'From a very early period in his life, certainly before the Crimea, Gordon made up his mind not to marry, and was in the habit of going even further and wishing himself dead. . . . Some years later he wrote, "There is a Miss —— here, the nicest girl I ever met; but don't be afraid, the dead do not marry". His own secret opinion seems to have been that marriage spoilt both men and women, and it will at least be admitted that if he had married he could never have lived the disinterested, heroic life which remains the marvel of the world.'

It is equally probable that had Gordon made a loving, lasting marriage, he would not have had to learn in such a hard school that, in spite of every conscious effort to the contrary, what is in the world is of it, and cannot be rejected or derided without paying a natural penalty. Like so many before him, Gordon the mystic was honestly and humbly dedicated to the impossible task of behaving as though he were already 'dead to the world', when, in fact, he was inescapably alive. Aware that they were opposites in many respects, he tried to be both saint and soldier. Aware of their conflict within himself, he sensed, in what would now be called the Unconscious, forces stronger than any available to the normal, waking personality. Anyone believing himself to be in the power of angels and devils tends to become a fatalist; for they lead and drive him where he would not go, until he looks forward to death as the only possible resolution of the conflict. But to seek death for the sake of peace he has first to turn his back upon the joys of living, which, ironically enough, are the natural peacemakers for embattled souls.

All this Gordon did. Though he retained a sense of humour, he was essentially a joyless person who believed himself led by a 'pillar', a manifestation of the divine will, and to be at the mercy of 'the Doles', 'Agag' and 'the Archers', pet-names for the moods which plagued him. All these children of darkness played a part in God's mercy, perhaps because they served to temper the uncompromising steel of his character, but also because over against them was the Light. And when it shone, then Gordon was filled with exaltation saying, 'Mahanaim: the hosts are with me'.

He was at once too proud and too humble to allow that he contrived his own fate, which, seen through a modern lens, seems more like the product of his deepest and most secret desires than an Act of God. Perhaps within the God of Gordon there was a godling 'Gordon', as lesser people also construct idols whom they serve. Of such a factor, for which there are many names such as the Self or the Shepherd, it cannot be said that it is either good or bad, for its rôle is to integrate the warring elements, 'not to destroy but to fulfil'; to achieve, as Gordon did, sublime distinction at the risk of psychic disintegration and material failure. A man sincere in his quest tends to become identified with the object of his search. No one has ever questioned Gordon's sincerity or his ultimate object, the imitation of Christ. Past all analysis and derision stands the heroic figure which Gordon at last achieved, of which Lord Tennyson, the Poet Laureate, wrote, 'This earth hath borne, no simpler, nobler man', and which Gladstone, the Prime Minister, referred to in the House of Commons as 'hero of heroes'.

* * *

In September 1855 the Russians quietly evacuated the battered fortress of Sebastopol and so brought the war to an end. Gordon was given the job of blowing up the harbour defences, and was pleasantly awed by the dramatic effect of the heavy demolition charges which had to be employed. He then settled down to his second winter in the Crimea, still with the theme in his letters home, that there was 'really no hardship'. He refused to accept the many comforts which his family would have sent out to him, and contented himself with trivial gifts— a pot of toothpaste, a bottle of cherry brandy. The only thing he did ask for—flannel shirts—could not be procured in England though the request seems very reasonable.

While awaiting developments, he seems to have paid more than passing attention to the rewards which the War Office began to announce. No doubt they were a ruling topic. Drily he noted that those who had earned decorations in the field seldom seemed to have been noticed at the time, while those with little battle experience but the right friends achieved all manner of distinction. It was rumoured that a Staff College was to be formed, and Gordon was anxious to attend it, for his profession had for the time being won the battle with that other half of himself, the ascetic. He had relatively little to say about religion in letters of this period, and the people round him accepted him at his face value—a cheerful extrovert, an efficient officer, a man of considerable personal charm and single-mindedness of military purpose. As such he was as welcome as spring to senior officers who had learned the lesson dramatised by the Charge of the Light Brigade and looked to a new professional spirit to imbue the modernised army they intended to create. Gordon had that spirit, and so every reason to look forward to a career very different from that dull sequence which he and Drew used to anticipate with such bored resignation.

On the 30th of March the following year (1856) peace was established by the Treaty of Paris, to which Sardinia was an allied signatory, and there followed the usual concern about the delimitation and 'rectification' of frontiers, particularly where Russia came closest to allied spheres of influence, in Transcaucasia and the northern border of Turkey. Instead of being sent home on leave, Gordon was appointed in May to an international Commission charged with the definition of the new frontier between Bessarabia and Moldavia, the focus of difficulty being the town of Bolgrad, some ninety miles north-west of Odessa.

In the twelve months he was there he had his first experience of diplomacy, which was particularly enlightening in that the French changed sides to support the Russians against their ally, Britain. Gordon was too junior to take part in high-level negotiations, and was chiefly concerned with map-making in the frontier area, which brought him into close contact with the local inhabitants. Though he had admired the courage and tenacity of Russian soldiers and at all times was singularly free from nationalistic bias, he found the Russian civilians avaricious, untrustworthy and inhospitable. This last should have reminded him that perhaps he was still regarded as an enemy, since hospitality has always been a Russian trait. But Gordon, having himself little capacity for bearing a grudge, saw nothing strange in the enemies of yesterday being friends today, and took exception to a snub administered to the Commission by the local Governor of Bessarabia, who, instead of giving the conventional dinner-party, asked only the French Commissioner to tea; and afterwards made him pay for the cards with which they had played.

The climate was worse than the Crimea, but Gordon had no complaint, though sherry froze in the bottle and he found neither the local wine nor the local delicacy, caviar, to his taste. He was glad to complete the survey and was due for home leave. Instead, in April 1857, he was sent on another Frontier Commission, this time based on Erzerum in Armenia, where for the first time he saw, or at least heard, something of slavery. From those bare, wild regions a stream of unfortunates flowed towards Stamboul; women for the harems, and men—often deserters from the Russian Army—for hard labour. Gordon expressed no view about the women, but he thought it rough on the men after having made their escape from one of the harshest armies in the world.

Perhaps of more importance to the development of his character was contact with the Dukhobors, that outrageously thorough sect of Christian idealists who, only a few years before, had been banished from Russia proper for failure to conform to State legislation. Gordon must have been touched by the intransigent faith of these 'Sons of Freedom'. Their capacity to endure the physical consequences of an antisocial creed would have attracted his abnegating mind, although he seems to have been too individualistic to belong to any group.

So, before getting his well-earned leave, he had to face yet another continental winter. He did not go home until November 1858, and had to return to Armenia in the May following. On the voyage out, which lasted a fortnight, was a young woman to whom he paid almost his only compliment. She was 'lively, volatile and very fascinating', but she was not serious-minded, and so did not possess the essential key to a heart already hardening at the age of twenty-five. His ideal state of mind seems to have been one of emotional detachment, almost of sterility, which was represented by what became his favourite biblical quotation, used almost as a motto, 'Be not moved', or, 'Be not thou greatly moved'. It could have seemed like a celestial inhibition for any kind of emotional response.

The glamour which had surrounded the idea of a distinguished military career was fast fading, particularly with an indefinite prospect of peacetime soldiering. The job of the soldier, he insisted, is to kill and be killed. If he is not doing that he is not fulfilling his vocation, which must, therefore, be understood as the pursuit of death rather than waiting for it. So, for the first time in his life, but by no means the last, Gordon found himself unwilling to go home. When the Commission's work was done he thought of offering his services to Turkey. But before anything could come of that idea he was posted as second adjutant of the Chatham depôt, a position with prospects, but for him without enchantment.

Again he arrived home in winter, took his leave, and in

May became a Captain. He was twenty-six. A new up-to-date army was being created out of what was left of the old one, and bright young officers with promising war service would be assured of a better future, in terms of promotion, than they could have dreamed when at The Shop. But Gordon no longer looked in that direction. The life of a peacetime officer would be beset by social occasions for which he had no use at all, and as in his first experience of a big Mess, he found that Chatham gave him few opportunities for being 'serious'. Fortunately destiny intervened to save him from such frustration. For the third time in twenty years England declared war on China. The object was to enforce the provisions of the Treaty of Tientsin (1858) which had been the result of China's failure to keep the provisions of the Treaty of Nanking (1842). China had then been forced to accept foreign trade at five ports, Canton, Amoy, Foochow, Ningpo and Shanghai—the 'Treaty Ports'. The Chinese authorities were particularly obstinate in their attitude to the import of opium, to force which had been a primary if indirect object of all three campaigns, collectively known as the Opium Wars; though France, England's hesitant ally in the last two, was not concerned with that pernicious commodity nor, to any great extent, with more legitimate trade. Her motive for joining in was partly a desire not to allow England to act alone in what might prove to be a far-reaching development of the Far East, and partly an affair of honour in that after a period of toleration, missionary persecution had broken out again and one priest had been murdered.

The opium trouble started as far back as the year Gordon was born; indeed, if Warren Hastings had been more scrupulous, the Hero of Khartoum might never have emerged. It was by Hastings' order that two ships tried to break through the Chinese embargo on the importation of the drug, which was banned in India. One of the ships was captured, but the other discharged her cargo, and afterwards the demand grew until, no matter what regulations were in force, increasing quantities were consumed. In 1859, at the risk of war, the Chinese froze stocks amounting to 30,283 chests. At that time the annual value of the trade to India, where it was a Government monopoly, was three million pounds sterling. Behind such practical reasons for conflict there was a fundamental antipathy. A British Ambassador, Lord Napier, also bearing the tactless title 'Superintendent of Trade', once referred to the highest official in the Empire as a 'presumptuous savage'. From the other side, 'It is plain', observed the Son of Heaven, 'that these barbarians always look to trade as their chief occupation and are wanting in any high purpose'. To which a tactful courtier replied, 'At bottom they belong to the class of brutes: it is impossible that they should have any high purpose'. The English conceived the furtherance of commerce as a 'high purpose' because upon it depended Progress, which was almost synonymous with God's will in the world and the means of establishing Christ's universal kingdom. Hence to reject the idea of Progress, which Chinese thought emphatically did, was to reject Christian civilisation.

The Chinese denied that there could be any civilisation but their own. Inevitably Chinese and British interests clashed whenever they met, and a series of incidents culminated in an affair of honour which England took very much to heart. On his way to Pekin to ratify the Treaty of Tientsin, Her Majesty's Minister Plenipotentiary had been forced to turn back. His ship was fired on by the Taku forts which guarded the Peiho estuary. Yet the Chinese had not refused to receive the Minister; they had merely required that he use an overland route, which, if it involved loss of face at all, had been good enough for the Americans whose treaty was duly ratified in peace. Pride now demanded the opening of the waterway and suitable compensation for the damage inflicted by the Chinese in defence of their own front door.

Opening the 1860 Parliament in person, Queen Victoria said, 'It will be very gratifying to me if the perfect acquiescence of the Emperor of China in the moderate demands which will be made by the Plenipotentiaries shall obviate the necessity for the employment of force'. In March, three months later, Mr. Bright, in opposition, 'traced the progress of the transactions in China from the war (*i.e.* the last one) which was commenced, he said, by the indiscretion of Sir J. Bowring; and after blaming the stipulation of the last treaty, he continued that we were as much in the wrong as we were in Canton, under the management of Sir J. Bowring. He denied that the Chinese were open to the charge of treachery; he insisted that the collison at the mouth of the Peiho was attributable to the folly and imbecility of our own Minister and the indiscretion of the Admiral, and he censured the Government for allowing a person so utterly unfit to conduct the negotiations as Mr. Bruce to continue to be our Minister in China. He could see no advantage to this country in requiring that our Minister should reside at Pekin which would inflict a grievous insult upon the Emperor of China and be an ungenerous act on our part. He warned the Government against a partnership with another power, and against making demands upon the Government of China, which, being based upon a disaster occasioned by the folly of our own Minister, we ought not, in the sight of God or man, to make.'

The 'disaster' became the excuse for a new war, basically undertaken for the sake of Mr. Bruce's dignity and organised on the assumption that there would be little fighting because the Chinese had already agreed to the provisions of the treaty. There was no reason for them to put forth more than a token effort, particularly since any serious resistance would be likely to prove more expensive than to pay the required compensation. Upon such a triviality the fate of the Manchu Empire was to hang; for the country had long been racked by civil war and any further loss of money or power was likely to tip the balance finally in favour of the 'Taiping' rebels, who were still widely, but quite erroneously, regarded as Christian peasants gloriously engaged in overthrowing idols and building churches—eighteen in every conquered town. It was only after the fall of Pekin in the same year that the real character of the rebels began to be appreciated. By then it was almost too late to save the ancient Empire of Cathay to which Sir Hope Grant's expeditionary force was about to deliver what amounted to an unintentional *coup de grâce*.

With enthusiasm Gordon volunteered for active service, was accepted, and sailed for the Far East that summer (1860) on the new P. & O. steamer *Valetta*. The ruling topic in her saloon was probably not China but the slavery issue in America, where Lincoln was President-elect and civil war imminent, because the South would rather secede from the Union than lose its slaves. Without compensation on a huge scale, abolition invited economic chaos. No doubt the British law of 1833 was quoted frequently and with approval. By it British plantation-owners had been compensated to the extent of £20,000,000 for their lost property, but the North was in no position to make such a gesture to the South. Though a convinced abolitionist, Gordon would have understood the realities of the American situation, which seemed to require a line of action at variance to that demanded by conscience. He must have sympathised equally with North and South. He must also have recalled, perhaps with a sense of foreboding, that one of the provisions of the Treaty of Tientsin was the protection of what was euphemistically called 'the coolie trade', by which operators could acquire yellow slaves in place of the black ones who had been bought out. But the 'coolie trade' was a small matter in comparison with the opportunity to open up the vastness of China to the wonderful promise of Christian progress. On that score Gordon had no misgivings, yet.

Because he had volunteered rather than been selected for the expedition, he left England too late to be incorporated in the main body of the force and this may well have been a factor of importance to his subsequent career; for upon arrival he was supernumerary, and was, therefore, an obvious choice for independent missions. He landed at Tientsin at one o'clock in the afternoon of the 17th September, and though he hurried to join the troops advancing towards the capital, in his own words, he 'arrived too late for the amusement', meaning the taking of the Taku forts which guarded the waterway to Pekin. Thereafter the allies pushed before them an enemy who consistently refused to be brought to battle. Both sides were prepared to open peace negotiations, the allies because the season was already far advanced. They had no wish to be pinned to the winter ground before Pekin as they had been outside Sebastopol, for the climate was more severe in China.

As the Chinese hesitated and havered, it became urgently necessary to force them either to give battle or accept defeat. The enemy's main force was still actively in being and constantly embarrassed the allies by its proximity while negotiations for an armistice were going on. One evening, when an assembly area had been agreed, enemy guns were found to be trained upon it, and the allies reasonably expected that there might be a treacherous attack. Envoys sent under flag of truce to expostulate became involved in an incident which made the Chinese think they were talking only to cover a surprise attack, so the envoys were taken prisoner. Hearing of this from officers who galloped out of the trap, General Hope Grant did attack, only to have the enemy withdraw without committing themselves irrevocably; and convinced, as subsequent events showed, that they had been tricked by the men they had taken prisoner.

As the armies moved forward towards Pekin without opposition the need for some provocative gesture must have been obvious. Was there nothing to be done that would bring the Chinese to battle or to terms? It was decided that the occupation of the Emperor's most revered palace would involve him in such loss of face as would achieve that end, and so the allied armies converged upon Yuen-Ming-Yuen, 'The Round Bright Garden', often called simply the Summer Palace, situated four and a half miles from the capital.

Both staffs agreed that the place represented a great temptation to the troops, but it was evidently considered that looting could be held in check. Unfortunately, during the last night of the approach-march, the French 'lost' the English and pressed on independently. They subsequently claimed that they did so only because their allies surreptitiously broke camp before the agreed hour, presumably with the idea of getting there first. Acting upon this rumour, two French officers promised a local guide 100 *taels*, about £5, if he would guide them to Yuen-Ming-Yuen before the English got there. They added that should he fail to do so they would feel obliged to blow out his brains. There had been considerable rivalry between the two nations, and these officers, acting without orders, probably had no other idea than the gay one of wiping England's eye over what was, after all, a symbol of victory as the Pole might be for two expeditions racing towards it.

Against all probability, the two Frenchmen succeeded in getting on top of the wall, only to be wounded by one of the few guards who remained. For the Son of Heaven, with his

Court, had suddenly decided to go 'hunting' far to the north in Jehol. Annoyed at what may have seemed uncalled-for offensive action, the next French detachment to come up forced the main gates, and so made looting inevitable. They went up a wide paved road, meticulously kept, and mounted serene steps to the Great Hall of Receptions, calm as a cathedral in the dawn. They broke in, and were faced by an ebony throne, magnificently carved. The *Illustrated London News* grudgingly admitted that 'it was quite a work of art' — high praise at a time when Chinese ideas of beauty were regarded as merely quaint. From there the troops fanned out to begin an orgy of destruction.

When the English came up they also caught the fever, and, whether on that first day or later, Captain Gordon acquired a throne which he eventually presented to his regimental depôt. Even at this stage the situation might have been brought under control had orders not been received that the troops were to camp within the walls. There is little point in making comparisons between the French and English, for, if there should be excuse for the subsequent burning of the buildings, the looting took place without official disapproval before there were any grounds for reprisal against the Chinese and while peace negotiations were still in progress.

The Round Bright Garden was by no means a single palace. It was rather an archipelago of palaces in a park some twelve square miles in extent, where for more than two centuries landscape gardening had continually improved upon the superb natural scene of woodland, hill and stream: the setting for some four hundred buildings of which forty were large palaces, many erected under the direction of Jesuit missionaries in the latter part of the eighteenth century. Most of the designs were classical Chinese, but there were a few European-style 'follies'. Building had begun in 1709, under the personal direction of the great Emperor K'an Hsi.

The Jesuits had been just as enthusiastic about Yuen-Ming-Yuen as were the Chinese. Père Atteret wrote in 1743, 'Each valley has its pleasure palace, small in relation to its enclosure, but in itself sufficiently large to lodge the greatest of our European lords with all his retinue'. No wonder that 'Old Buddha', the Empress Dowager Tzu-Hsi, according to her lady-in-waiting, 'never ceased to bewail the destruction and the fact that it could never be replaced'.

When looting was already far advanced, the two commanders met in the one room which seems to have been guarded. It must have awed even the wreckers, for the very walls were encrusted with jade. Here Generals Hope Grant and Montauban selected presents for their respective sovereigns, Queen Victoria and Napoleon III—two matching staves-of-office in gold and jade. What made Yuen-Ming-Yuen so fantastic a prize was not the range of treasure, which might have furnished any well-found Chinese palace, but its quantity. Many of the buildings had long been used as elegant storehouses for presents which poured in from distant parts of the Empire and even from the countries of the 'barbarians-beyond-the-seas'. Soldiers spread silks and antique embroideries a foot deep upon the polished floors of the great halls. Fine silk was used as common packing material. Jewelled watches were handled by the sackful. Gordon wrote: 'You could hardly conceive the magnificence of this residence, or the tremendous devastation the French have committed. The throne and rooms were lined with ebony, carved in a marvellous way. There were huge mirrors of all shapes and kinds, clocks, watches, musical boxes with puppets on them, magnificent china of every description, and as much splendour as you would see at Windsor; carved ivory screens, coral screens, large amounts of treasure etc. The French have smashed everything in the most wanton way. It was a scene of utter destruction which passes description.'

And he would have seen only part of what was going on. The French found, 'Or, argent, bronzes niellés, émaux cloisonnés, jade vert, jade antique, jade blanc, cornaline, améthyste, pierres dures de tout genre, bois précieux, ivoire, incrustations de nacre, soieries brochies, porcelaines admirables, tapis précieux, fourrures inestimables, laques anciennes. Rien ne peut donner une idée des merveilles.'

Such was the profusion of treasure that the soldiery did not believe that it could all be genuine. Gold was treated as brass, pearls as common beads, jades as so much glass. There were also some curiously incongruous items, English carriages, for example, and a pair of brass guns with ammunition, the gift

of England's first ambassador, Macartney. Gordon wrote:
'Imagine D giving sixteen shillings for a string of pearls which
he sold next day for £500. The people are civil but the
grandees hate us, as I think they must.' He adds that his own
share of the prize-money was £48 as an officer. Each private
soldier received £4: for the General had ordered all private
booty to be surrendered so that it could be sold at public
auction and the money fairly divided. He did not mention
that the effect of holding the auction was to let the treasure go
at ridiculously low prices into the hands of local merchants,
who were glad to do business even at the risk of losing their
heads, the penalty imposed by their own countrymen. As to
the fairness of the auction, though the principle may have
been sound, there must have been anomalies; with the neck-
lace Gordon refers to at one extreme, and at the other a single
cup of the imperial yellow which fetched £22. The auction
could have had sad results for a connoisseur required to surrender what he had rescued. Still, there can hardly have been
many connoisseurs, though a number of pieces, particularly
of jade, found their way to England.

*   *   *

The Chinese still havered after the news of the wrecking of
the Round Bright Garden, and, instead of being more con-
ciliatory, they tried to bargain with the lives of their prisoners
for a token withdrawal by the allies. Such blackmail had to be
refused, if only because time was on the side of the enemy.
Accordingly, an ultimatum was despatched, calling for the
surrender of the capital and the return of all prisoners, failing
which the city would be taken by storm. As part of this policy
Gordon was ordered to prepare positions for eight-inch guns
opposite the Anting Gate. His work done, he went, on a Sunday afternoon, to inspect the defences and concluded that
'the place is very weak and could not hold out two days', a
surprisingly optimistic conclusion in view of the extraordinary
strength of the walls, which were so wide, even on top, that
General Hope Grant estimated that 'with a little management' five coaches-and-fours could be driven abreast.

Neither Gordon's appreciation of the situation nor his
guns were put to the test, for a few minutes to the noon hour,

when the ultimatum expired, white flags appeared on the walls and the great gates slowly opened. In accord with an undertaking that the troops making a formal entry would not exceed in numbers a proper escort for the two ambassadors, French and English, two hundred men of each nationality moved forward cautiously, passed under the gate-tower and entered the town. According to plan the British detachment climbed the tower to hoist the Union Flag. The French should have joined them there. Instead, they marched a mile into Pekin, southwards towards the Tartar city—a brave showing and perhaps a foolhardy one; but they, the 101 de la Ligne, made the gesture without loss and returned to the gate, expecting that the British would be waiting for them so that the allied flags could be hoisted together. But the British had not waited—'*Une altercation très vive s'éleva entre lui (Général Montauban) et le Général Napier, qui s'excusa de son mieux*'. Dignity restored, flags flying and the campaign ended, the allies withdrew from the open city, henceforward to be entered on diplomatic business or on leave passes only to be obtained by 'non-commissioned officers and very steady men'.

Yet the Imperial City had not, in fact, surrendered to the foreigners so much as to the panic of its own merchants. They represented to the authorities that it would be better to yield to the foreign devils than to the Taipings. The foreigners, with all their faults, respected and protected trade. The rebels cared nothing for it. The foreigners were neither treacherous nor bloodthirsty and they usually respected—in spite of the fate of Yuen-Ming-Yuen—the property of peaceful citizens. The rebels were quite otherwise. Had they not put to the sword almost the entire population of their new capital, Nanking? It had been to such entreaties rather than to the threats of the allied generals that the Imperial Council had listened, being no doubt convinced that Pekin could have stood siege, and that in winter the supply of a foreign investing force would have been extremely difficult—an idea which must have haunted the allies also.

Chapter 2

WIDE DARK WASTELAND

BEFORE the allied troops could celebrate their bloodless victory came the news of ill-treatment of the prisoners, all of whom had suffered—some within the grounds of Yuen-Ming-Yuen — and six had died. One was a brother officer and personal friend of Gordon's named De Norman. His arms and legs had been tied behind his back and water poured over the ropes to shrink them. He was then left in an open courtyard where he was beaten at intervals and for three days given nothing to eat or drink. The limbs became gangrenous, the fingers burst and fell off. His wounds and sores were flyblown and maggots entered the body cavities. Lord Elgin, Minister Plenipotentiary, and the General felt that some decisive step should be taken 'to mark England's horror', and it was decided to burn to the ground the palaces of Yuen-Ming-Yuen. The French refused to cooperate, though there had been one of their people among the bloated dead, and so the British took the initiative, ordering Captain Gordon to take charge of the operation.

In spite of his own sense of indignation and bitter fury, the greater because it was not then known that there had even been the paltry pretext of an alleged act of treachery on the part of the prisoners, Gordon went to work without enthusiasm. 'You would scarcely conceive the beauty and magnificence of the palaces we burnt. It made one's heart sore to burn them; in fact, these palaces were so large and we were so pressed for time that we could not plunder them carefully. . . . It was wretchedly demoralising work for an army. Everyone was wild for plunder.' Even the skilled and methodical Sappers could not in two days manage to consume more than three or four of the palaces, but in the ensuing national chaos no one thought of affording protection to what remained, and bandits disposed of it until there was nothing left standing. Meanwhile Gordon himself had lost something in the fire he had started, which, among the rest of

C   25

the fabulous treasure, had destroyed a history of China kept personally by successive Emperors for a thousand years. He had lost a sense of rectitude, of conviction in the inevitable rightness of the West. Doubts which he thought he had conquered came up like weeds among the ruins. How much suffering did the Gentle God require? What had De Norman done to deserve such a death? Would he have approved the burning of the Round Bright Garden or seen the act as irrelevant barbarism? Do two wrongs ever make a right, or wrong means make right ends? Does vandalism become the Soldiers of the Queen, or vengeance help Christians onward?

Though circumstances often forced upon him means which were contrary to his ideals, Gordon never seems to have rationalised the problem, though to the eye of the spirit may have come that illumination which is itself an answer. He was entitled to it, for no one ever attributed to him a base motive or a greedy attitude. He never sheltered inside his uniform from responsibility for his right and his wrong, but took at all times a personal as well as an official responsibility for his actions, before God as in the sight of men. Until it killed him, he wrestled with reality, though he could so easily have found comfortable refuge under the stuffy wings of Victorian hypocrisy.

Following the surrender of Pekin the situation was a delicate balance of power in which the initiative lay with the British as between the Imperial Government of China and the Taiping rebels. An Imperialist army occupied an entrenched camp only a few miles from the capital, from which they had fired upon an English reconnaissance party. A rebel army was also in the area and presumably no less capable of joining forces with the Imperialists against the invaders than of sacking Pekin, as the merchants feared. In such a context there seems every reason why the Imperialist general Sinkolinsin refused battle once the Taku forts had fallen. He must have been aware that diplomatic overtures were being made to gain British help against the rebels, and also that they had met with no success for the understandable reason that the foreigners, as a point of honour, must first achieve the object of their expedition, the enforcement of the provisions of the Treaty of Tientsin.

GORDON'S CHINA

0   Miles   300

J E H O L

Great Wall

Yuen-Ming-Yuen

Pekin

Tientsin

H O P E H

R. Tzaya

Takû

Gulf of Chihli

K O R E A

Y E L L O W S E A

K I A N G S U

Grand Canal

Nanking

Fushan

Chanzu

Soochow Taitsan

Taiho Lake

Quinsan

Shanghai

Sunkiang

Hangchow

R. Yangtze

E A S T C H I N A S E A

Canton

*Canton to Hangchow
is about 600 miles*

On the 24th of October 1860 the redrafted treaty was
signed in Pekin between Lord Elgin and the Sixth Prince,
Kung, acting as Regent while the Emperor's 'hunting' was
prolonged. All the concessions about the Treaty Ports,
opium and missionaries, were confirmed, and in addition an
indemnity of £2,666,666 was levied for the expenses of the
campaign, the odd figure being due presumably to the conversion from Chinese currency. Of more interest, however, is
a comparison of worth, which may be illustrated by the cost
of total castration, which a man would undergo at a fee of six
taels, about six shillings, and often be so poor that, if he survived the operation, he undertook to go on paying the surgeon
instalments out of the wages he expected to get as a eunuch.
For such a small payment, however, he would not be allowed
to keep the discard, and when he died his relatives would be
obliged to purchase it or the equivalent; unless they could be
so callous as to care nothing for family honour beyond the
grave. By way of contrast, a sum of 500,000 *taels* (£25,000) was
demanded as compensation for the relatives of the murdered
prisoners.

That the Imperialists so readily agreed, particularly in
view of what had happened to the Round Bright Garden,
may have been due less to the conviction that they had lost a
war than to the belief that it was a small thing if, in exchange
for concessions, they could get the foreigners to fight the rebels.
They may even have thought that the foreigners would have
much the same idea, for it would give them a chance to
become masters of the whole country instead of merely traders.
For whatever reasons, both sides decided to make a great
show of the formal exchange of copies of the treaty, which
took place on the following day in spite of the fact that
General Hope Grant had reason to suppose that an 'under-
ground' movement was at work in the city and might take
the opportunity to create trouble. The French were to take
no part, preferring to sign their own treaty in their own
way.

British troops lined the street from the Anting Gate, on
which Gordon's guns remained trained, to the Hall of Ceremonies. Lord Elgin's chair, borne by sixteen men in scarlet
robes, was preceded by a military band, and succeeded, after

other chairs, by a second band, with due place for the escort of a hundred cavalry and four hundred infantry. Gordon would have approved the pageant and enjoyed the sense of hidden danger. He may even have forgotten the ethical problems which had come back to plague him, and for the time being put on one side a natural concern as to what would happen now that the shooting seemed to be over. The bands played, the gold glittered. Prince Kung came to the threshold of the hall to receive his guests, and with extreme formality, surrounded by five hundred officers of state, handed to Lord Elgin his copy of the treaty, engraved upon plaques of gold. In view of the magnitude of the indemnity, the gold was a gesture for 'face', and the Chinese must have been gratified to note that the English copy was only on parchment. The barbarians might be as skilled in war as in trade, but it was as well to let them realise that they remained barbarians.

* * *

A month later the fall of Pekin was history, but, far from staying to keep the peace, the allied forces withdrew. Already the weather was bitter (Lord Elgin went down with influenza) and, if they had not hurried, they might not have been able to get away by sea until the spring. Meanwhile an overland mail continued to function. By it Queen Victoria sent her congratulations, the *Illustrated London News* received sketches from its correspondent and Lord Elgin submitted his suggestion for a campaign medal, one of which went to Gordon.

So, except for diplomatic contacts, China was left largely to itself and to civil war. The only British troops to remain were two and a half batteries Royal Artillery, one company Royal Engineers (Captain Gordon), Fane's Horse, three Line Regiments and the Military Train. These were quartered at Tientsin, while at Shanghai would remain temporarily two Indian Infantry Regiments and one half-battery R.A. The rest of the Expeditionary Force went home, and it was this circumstance which next led Gordon towards an independent command for which, in the ordinary course of events, he was still too junior.

What makes the broad picture so puzzling is that the withdrawal was made in the light of the belated knowledge that it was doubtful whether the Imperial Government would now be able to prevent the complete victory of the rebels, who were at last recognised as a threat to Western interests in the country. Merchants did their best to raise a 'home guard' for local protection, but the menace was continually growing; and yet the diplomats apparently continued to believe that the Taipings were reasonable people and would consider themselves bound by the treaty forced upon their Imperialist enemies. All of which was far above the heads of the officers and men whose bad luck it was to remain behind to see that the provisions of the treaty were carried out. All they wanted to do was to get home in the wake of their comrades, and meanwhile to pass the dreary months as agreeably as possible under the circumstances. It was a dull prospect, especially for that active Engineer Captain who had already acquired a distaste for peacetime soldiering in England. Though living at Headquarters, he did not find Tientsin dull, because he took to studying the countryside with his usual thoroughness. He used to go for long solitary walks or rides, often with a notebook and sketching materials, keeping his eyes and ears open to the state of the people, for whom, caught between three fires—rebel, Imperial and foreign—he had the liveliest sympathy.

Some time during the early part of 1861 all these observations coalesced and made a pattern in which Gordon saw the next stage of his destiny. He decided, not without grave consideration, that the 'Christian' Taipings were worse than the pagans, whether peasantry or Government. That being the case, it was his—and England's—duty to oppose them, as much for the sake of the common people as for her own merchants and those of other foreign powers. Whether Gordon formulated his own rôle is doubtful, but he did come to the conclusion that it was urgently necessary to take steps to defeat the rebels, a task manifestly beyond the capacity of the Chinese Government alone. It is possible that, had there not been a regulation against such an act, he would have taken service with the Imperialists; for the people, he thought, cried out to him, or rather, to the representatives of civilisation, whatever their country or their colour. He wrote: 'The hardest heart would have been touched by the misery of these poor, harmless people, for whatever may be said of their rulers, no one can deny that the Chinese peasantry are the most obedient, quiet, and industrious people in the world'.

Nor was he content only to feel pity and to dream of intervention. He was instrumental in collecting nine hundred dollars for the poor, many of them starving because of the loss of their homes to the rebels. The local magistrate was asked to supervise an equitable distribution but refused, perhaps because he would have lost face by accepting money from foreigners, even to comfort his own people. Consequently the crowd got out of hand. Gordon wrote: 'There were about three thousand beggars and, in the crush, seven women and one boy were killed. The poor women on their little feet, on which they are never very safe, were thrown down and trampled upon.'

Another more florid hand wrote of the refugees: 'On they go, the blind and the lame, the women with babes in their arms, and very small children clinging to them, led faltering over bridges, the whole face of the country alive as though a human ant-hill had been disturbed, all rushing madly towards the creeks and rivers, followed by a belt of smoke consuming the produce of their industry and many of the inhabitants'. This description was of a single occasion, but it applies to the whole ferment in Northern China, where the rebels, having fully consolidated their gains in the south, were about to make another bid to reach the sea, convinced in the divinity of their Heavenly King (Tien Wang) who had established his 'Heavenly Capital' at Nankin in 1853. There he still kept pseudo-imperial state, attended by other 'kings' —for he conferred the title freely upon his intimates. Among such were Faithful Wang, Eastern Wang, Western Wang, Warrior Wang and Attendant Wang, supported by some less eminent characters with equally picturesque appellations, Yellow Tiger, One-eyed Dog and Cock-eye.

Tien Wang had already fought for a number of years to achieve his exalted position, and his history is relevant, not only to the state of China but to the temperament and philosophy of Gordon, for whom he constituted the first of two great enemies. The second was a like fanatic, the Mahdi of

Allah, who also came from an obscure origin to sow the wind of power, not in men's heads but in their hearts, and to reap the whirlwind.

The boy who was to call himself the Heavenly King came from the *Hakkas* (Strangers), a hill-dwelling people analagous to the gypsies of Europe. His family lived in the area south of Canton and their name was Hung. It was in 1833, the year of Gordon's birth, that this boy, Hung-Seu-Tsien, went down to the city to seek his fortune. He was dissatisfied with the traditional primitive, poverty-stricken life of his people and desired a position of authority, such as a schoolmaster's. But before any post could even be applied for he had to take the Civil Service examinations, which required a memorised knowledge of the Confucian classics. To have cut his domestic ties and ventured out into the world beyond the hills, Hung must have had both courage and ambition, but he does not seem to have had brains to match. In 1837 he failed the exam, though later his supporters claimed that the result was not due to lack of marks—they said he had been placed well up the list—but to lack of ancestors.

Whatever the reason for this rebuff, he returned to the hills, where his bleak prospects in this world made him look to reward in the next. In pursuit of this conviction he went so far as to speak openly of Heaven in the light of what little mission teaching he had absorbed while studying for his exam. Surrounded by superstitious people living in want and in fear, he soon attracted notoriety, upon which he throve. He either experienced, or claimed that he experienced, visions and revelations, possibly in association with a severe illness which he suffered about this time, quite apart from the epilepsy with which he was probably afflicted and which would be an additional attraction; for those with the 'falling sickness' are traditionally favoured of the Gods.

The next, almost inevitable development, was the formulation of a doctrine and the establishment of a rule. The rule was the obvious one of austerity, for it tends to convince the disciple that the master has no ulterior motives. The dogma inevitably focussed upon a messianic claim—or so it became—though it is probable that at this stage the whole pattern was relatively innocent; for otherwise, when Hung again went down to Canton in 1846, he would hardly have been received as a catechumen by the American missionary Baptist, Issachar J. Roberts. Mr. Roberts soon became uneasy, and at last dismissed Hung, presumably unbaptised; though not before the man had received the ammunition he needed for his own ministry; that same high-explosive which among a Palestinian people not so unlike the Hakkas, had proved strong enough to rock the world.

By 1850 the Imperial Authority had to take notice that Hung's movement was threatening the peace; but so did a powerful secret society, known as the Triads, who had long been looking for a figure behind which to rally the forces of rebellion against the Manchu régime. The fact that the Triads stood for the purity of Buddhism against the corruption of official Confucianism did not prevent them from making use of the pseudo-Christianity of Hung; until they also detected the crazy streak in him. Then they denounced him, and eventually went over to the Government cause. Their leader was rewarded with a high military command, as was only fair since the Triads were an old-established secret society in the ancient tradition, a dignified set of people with a modicum of culture. There was no dignity and less culture about Hung and the men he gathered round him to fight for Eternal Peace, which is the sense of the word *Tai-ping*.

Luckier than most prophets at the outset of their careers, Hung had almost a ready-made army at his disposal, for many ex-soldiers were idling around, careless of the issues involved and prepared to sell themselves for loot. In the absence of any system of pay, booty was the practical object of each successive phase of the Rebellion, and so produced one of the most cynical hordes of 'holy' warriors that the world has ever seen. Like locusts they swarmed and like locusts they behaved. The infernal fire usually takes time to spread. This outbreak was an exception because times were very hard, and men without hope are easily led. Not that all his troops were male. Two amazons brought to him a following of four thousand, an extraordinary event in a country where women bound their feet and the profession of arms was the lowest in the social scale.

To distinguish themselves from the shaven-headed or pigtailed non-combatants and Imperialists, the rebels affected long hair. They wore, most of them, a robe or tunic in white bordered with yellow, not so very different from the Dervish dress which was evolved under somewhat similar conditions. When they overran a town or a province they destroyed what they could not carry off. The remaining inhabitants were left to starve. A missionary, J. L. Holmes, wrote: 'To rob and murder an adherent of the Manchu dynasty is a virtuous deed. To carry away his wife and daughter for infamous purposes, or his son to train up for the army, are all legitimate acts. . . . Wherever their armies had overrun the country, they had captured the boys and led them away with them. The large proportion of comely-looking women to be seen looking out at the doors and windows showed the summary way in which these celestial soldiers provided themselves with wives.'

Because the rebels had to get arms as well as feed off the country, their strategy became a drive towards the ports where arms could be obtained. For the same reason they laid siege to large towns, particularly those under foreign influence. Nor did all the weapons have to be looted. There was a brisk trade in them through the Treaty Ports. Gordon had to face guns made in England.

*   *   *

When the hard winter of 1860 locked up the good earth, Tien Wang was as usual in his palace hard by the Porcelain Tower of Nankin, while his northern army observed from a discreet distance the withdrawal of the victorious invaders from the cowed Imperial city of Pekin. The Son of Heaven had died of debauchery during his 'hunting trip', leaving the people without that mystical link between Earth and Heaven upon which the welfare of the Empire was held to depend. For in China the head of the State was more than an Emperor in the ordinary sense. He was the channel through which Heaven worked its will on Earth. He was the god-man, so sacred that the commonalty must not look upon him. When he left his palace a great gong sounded in the streets and the shutters had to be put up as they were for Lady Godiva; and basically for the same deep reason, that both the naked woman and the god-man are charged with 'mana', that mysterious power which under different names all over the world has been revered and feared as the greatest driving force for good or evil, according to the channel through which it flows and the purpose to which it is directed. 'Taboo', the surrounding of 'mana people' and 'mana objects' by ritual restrictions, is equally universal, based upon the common-sense idea that such power is dangerous unless clean and ethically directed. Hence the restrictions imposed upon the Son of Heaven. Hence, perhaps, the peculiar miseries of Gordon who had no such protection. Though it did not seem to occur to him, it certainly did to primitive people, that he himself was such a person, a man of *mana*, of power beyond their, or his, understanding.

It had been naïvely assumed by the British that the Treaty of Pekin would be honoured by Tien Wang, but on being presented with a copy he is said to have been displeased, having expected the document to contain recognition of his status as the younger brother of Jesus Christ, a central claim which he had promulgated in these words:

The Heavenly Father sits on the throne above.
The Heavenly Brother Christ is the next honourable, sitting
    on the right hand of the Father, excelled by no man.
By the Grace of the Father and Brother we sit on His left.
United as One we reign.
Disobey the Heavenly Will and you will be ground to
    pieces with a pestle.

In such a context it should not have been surprising that when, seeking to control coastal waters, Admiral Sir James Hope sailed down to Nankin to arrange for a gunboat to be stationed in the Yangtze, Tien Wang sent a message to say that he would gladly have conferred his protection upon such a vessel had not the Father appeared to him in a vision and told him not to. Later he had another vision which permitted the gunboat. He also proposed a truce as between the Tai-pings and the foreigners to the effect that the rebels would engage to keep a distance of one hundred *li*, or thirty miles, from Shanghai. He said nothing about Pekin, near which his warriors patiently waited, hung about with sheep-skins against the cold.

They had reason to hesitate on that account, for there was considerable diplomatic activity behind those towering walls. The Russian Ambassador with his French colleague seems to have invented an English plot to overthrow the dynasty, now technically under the guidance of a weakling child, the late Emperor's heir, while young Prince Kung ruled as Regent. He was twenty-five. The alleged British plot, so Kung was informed, was to support the rebels; but the Regent's own intelligence service seems to have been otherwise informed. So Kung still acted as though he believed in the solidarity of the allies. Then he received a private offer from the French to put down the Taipings without any help from the English. This he refused, realising that it would have the same effect as the opposite course. In either case the Empire would come under foreign domination. The Russian Ambassador, perhaps feeling there might be some undiplomatic frankness between his colleagues, to whom he had kindly supplied the only detailed plan of the city known to be in existence (it was photographically reproduced, for the benefit of the troops taking part in the operation, by an Italian named Beato who was attached to Headquarters), took the opportunity to leave the capital on holiday. The Regent, advised no doubt by his Commander-in-Chief, Sinkolinsin, that the Imperial armies were intact and battleworthy, decided to wait in the hope that the foreigners might fall foul of Tien Wang and so have to take action against the Taipings without reference to the Imperial Government, an excellent solution to what must have seemed a most desperate problem.

It seems typical of our mole-like methods (the mole is a haphazard digger of tunnels) that it was in the end the English who, without any direct intent, had the opportunity to dominate China, and did not take it. Yet an Englishman, or rather a Scot, with very little official encouragement, rescued the dynasty whose palace he had destroyed, and became a primary person in a country which execrated foreigners. Had he been supported, a peaceful future might have unfolded not only for the East but for the West, since the emergence of China as a pro-British Great Power might have deterred Germany from launching the Kaiser's war in 1914.

Through the spring and early summer of 1861 Gordon continued to spend as much time as possible away from the army, usually on private reconnaissance, though sometimes he seems to have gone out only to test his endurance, as, for instance, to ride to the Taku forts and back in the day, a distance of eighty miles. On one occasion he records the severity of the weather in which he made such a journey: 'Two officers of the 31st Regiment were *en route* for Taku by boat, and one of them started to get a coat when the storm began. He lost his way, fell into every ditch he could find in the neighbourhood, and had to sleep in a grave all night. He was brought in quite wild and blind next morning. The thermometer fell to 25° from 60° during the night, so we did not have a comfortable time of it.'

His constant preoccupation must have been to pursue a line of action which would protect British interests from the rebels and, at the same time, mitigate the miseries of the people, which had been increased as the result of the weakening of the Imperial power at the hands of the allies. His ideas seem to have crystallised that summer, when he went to stay with the Minister, Sir Frederick Bruce, a brother of Lord Elgin—who had sailed for India to become the first of the Viceroys. No doubt Sir Frederick sympathised in a general way with Gordon's detestation of the Taipings, but he would have pointed out the official policy of 'no commitments' and the democratic pressure behind that policy. For in England not only the missionary and general religious view, but also that of the Liberal Opposition, was favourable to the rebels and critical of the Manchu administration as incompetent and tyrannical. Both charges were true but, by comparison with the terror which the Taipings had become, they were trivial. Nor was the crazy theology of Tien Wang appreciated at home. Its perversity may be illustrated from a publication in the *North China Herald* on the 20th of September (1861): 'We are the Supreme Lord, the Brother is the Saviour of the World. We are the True Lord and Our Son is the True Young Lord. Let many copies of this be struck and promulgated over the World.'

Gordon must have reasoned that ordinary diplomatic relations were out of the question with such a madman, who was obviously dangerous and could only be dealt with by armed

force. Once his mind was made up Gordon was not a man to
set the candle of conviction under the bushel of discretion.
The very fact that the diplomatic situation was delicate may
have encouraged him to set out his views with fierce frankness
that may not have been well received. For thereafter Sir
Frederick does not seem to have been a warm supporter of
Gordon. Another man might have sought his own advancement in such a situation, but Gordon had already set his
face against even the most indirect gains from 'good words'
put in for him at high level. He probably contented himself
with two practical suggestions: that permission should be
sought at once to allow English troops to be used against the
rebels, or that officers should be loaned to the Imperialists for
the purpose of creating a Chinese force adequate to defeat
them. Even these suggestions were not likely to have been
enthusiastically received, for people at home could hardly be
expected to understand why, having beaten the Imperialists to
their knees in a short and brilliant campaign, we now wished
to prop up their rotten régime.

Gordon went back to his post and soon afterwards the troops
were withdrawn from Tientsin and sent to Shanghai to hold
the perimeter which had been agreed with Tien Wang. As
Officer Commanding Royal Engineers, Gordon immediately
began to plan and build fortifications against a possible attack
on the city, and as soon as this was completed he was ordered
by General Staveley to make a survey of the area within the
perimeter, on the same lines as the private reconnaissance he
had been doing at Tientsin.

This he did in great detail and at considerable risk, earn-
ing the general's admiration in the process. Staveley was no
office-general. He frequently accompanied Gordon on his
surveying expeditions and evidently formed a very high
opinion of him, the one thing still necessary to open the way
to fame. Staveley wrote that in his eagerness to get accurate
details of a moat round a village held by the rebels, Gordon
pressed forward under fire, pointedly ignoring his superior's
shouts to come back. Arrived under cover, he then made a
leisurely sketch before returning to the general—not a liberty
to be taken by most junior officers with most generals, but
then Staveley was Henry Gordon's brother-in-law. The in-

cident is typical of the man's calculated courage, and the practical efficiency which underlay his idealistic faith, giving balance to his wildest notions.

Periodically the rebels would surge up to the thirty-mile boundary, driving before them the wretched inhabitants of the desolate province on the other side of the line. As many as fifteen thousand homeless, hungry people came within Shanghai's walls, where they existed in an abjection of poverty or starved to death. Harrowed by so much misery, heightened by contrast with the affluence of the European community, Gordon took leave, and with a companion rode away through the rebel-dominated territory to inspect the Great Wall, passing on his way through regions where a white face had never before been seen. It was winter again and so cold that fresh eggs froze hard. The long journey passed without incident except for a fracas over a bill at an inn. Gordon paid only what he thought was fair, but the landlord, supported by vociferous local opinion, took a different view and haled his guests before a magistrate, or rather they were taken to his *yamen*. Arrived there, the two officers jumped onto their horses, which they had been leading, and galloped away. Whether it had any bearing on this incident or not, there was also some trouble over their baggage cart, the driver of which Gordon admits to having treated roughly. They awoke one morning to see the cart leaving the inn-yard, and it took them a long time to catch up with it, presumably because the contents were removed and hidden. In the end they returned to Shanghai fourteen days over their leave. There does not seem to have been even a private reprimand, which would indicate in another way how high Gordon stood with his superiors.

Early the following spring Gordon suffered the only acute illness of his life. It was a mild attack of smallpox, and the probability is that he had been vaccinated since the procedure had become compulsory in England in 1853. Nevertheless, there was a considerable effect upon the personality. Gordon wrote to Augusta in March, 'I am glad to say that this disease has brought me back to my Saviour, and I trust in future to be a better Christian than I have been hitherto'. It was as though he decided that he had rendered too much to Caesar, for the letter contained a warning to his sister not to show it to anyone, perhaps because she often passed on his news to Henry, who was at the War Office. He might have become anxious that the rekindling of the mystical flame would be followed by a falling off in professional zeal. On the contrary, the new impetus raised Gordon's military effort to the level of a crusade and sustained him through a set of circumstances so trying that without the conviction of divine inspiration— if only occasionally, even he might well have faltered. Certainly the 'new conversion', as it has been called, did nothing to impair his judgement in the field. If the cynic suggests that he merely suffered a psychological reaction from acute infection, the fact remains that he won the campaign which began the following year, 1863, after Shanghai had withstood six weeks of siege by the rebels during the winter.

*   *   *

The war began with an announcement from Tien Wang that he considered the truce to be at an end and proposed to take Shanghai. There were at this time quite two thousand English, French and Indian troops in the walled city, supported by half a battery of artillery and a small naval squadron; but because of the diplomatic situation what action had already taken place fell to an irregular force of volunteers, mostly Manilla-men and Spanish half-breeds, officered by soldiers of fortune whose characters are set in relief against the record that in one month eleven of them died of *delirium tremens*. . . . Though this, it must be admitted, was when the establishment was larger!

Gordon's survey was complete: 'I have now been into every town and village in the thirty-mile radius. The country is the same everywhere—dead flat with innumerable creeks and bad pathways.' The Imperial Government had met the threat to the city by taking over the volunteer force, which had up till now been paid by the merchants, arming and expanding it. The commander was an American adventurer called Ward who had gained his considerable experience of war and tempered his undoubted courage in the tough school of Central America. Yet when he was killed, gallantly leading his men into a breach, the prevailing opinion was that it was just as well, for he had proved too boisterous even for the Europeans, who were the first to benefit from his operations, and was equally unpopular with the senior Army and Navy officers for the old reason that the pay and prospects he offered were better than those of the Queen, so that soldiers and sailors were continually deserting.

Probably because he felt he could not hold the force together, the second-in-command refused to step into Ward's place, but the quartermaster, another American, called Burgevine, was more confident, though he did not have the necessary qualities of leadership. Incapable of instilling discipline in the force, which had now been inappropriately named by the Chinese 'The Ever Victorious Army', he did not hesitate to try to dictate to the authorities. A blunt man of bluff and bluster, he could hardly have been a greater contrast to his immediate civil and military superior, the Provincial Governor. This officer was a calligraphist and scholar of the old school, who had been hardened by the loss of his wife and children, presumed killed when they were overrun by the rebels. It is probable that he also had then been taken prisoner. A story was current that he had escaped torture and death by putting his elegant brush and exceptional learning at the disposal of his illiterate captors. His name was Li Hung Chang.

He had scant respect for the Ever Victorious Army, and must have despised Burgevine. Small wonder then that he was inclined to pay by results. In the unlikely event of the Ever Victorious Army living, even briefly, up to its name, the soldiers could be recompensed, as were the rebels, by loot. If they did not win a battle they were not worth paying. Burgevine did not see it like that, and took a strong if foolish line. With an armed party he forced his way into Li's pay office, a bank, forcibly removed some forty thousand dollars representing arrears, and even assaulted the wretched banker, so creating a humiliating situation which to the Chinese eye was more serious even than the loss of the money. Li was honourbound to deal hardly with Burgevine to recover 'face' for Takee his banker. So the American found himself dismissed with ignominy from the Chinese service, and the Ever Victorious was again without a commander, a post for which no one could now be expected to display any eagerness. Already suspicious and patronising in dealing with foreigners, Li-Hung-Chang became convinced that they were all little better than bandits. But even the usages of courtesy are less important than life and liberty, so he acceded when General Staveley appointed his chief-of-staff, Captain Holland of the Royal Marines, to succeed Burgevine. Permission to make such appointments had recently been received from England.

Because of the need to give the Ever Victorious something to do, to pull it together and regain the respect of the authorities, Holland went over to the offensive. He did so without adequate preparation, beyond the thirty-mile boundary, and before the truce came to an end. The result was a farcical defeat which gave the rebels superiority not only in men but also in morale. Previously they had been not a little in awe of foreigners in battle, following the storming of the Taku forts and the subsequent discomfiture of Sinkolinsin. Now all that evaporated. One of the Wangs wrote: 'Oh, how we laughed on the morning of the assault, as they advanced nearer to the creek which they had brought no bridges to throw over! How we laughed as we saw the ladder they had thrown over getting weaker and weaker beneath them, and at last fall into the creek, leaving half the party on one side, half on the other. "What a general is he," cried our chief, "who sends his men to storm a city without first ascertaining that there is a moat?" So we laughed and we jested and we saw the slaves of the Tartar usurper advancing to destruction. . . . And we arose as one man; the cry of "Blood!" was in our mouths and the thirst for blood consumed us. We sallied forth on the "ever-victorious" troops and behold they retired as soon as they saw the brandishing of our spears. . . . There were English officers too. O recorder of events, how they ran! One of them flung away his pistol and his sword and swam the creek in haste. Another also lost his sword, which the Sung-kiang men picked up, and, I am told, have it now in Sung-kiang. But they needed it not. We know the policy of your nation, not to attack beyond the thirty-mile boundary, and we should not have hurt them, knowing that they only came to witness our prowess. We know likewise full well that the English *Chuntai* did wrong in overstepping the boundary but he has suffered for it; let him rest. . . .

'Mightily were we surprised, O recorder of events, at the conduct of the English *Chuntai*. Can you believe it, he removed the smaller guns first, instead of leaving them to the last to protect the removal of the bigger ones. Then, too, we were surprised to see him leading the retreat in his boat. We know that such is the practice of the impish mandarins; but we thought that the English officers always sought the post of danger. We thought, truly, that he would have brought up the rear. . . .'

*　　*　　*

It was soon after this grim comedy that Gordon was relieved of his survey to replace Holland at the head of the Ever Victorious, now a sizeable force of between three and four thousand men with a hundred and fifty officers, among whom his own staff were English, the rest mixed European and American. The ranks were mostly Chinese dressed in Western uniforms, which made another joke for the Wangs who referred to them contemptuously as 'false foreign-devils'. Their arms were varied, firelocks and other smooth-bore guns, a few Lee-Enfield rifles for marksmen. Artillery included smooth-bore guns, but there were also some of the new breech-loaders, which were rifled.

Discipline was non-existent and Gordon's immediate worry was how to create it without risking mutiny, melting away or desertion to the enemy, now confident of success because Tien Wang had proclaimed the truce to be at an end. Accordingly he went from his headquarters to the *yamen* of Li Hung Chang, who could not have anticipated the visit with any enthusiasm. Li had no place for foreigners in his background, and no use for them in terms of personal experience. His was the heritage of the suave, sophisticated, cruelly self-sufficient ministers of immemorial Cathay. His learning was the Confucian classics, an arid discipline by which he had acquired a facility for reciting whole books backwards. His calligraphy, and his ability to improvise verses upon almost any theme—his essays were not quite so good but his memorials were highly thought of—had already gained him a place in the

Forest of Pencils, the Hanlin, as a Second Class Recorder. Yet he was by no means a recluse. On the contrary, his acrobatic intellect had, as his tutors intended, an ability to hop with disconcerting efficiency from one subject to another, in real life as among the scrolls of his library. Behind the façade of superiority as a cultured gentleman among clods, was a cynical, disillusioned power-seeking; and behind that again the hurt of his lost family and a lust for revenge against the Wangs; particularly since they who had presumed to lay hands upon his wife and children were not educated persons. He was, as one writer put it, 'panoplied in the suave certainty of his own ineffable superiority'.

If Li Hung Chang had dignity, so had Gordon, though the quality was in a different mode. Both used speech as a weapon: Li like a rapier, Gordon like a broadsword. Li had no morals but honoured the ancient rules. Gordon obeyed no man-made rules but held certain principles sacred. Li sailed to his destination, tacking with every wind, contradicting himself, switching loyalties, doing everything that a western gentleman must never do. Gordon drove to his objective as though by steam, not deviating from his course, not cringing to the weather, changing neither his mind nor his loyalties.

It might have seemed to Li that in the end both methods produced the same results. Heads still fell and friendships failed. Anger and despair were not diminished, nor was the character of a man changed by reason of his belief, or disbelief, in the intangible. Had not Confucius said that while ignorant persons can only be loyal to parties, people of culture should be loyal to individuals? According to his element and his life-line, a person is crude or cultured, benign or malignant. What he professes with his mouth, even the secret efforts of his mind, cannot alter his nature, which must by the Law of Heaven continue to work itself out within the combinations and permutations of the sixty-four Trigrams. For that reason the Master also said that no man can be changed once he is set (after forty years of age), and that a gentleman never competes.

Perhaps that was why Li never seems to have tried to set against Gordon's evangelical Christianity his philosophy of far older origins, and so left the Englishman with an unim paired sense of rectitude. It would be interesting to consider what would have happened if Gordon had taken to the study of the Trigrams and their associated literature. There was one lesson in particular which he needed from them: 'He who wishes to govern the world must first regulate his own household, and he who would regulate his household must begin by controlling his thoughts'. Apart from the defence of Will against Temptation, Gordon would neither know nor care about his thoughts. Still less would he have realised that the direct action of Will against emotion is dangerous if long continued. For the effect is to create repression which, like steam pressure, increases as Will holds down the safety-valve. Gordon's boiler was often on the point of bursting. If that had happened, and it nearly did, Li might have quoted the root cause in the lines, 'He who knows the male yet cleaves to what is female, receives all things under Heaven'.

So Li and Gordon had nothing in common except strength. This, in each other, they recognised and respected, so that in spite of their oil-and-water temperaments friendship was established on a basis of mutual respect; but that did not prevent Gordon's 'steam pressure' from mounting eventually to a point where he nearly killed the Chinaman. The Mandarin's respect is evident in his own comment, made early in their association: 'Gordon is superior in manner and bearing to all the foreigners I have come into contact with, and does not show outwardly that conceit which makes most of them repugnant in my sight. Besides, while he is possessed of a splendid military bearing, he is direct and business-like. Within two hours after his arrival, he was inspecting the troops and giving orders, and I could not but rejoice at the manner in which his commands were obeyed.'

Thus was the Ever Victorious Army set to earn its title, and young Gordon entered on that alien service of which his father so much disapproved. He must have been wonderfully elated as he began the shaking-up of his command, knowing that ahead of him, instead of a dreary sequence of barracks, was not only action, but independent action. He cared nothing for rewards in the eye of the world—his own phrase was 'a high name'—but he realised that he would not have been happy as a peacetime regimental officer, which now he might never have to be. He wrote home: 'You must not think that I am going to be rash in this matter. I have thought well over it and consider that I should not act wisely in refusing the same. I wish you to be satisfied that I will not D.V. remain out very long and I am sure, when you consider all things, you will think I have done right.'

Chapter 3

TREACHERY

WITH the efficient enthusiasm of an old-style school-master confronted by a class which has got out of hand, Gordon set about the Ever Victorious Army. From a military point of view there was as yet no great urgency in the situation, but he desperately needed a material enemy against whom to project the pent forces of his soul. So he drove himself and his men hard. For plans and parades, directives and discipline, there were not enough hours in the day. He worked also at night and took no regular meals.

His object, it seemed, was simply to destroy the enemy, an elimination of flesh-and-blood rebels; but he also thought of himself as confronted by 'principalities and powers' which, on the basis of 'fear not them that kill the body', were far more dangerous. He had a contempt for the fear of physical death, but he was scared of sin, and sin was creeping up on him. Unsupported by his own country's Minister, the object of official jealousy and scheming opportunism, betrayed by his officers and deserted by his men, Gordon drove on to victory up a road increasingly devious until, in loyalty to some of his enemies, he also became a man of violence, seeking vengeance against his superior officer for a blood-guilt which, if it existed at all, was certainly not Gordon's.

On the 31st of March 1863 he led into battle, from the deck of a paddle-steamer, his first independent command. His official position was so anomalous that it would have worried any-one with a less fanatic concept of duty. He was a Captain R.E., Brevet-Major in Army rank, acting Lieutenant-Colonel, behaving as a General and taking his basic instructions from Her Majesty's Minister in Pekin. He was also an officer (Mandarin) of the Chinese Government, and as such was under the orders of the Provincial Governor, who had every reason to differ from H.M.'s Minister and had no love at all for foreigners. He was an undenominational Christian fighting for pagans against heretics. He was an individual who tried in matters of honour to be such a paragon as was Rostand's *Cyrano de Bergerac*, yet lived among people who seemed to him to have no scruples of any kind. There was not a single person, European, American or Chinese, whom he could call an intimate friend. That isolation, which was to be at once the spur and the curb of his life, had begun. It would never leave him, whether at home or abroad, socially or officially.

The area of operations was some thirty thousand square miles, most of it highly cultivated, and so intersected by waterways that they carried as much day-to-day traffic as did the roads, which usually ran alongside them. There was one *massif* of considerable hills, but high ground usually consisted of little more than conical hummocks, bare and brown even in summer, and now with the frost hardly out of their friable sides. North and south ran the Grand Canal. East and west was a deep-water connection between Headquarters at Sung-kiang, Shanghai and the sea. In the middle of the area was Taiho Lake, as big as an inland sea and a natural hub for all the waterways.

The immediate objective, agreed with Governor Li, was a typical walled and moated town called Fushan. Gordon's two new-fangled iron steamers, followed by a straggle of local sailing boats, secretly landed his Ever Victorious Army on the 2nd of April. It may be imagined that the troops were far from enthusiastic, for the last action in the area had been Holland's ill-fated attack against Taitsan, which had caused the local Wangs so much amusement.

The following day Gordon spent in reconnaissance. That night he dismayed officers and men by having his one big gun moved up to a position where it was vulnerable to attack and difficult to withdraw. At seven in the morning it opened fire on the walls, and three-quarters of an hour later the attack went in against an enemy already breaking. Gordon's losses were two killed and six wounded.

Leaving three hundred men as garrison, he re-embarked without giving his troops time to rest, let alone to loot, and was soon steaming towards the next objective, Chanzu, where loyal defenders were being besieged. It was particularly important to raise the siege because not so long ago these defenders were themselves rebels. It would not encourage others to turn their coats if they were left to an unkind fate by their new friend, Li, who had been too slow to save Fushan and so had been forced to capture what was recently his own.

Gordon saw some of the men who had changed sides and been caught. When they had gone over to the Imperialists they had shaved their heads and so there had been no hope of concealing their sympathies. There were thirty-five of them just off the road which ran beside the waterway. Each had his own rough cross on which he had been toasted and sliced.

There were stakes sunk into the bed of the canal, and these had to be heaved out by tug-of-war teams on ropes, covered by a screen of riflemen. The ragged squadron pressed on, seeing the stockades before the town, beyond which rose the usual brown walls. At least the town had not yet fallen.

Since the stockades were built for the protection of besiegers from the town, they afforded little or no defence against the relieving force which, behind the big gun, now mounted on the leading steamer, blasted its way forward with a shower of grape-shot and musket-balls. Directing the clash of forces, Gordon may have had time to remember that over those walls in front of him were tossed, not so long ago, the heads of three European officers who had been members of Holland's force. The besieging Wang had had the happy notion that the dramatic presentation of such trophies would incline the defending turncoat to turn again and open the gates. Instead it made him cut off the heads of three hundred of his own troops so as to make his message to the rest quite unmistakable. It was, 'Fight on!'

They had done so to such good effect that not even the fall of their neighbour Fushan to the Wangs had weakened their determination not to be crucified. Now that they could see the Ever Victorious trying to live up to its name, they began to fire like fiends and then to sally. The besiegers broke and fled before Gordon's force was fully engaged. Typically, Gordon paused as briefly as possible, then turned back for his headquarters.

Governor Li was overjoyed. It seemed at last that Heaven was smiling again, perhaps because the dissolute Emperor was now officially dead, months after his actual decease. There was evidence of Heavenly justice, touched with humour, in that the barbarians who had humbled the Dragon Throne had not only failed to take military advantage of the situation, but had given the very man who had burned the Round Bright Garden to be the military servant of a Provincial Governor, in whose name—not England's—he would destroy the Taipings and restore 'face' to Pekin.

Li's amusement and satisfaction stemmed only from what came within his personal knowledge. He did not realise the full irony of the situation in that the War Office would neither take responsibility for Gordon and his force, nor would it recall him. Six months earlier Sir Frederick Bruce had written home to say he thought the appointment of British officers to the Chinese Service unwise. But the overland mail was unreliable and there was no cable station nearer than Suez. Then his despatch had almost sunk with the ship that carried it. Eventually it reached London. Meanwhile an Order in Council had confirmed the authority under which Gordon had been appointed, in a purely military capacity, by General Staveley. But Staveley was now on his way home and General Brown was taking over, while Bruce, having interviewed the sinuous and disgruntled Burgevine, agreed with his colleague, the American Minister, the Honourable Anson Burlinghame, that the man should be reinstated. Bruce accordingly wrote to Prince Kung, 'Sir Frederick Bruce must decline to allow officers of Her Majesty's Army to take any part in military operations further than may be necessary for the protection of British interests, and his first step, consequently, will be to desire that Major Gordon, and others serving with him at Shanghai, shall not pass the boundary described by the thirty-mile radius'.

Meanwhile from England a new hair-splitting achievement was coming out in the form of a letter from the Foreign Secretary, Lord John Russell, which read: 'The only rule Her Majesty's Government can lay down for the Chinese Service is that those officers who choose to go on half-pay with the Queen's licence should be at liberty to serve in any part of China they please; but the officers who retain their regimental rank should keep within the thirty-mile limit'. In due course this was going to reduce Gordon's establishment of English officers to two, for none but himself would lightly go on half-pay between the devil of the War Office and the deep blue sea of Li Hung Chang, but it came just in time to rescue him from an impossible position. For when he got back to headquarters and began to pull the Ever Victorious into a disciplined shape he was confronted by the challenge of an Imperial Commissioner accompanied by Burgevine. They presented themselves to Li and the Commissioner told him to get rid of Gordon and reinstate Burgevine. Anyone other than a Chinese scholar might have concluded that an order from the Throne ought to be obeyed. But Li recalled that in the Imperial Authority, as delegated to Provincial Governors, there was no provision for overruling the general competence of the Governors. Either they enjoyed the Royal Favour or they did not. If they did they ruled almost as kings within their allotted boundaries. If they did not they were banished or lost their heads. Li told the Commissioner that he refused his request, and put this decision in writing.

Gordon went on drilling and Burgevine returned to Shanghai, full of spleen and rancour. Li could afford to smile. It had been pleasant to be able to humiliate again the man who had laid hands upon his man of affairs. His cup would have overflowed had he known that the outer barbarians were quarrelling among themselves. In defence of the diplomatic hesitation and general infirmity of policy, it has to be admitted that for England to have been committed to further operations in China might have been a serious handicap to other far-flung enterprises. One of these even had a direct bearing upon the official attitude to Burgevine, who, as an American, was a person not to be offended while the United States remained testy over the effective help being given by the cruiser *Alabama* to the Confederate cause. The ship was not officially English, but it had been established that she had sailed to American waters from Liverpool.

The Maori war had broken out again in New Zealand and the force necessary to complete the pacification of that country was still uncalculated. War had begun with Japan, on a point of honour—the execution of an Englishman—and with much the same commercial objects in view as had led to the Treaty of Pekin. As if that were not enough, there was fear of war, even two wars, in Europe, by which England might be involved, through her usual hard-headed quixotry, in defending Denmark from Prussia and Austria, and the Poles from Russia.

*   *   *

At the beginning of May the Ever Victorious again went forth to battle, this time cooperating with General Ching, who had once been a Wang, and a brother of Li's called Santagen. The general idea was that while Santagen received the promised surrender of Taitsan, Gordon and Ching should take Quinsan. This time the Ever Victorious set out in good heart. Pay was regular and the rate acceptable at £4 : 10s. a month for privates and £30 for Lieutenants. Uniforms, dark green with dark-green turbans, were to be issued. Ships and guns were coming in under Gordon's continual pressure on the authorities at Shanghai. It seemed as though the operation would be cheap and glorious.

Taitsan was a big place as such towns went, with a garrison estimated at ten thousand. On its surrender there was every expectation that other towns would follow and the rebellion fade out with little more fighting. As usual, the plan of the place was a square with rounded corners defined by a wall and protected by a moat. There were only four gates, one for each of the cardinal points. By agreement with the garrison, one of these was to be opened to allow Santagen with his force to take over. They entered, and then the gates were shut behind them. This was odd, because presents had been exchanged between Li and the commanding Wang, and, therefore, treachery should have been against even the Taiping rules. Santagen escaped with a wound in his back, but most of his men had their heads chopped off.

The news of the massacre reached Gordon on his approach-march to Quinsan. He promptly changed his plans and went for Taitsan to avenge not only Santagen but Holland, whose abortive attempt had been made against that place.

His conduct of the operation, in spite of the emotional spur, was in marked contrast to Holland's. The column marched beside the waterway, but it was preceded by a well-designed steamer, *Hyson*, which, though sixty feet long and capable of carrying more than two hundred men with a pair of guns, one thirty-two and the other a twelve pounder, drew only three foot six of water. She even had a set of wheels to ease her along the soft bottom of a creek should she lightly ground. Her captain was an American called Davidson.

Gordon's reconnaissance was faultless. He knew the width of the moat to a foot, and its depth to an inch. He had plotted the position which his guns could occupy when disembarked, and had protected their crews with wooden mantlets which were quite sufficient to stop a ball from a smooth-bore gun. He had even calculated the trajectory of his howitzers so that they could drop shells behind the walls where past experience told him the mass of the enemy would be. As usual, he maintained personal control of the entire action, which was in itself a feat; for, on this occasion, there was no walk-over. The rebels must have had a shrewd idea that they might be treated impolitely if captured. They fought, therefore, in desperation, but also with skill. Twice the assault failed, and once again the close-packed rabble scrummaged in the breach. The guns were silent. Even rifles could not be brought to bear. This was the rebels' own style—blade and brute strength. Gordon appeared with his usual weapon—a 'swagger pole', a short cane. He never carried anything more lethal and so earned the repute of a charmed life and magical efficacy. Waving his swagger pole the 'General' pressed into the *mêlée*. The enemy wavered and broke. The Ever Victorious pursued them down the dirty, earthy streets, through the broken houses. Taitsan was won.

Gordon wrote home: 'I left Sung-kiang with some 3000 men on the 24th April and intended to attack Quinsan. However, before I had arrived at the place, intelligence reached me that the Taiping forces at Taitsan, who professed to come over to the Imperialists, had treacherously seized the party sent to take possession. I immediately changed my route and marched on Taitsan, attacked the two large stockades on one day and the town on the next. The rebels made a good fight but it was no use and the place fell. . . . I am now a Tsung Ping Mandarin (which is the second highest grade) and have acquired a good deal of influence. I do not care about that overmuch. I am quite sure I was right in taking over command, as you would be if you saw the ruthless character of the rebels. Taitsan is a large place and was strongly held. It is a Fu, or capital city.'

Within Taitsan some discoveries were made, which Gordon did not mention—presumably because they reflected upon his countrymen. The place had been a rebel arsenal, of which the stock betrayed the extent to which Europeans had been smuggling arms, ammunition, stores and even field pieces. They had set up their own shot-factory and armouries. No wonder an English wounded prisoner, brought before Gordon, expected the firing-squad. The order for it was given for all to hear, but in a lower tone Gordon gave instructions that the man be sent back to the doctor.

Native rebels, captured by their own countrymen, were not so lucky; though the majority of them escaped the fate they expected by displaying enthusiasm for the idea of joining the Imperialist forces. Seven 'examples' were made, for which barbarous executions Gordon did not escape blame, though it is difficult to see how anyone could seriously have believed him guilty. He had no authority over 'General' Ching, who, as an ex-rebel himself, was the obvious source of the order as the result of which the seven men 'were tied up and exposed to view for about five hours previous to decapitation, with an arrow or two forced through the skin in various parts of the body, and a piece of skin flayed from one arm'. The biographer's style succeeds almost in suggesting that the process was merely uncomfortable and the sentence whimsical; but the incident stirred up such a storm that Official Channels, from the Foreign Secretary downwards, became involved. General Brown wrote to Governor Li that if anything of the sort happened again, England would cease to support the Imperialist cause. The Press invented details to please sadistic readers, and followed up this incident with others, whether real or imaginary. At last Gordon, who hated print almost as much as sin, had to write in the *Shanghai Shipping News*, 'I am of the belief that the Chinese of this force are quite as merciful in action as the soldiers of any Christian nation could be; and, in proof of this, can point to over 700 prisoners, taken in the last engagement, who are now in our employ. Some have entered our ranks and done service against the rebels since their capture. But one life has been taken out of this number, and that one was a rebel who tried to induce his comrades to fall on the guard, and who was shot on the spot. . . . If "Observer" and "Eye-Witness" with their friend "Justice and Mercy" would come forward and communicate what they know, it would be far more satisfactory than writing statements of the nature of those alluded to by the Bishop of Victoria.'

This letter, however necessary, seems odd in view of what Gordon must already have known about the play of Chinese. He was never intentionally insincere, and so one can only conclude that he had successfully repressed the disagreeable notion that the people with whom he was fighting were hardly chivalrous. If this be the case, later outbursts of his become explicable—in our terms. But they must have been out of Gordon's knowledge, or control, for he had little or no insight into his own mind, still less into his heart. It would no more have occurred to him that he was heading for a nervous explosion than that the letters were only sadistic phantasies having little or no connection with fact—which they probably were.

* * *

Gordon marched, or rather sailed, on Quinsan and proceeded forthwith to arrange for its capture, driving his brave, tired troops without respite, in punishment for their looting of Taitsan. Such discipline was an unheard-of thing to a force which had long relied upon booty, if not for pay, then at least for allowances; but Gordon remembered Yuen-Ming-Yuen. So shaken was their newly-born *esprit de corps* that Gordon called off the battle and marched them smartly back to headquarters. By doing so he lost the tactical advantage of the impetus and the prestige gained by his recent resounding victory. Nor did the unrest subside; instead it was fanned even by regimental, *i.e.* unit, commanders, ostensibly because of the appointment of Lieutenant-Colonel Cooksley to be in charge of stores, arms and commissary. Hitherto unit commanders had evidently found it profitable to divert to others some of the material drawn for their own troops. They may even have been trading in arms and ammunition with the rebels. By putting in a senior officer—and an Englishman—Gordon made further profits unlikely along those lines, and at the same time gained a second-in-command whom he could trust. But he also provided the detonator for an explosion. On marching orders being posted, the majors presented a demand that they all be promoted to Cooksley's pay and rank. When Gordon refused they handed him their resignations. These Gordon had to accept because there was no international military discipline outside the Ever Victorious itself. He did not accept their magnanimous offer to accompany him for one last battle, and he insisted that the force should parade as ordered, less those officers, at eight o'clock the following morning.

When the hour came round the only men on parade were those of Gordon's bodyguard, which then consisted of just six stolid Chinese. They included a sergeant who wore four stripes and a whistle, a corporal with a proper pair of stripes, and a heavyweight private soldier who affected a much larger and darker turban than the rest. No doubt the majors thought there would be nothing Gordon could do about the situation they had created. Having accepted their resignations for immediate effect he could not arrest them, and with so few loyal men he would be powerless to deal with the rest of the force. Gordon sought out the N.C.O.s of the First Regiment, whom he suspected of being the ringleaders. In any case they would have ranked senior to the other regiments according to the universal convention of the time, which would put them in battle on the right of the line. His bodyguard arrested them and put them in chains, Chinese fashion.

That gesture completed, there should have been another impasse, but the officers now showed signs of weakening. Perhaps they thought that Gordon would shoot his prisoners and that the anger of the men would turn on themselves. At all events the majors reappeared and offered to withdraw their resignations, no doubt with the idea that if the proposition were accepted they would become the real masters of the army. Gordon told them coldly that his orders still stood as they were written. The Ever Victorious, presumably consisting only of Cooksley, himself and his bodyguard, would proceed towards Quinsan. They would, however, halt at a place about half-way to their objective and there call the roll. Those answering to their names would be reinstated and no proceedings would be taken against them. Others would be dismissed.

The officers gave in. Gordon tore up their resignations. The prisoners were unchained. With a full complement the army took the road to war, in which all ranks displayed every evidence of loyalty and were brave beyond the demands of duty. Victory was their reward. When night fell the *Hyson* was churning along in the wake of a confused mass of seven or eight thousand rebels—the fleeing garrison. These unfortunates were confined to the single escape route offered by a road alongside the canal, for to attempt to go across country involved swimming the frequent water channels which ran into the main waterway; and few Taipings could swim. So complete was the demoralisation of this retreat that Gordon ordered the steamer's fore gun not to fire except when the rebels showed signs of returning morale. Otherwise they could have been massacred by a scythe of grape-shot cutting into the compact mass of scared men. They were afraid not only because they were in flight. There was a devilish power about the steamer, whose red and green lights, plume of smoke and steam, and plashing paddles, awakened in them the superstitions which all primitive people share. The steam whistle, which *Hyson* blew continuously, clinched the matter: Gordon and his 'false foreign devils' were devils indeed.

The casualties were exemplary: Enemy, fifteen hundred, with a further fifteen hundred prisoners: Ever Victorious, two killed, five wounded, no prisoners. Nor was this due only to the magical effectiveness of the steamers. The convoy included as many as eighty vessels, flatteringly called 'gunboats', which were rather troop transports. From these the lately mutinous soldiers disembarked for a series of short actions as obstacles presented themselves or parties of the enemy appeared upon the flanks. So great was the moral victory that local authorities ordered up from Shanghai a quantity of Army boots. These they issued under such circumstances that the spoor of foreign devils, typical as that from cloven feet, would everywhere remind waverers where lay their loyalty, hearten honest men, intimidate cravens and bewilder spies.

* * *

E

On withdrawal of the Ever Victorious to their headquarters, General Ching garrisoned Quinsan, but not before the civil population had wreaked their own vengeance to the extent of several thousand casualties, to which must be added a large number drowned. With them, as with Governor Li and authority in general, Gordon was now most honourable, in token of which he was raised to the rank of Red Button, equivalent to Brigadier; 'but I do not wear the dress, as you may suppose'. In the same letter he said that scurrilous rumours were being circulated, for instance, that he had accepted £2000 not to take Quinsan, and in another context, 'I dare say I shall be loudly attacked in the House of Commons'. The question of harshness to prisoners was still worrying him: 'You may hear of cruelties being committed. Do not believe them. . . . If I had time I could tell such extraordinary stories of the way men from distant provinces meet one another, and the way villagers recognise in our ranks old rebels who have visited their villages for plunder; but I really have no time for it. I took a Mandarin, who had been a rebel for three years, and have him now. He has a bullet in his cheek, which he received when fighting against the rebels. The rebels I took into my guard were snake-flag bearers of head chiefs, and they are full of the remarks of their old masters. The snake-flags are the marks of headmen in both armies. Whenever they are seen there is a chief present. When they go, you know the rebels will retire. At Taitsan the snake-flags remained till the last, and this accounted for a very severe fight.'

There follows a note which suggests that, in spite of the promised new uniforms, not much progress had yet been made in the clothing of the troops: 'I have some four English officers with me; we wear anything we can get, and the men are almost in rags'. Yet they were better off than many of the rebels who were lucky enough to escape a worse fate at the hands of the liberated populace. These were utterly stripped, and could be discerned creeping about the countryside, or inadequately concealing themselves in the new grass.

The Ever Victorious shared little in the general rejoicing. They had again been denied loot, and now Gordon ordained that they should shift headquarters to Quinsan, where they would have none of the home comforts which they had gradually acquired in the long stretches of easy life at Sung-kiang between the infrequent and short operations which had been the rule under Ward and Burgevine. The general feeling was further embittered by a cumulative jealousy on the part of the Imperialist troops of General Ching, who had shared none of the glory of the campaign and so had lost face. On the other hand they had been much more comfortable, of which the Ever Victorious were jealous.

The enmity soon flared up. A detachment of Gordon's troops, conspicuous with one of the big flags which regiments were accustomed to carry on parade and into battle, was fired upon by some of Ching's men. Gordon protested, only to have his fury increased when Ching, that ex-Wang, dismissed the incident as a mistake or a joke. To 'fire on the flag' was not a thing Gordon could take lightly, and he threatened to turn his force against Ching's to avenge the insult, which would have put him in the impossible position of fighting both the Imperialists, who were, after all, his employers, and the rebels. Fortunately he soon thought better of his rash threat, but the incident remains as a hint of the way in which he was feeling the strain, and as a precedent for a kind of irresponsible action which later on was to have serious consequences. He was already a man divided against himself. The repression of his boiling emotions by duty in terms of a fierce and friendless discipline, was continually being increased, not only by the contrariness of his nature but also by the assault of cruel experience upon his kind mysticism.

While the common people starved to death he had seen rebel leaders clothed in fine raiment, pearls in their turbans. He knew their Supreme Lord, Tien Wang, now hardly left his harem in Nankin. He had also seen a girl in a village whose hands had been tied behind her, her breasts cut off and her belly ripped. He had resonated to the misery of the innocent while opportunists turned their coats by the moon, and no man was safe from the traitor and the spy. Some villages even had two headmen, one for the rebels and one for the Imperialists, each paying the taxes demanded by his appropriate authority. In the icy loneliness of command, surrounded by officers who themselves, with one or two exceptions, were no better than his traitorous N.C.O.s, Gordon must have questioned to the point of desperation those over-simple dogmas which had served him well enough in easier times. Having come to believe that a God of infinite mercy is the ultimate agent for all actions, there is something more than shocking about a group of children with their throats cut.

No wonder he drove himself and others harder than was necessary or reasonable. Brother officers wrote: 'He told us that it was a great source of wonder to many around him how his life was sustained, for he said it was generally at night that he would pay a visit to the larder or commissariat, when he would suck ten or a dozen eggs and so satisfy his need'.

'Gordon's activity, zeal and energy were wonderful; for work he was a perfect glutton. . . . For months on end he hardly took his boots or clothes off at night. He would go to his boat and turn into a couple of blankets sewn up in the form of a sack.'

*   *   *

So, in spite of more regular pay, the virtual certainty of win-ning their war, glory and the promise of reward, another mutiny, more serious than either of the preceding ones, became inevitable. This time it was planned so as to leave no loophole through which the General could fire his moral courage and exercise his penetrating will-power, which at times could be almost hypnotic. The officers may have been at the bottom of the plot, but the N.C.O.s again took action, this time backed by the men. A proclamation was drawn up and posted in camp. It called upon Gordon to rescind his order about moving headquarters or the gunners would blow him to bits together with his loyal officers.

When ordered to parade, the troops refused, but the N.C.O.s came forward in a body to press their demands. Gordon listened, then told them coldly that his orders re-mained, and that they would be carried out. The mutineers must have realised that by material power they were now domi-nant. Perhaps his impotent fury struck them as ridiculous. At his words a loud groan of derision arose from among them. Gordon's self-control snapped. Perhaps he allowed it to, for the situation was beyond argument. He laid hands upon the loudest groaner and dragged him from the rest. He said to a loyal soldier, 'Shoot him'. In an instant it was done. The dying man fell at the feet of his friends, and over the twitching body Gordon's pale eyes blazed into the stolid Chinese faces. A few minutes later the N.C.O.s were all locked up with an ultimatum. Either they gave the name of their ringleader—the person responsible for the proclamation—or, at the end of twenty minutes, one in five would be shot. Within the allotted time a name was given, and whether by coincidence or out of expedient tact, it belonged to the man who had been shot. Gordon accepted it. The mutineers were presumed to have been mere dupes and were released. The moving of headquarters was carried out in good order and with military discipline.

Gordon began to plan offensive action, as much to give the force something better than mutiny to think about as to exploit the success already gained. Victory was his, but it did not turn the disgruntled troops into guardsmen. They began to melt away, until only half the force was left in the new headquarters, where the officers were plotting again; and Ching, smarting under Gordon's rebuke, was intriguing with Li Hung Chang against him. Li contributed to the demoralisation of the force by his old trick of holding back pay and refusing to settle accounts for shipping and other equipment. Nor was he acting on his own authority, for the success of the Ever Victorious had been too much to the credit of Gordon, so that in high places, even perhaps with the consent of Prince Kung, it was now policy to hamper him.

In Shanghai there were other plots. Having failed to regain his post by intrigue, Burgevine was secretly recruiting a new force which he intended to place at the disposal of the Wangs. Gordon got wind of this and would have been able to stop it if Burgevine had not taken the trouble to write personally denying that there was any truth in the rumour. Gordon believed him. Even so, he felt that the general circumstances of his command had become intolerable in spite of all his brilliant endeavour and his good success. He wrote to Li Hung Chang: 'Your Excellency, In consequence of monthly difficulties I experience in getting payment of the force made, the non-payment of bills for boat-hire and necessities of war from her

Britannic Majesty's Government, who have done so much for the Imperial Chinese authorities, I have determined on throwing up the command of this force, as my retention of office in these circumstances is derogatory to my position as a British Officer, who cannot be a suppliant for what Your Excellency knows to be necessities, and should be happy to give. As my resignation of this command will necessitate the knowledge of the British Minister and General, I have forwarded to them copies of this letter and have to add I will remain in command of the force till such time as I have received their replies.'

Disillusioned and deflated, Gordon took ship for Shanghai where he would justify his action to General Brown and the Minister. It could have been only bitter consolation that he now saw each side in the war as equally ignoble. 'Let them stew in their own juice' must have been his dominant thought as the drab banks slid by to the rhythmic splosh of the paddle-wheels. What could one do for such people? One did one's duty, and as to that he had still an unclouded conscience.

The same evening the man who had warned Gordon of Burgevine's plot was also waterborne. His name was Doctor Halliday Macartney. He had found the life of an Army surgeon dull and profitless, so had entered the Chinese service under Li, for whom he ran an arsenal while commanding certain of his forces.

He saw the screw-steamer *Kajow* tied up to a quay; and as he casually noted that she was fitted out for war, a bunch of men rushed her gangplank and took possession of her, casting off and steaming for rebel territory. Macartney had his own boat brought into the bank, leaped ashore, borrowed a horse and went galloping after the *Kajow*. If he had any doubt about the sinister way she had sailed it was soon dispelled by the fire which was opened upon him. He kept on, however, passed her, and tried to induce one of Li's boats to block her way. The boatmen, valuing their lives, refused to help and the *Kajow* churned past, carrying Burgevine on his way to take up an even odder position than Gordon's. He was going to be a Wang, and behind the title of doubtful distinction he cherished a dream of power as ambitious, and as ruthless, as that of his late enemies.

So delicately poised were the factions, that Burgevine's theatrical departure with his thirty-odd henchmen caused something near panic in Pekin, where it was believed that the Ever Victorious, or what remained of them, would soon follow, and so give the rebels a decisive superiority not only in men, which they already possessed, but in arms, discipline and initiative. In that case Gordon's campaign might never have been fought, and then, if the new masters of China took advantage of the international situation, the same might have to be said about the Anglo-French campaign also. Sir Frederick Bruce wrote to Lord John Russell: 'A man who might have been a friend has been converted into a danger- ous enemy. Major Gordon and the Chinese are now put on the defensive. Burgevine may organise an expedition to Pekin. There is a possibility that he may receive support from the brigands in Shantung, and, if he were successful at Pekin, it would certainly mean the overthrow of the present dynasty.'

In this emergency Gordon's resignation could not be ac- cepted and he rode back urgently to Quinsan to try to stop the rot. It must have seemed to him there that there is no end to man's treachery and that his work had been deprived of all moral significance. Each of the European powers had in- trigued secretly against the others. All had been played off, one against the others, by the Chinese. Among the Im- perialists the war had become an occupation, not a crusade. Even Governor Li made a business out of it, to his own financial advantage. Among the rebels the same thing was true, though their military opportunism was even more marked in contrast to the religious pretensions of the Wangs, who were now living in palaces. The unkindest consideration of all to Gordon must have been that his knightly rôle had degenerated into that of Li's catspaw. His force had done the fighting, sustained the losses, while enormously superior Im- perialist armies stood around, for instance, at Nankin, and watched with patronising professional interest the strategy and tactics of the first and only barbarian Tsung-Ping.

The necessary steps were taken to minimise the effects of Burgevine's defection. General Brown assumed responsibility for all the military forces, including the Ever Victorious, whose headquarters he removed to Taitsan where there was

less risk that a mutiny would result in further reinforcements
to the rebels. Gordon was still in command, but was ordered
to take no offensive action. His position was, therefore, even
more stressful than before, his loneliness and sense of futility
greater. Some of the officers left to him were friends of Burgevine, with whom they were probably in communication,
plotting against Gordon. In such circumstances he could find
refuge only in faith. It alone could keep him unconquered and
incorruptible. Inevitably in his spiritual exercises he must
have turned further away from the world of which he already
had such a low opinion, and thereby increased, not de-
creased, the ultimate weight of his loneliness. For his inspiration came from that austere and solitary contemplative,
Thomas à Kempis, a man who had written, or at least inspired, a textbook of that branch of mysticism which negates
the second Great Commandment by substituting for its
splendid simplicity, 'Love thy neighbour', a negative set of
rules, the object of which is to cut off this world; which inevitably includes the neighbours and thyself.

In defence of asceticism it is implied that some individuals
outgrow the needs of common souls, becoming in their neigh-
bourless seclusion a channel for grace. Such individuals appear in all cultures, but they are rare and Gordon certainly
was not one of them, even if à Kempis was. Being in this
world, and very much so because of his profession of arms,
Gordon's effort to reject it was a painful psychological futility.
It was even dangerous because of the associated repression,
only occasionally relieved by such a spontaneous gesture as
the rescue of a little boy from a ditch, 'his muddy paws all over
my jacket'. The world appeared to Gordon desperately
wicked. He would have no part in it. He would tear out all
the teeth which it had sunk in him. He would build round the
live coals of his *mystique* a wall of ice to cut him off from all
that body hungered or soul yearned for.

And so he was driven to try to imitate his Master, who
saved the world by loving it and was the friend of all sorts and
conditions of men, by hating the world and allowing neither
man nor woman to touch his heart. Therefore he had to
travel, in all humility, a barren path of spiritual pride, on
which the only signposts were chapter-headings from à

Kempis, grim concepts from a creed which fails to recognise that there are no negative virtues:

> Contempt for Worldly Vanities
> Inordinate Affection
> Avoiding Familiar Intercourse with the World
> Superfluous Talking
> The Consideration of Human Misery
> The Meditation of Death
> Self-Abasement
> Self-Denial and the Renunciation of Animal Desire
> In Man there is No Good
> Contempt for Temporal Honour
> The Vanity of Learning

*   *   *

For two months this tense interlude lasted, and then General Brown released the Ever Victorious for further action with the object of taking the rebel capital of the north, Soochow. Gordon leaped at the task with all his old enthusiasm, though he had under his command less than four thousand men. The Imperial Troops numbered some fourteen thousand, under Ching, who could only be relied upon to let Gordon do all the hard work, and even to intrigue against him out of jealousy. The rebels had forty thousand men in and round Soochow, with another thirty-eight thousand potential reserves.

Gordon's minor successes apparently went unnoticed by the high command of the Wangs, though General Brown, with Li Hung Chang, could heave a sigh of relief. Gordon now found that Burgevine's friends in his own force were more of an advantage than otherwise, for through them information freely passed.

Burgevine's reception by the Wangs had been regal, but his propensity for talking much and doing little had soon got him into difficulties. Through his contacts in Shanghai he had undertaken to procure quantities of warlike stores and had been given a large sum of money with which to pay for them. He journeyed in disguise and arranged for the purchases through American channels. Gordon wrote: 'Burgevine has been down at Shanghai, and escaped by a very little being captured. The United States Marshall, who has a nephew in this force, was seized in a lorcha with nine others. Two other boats with arms were captured, and Burgevine jumped into the river. This shows what men these Americans are! This United States Marshall pretended that no one was on board the boat, but the men were found below.'

Burgevine escaped. Back at Soochow with neither money nor arms, he was promptly put under arrest by the Wangs, who also began to be impolite to the Europeans he had brought over with him. Unabashed, he was soon plotting again, this time to persuade Gordon to join forces with him and take on both the Imperialists and the rebels. To a man with Gordon's code of duty the offer was nothing but magniloquent eyewash; yet there may have been a grain of sense in it. China was at the time a splendid subject for the old prescription 'divide and rule'. Both sides were exhausted and foreigners were not now going to make a decisive intervention. Round the nucleus of the Ever Victorious and the hard core of Burgevine's veterans there was a vast potential, to be recruited from the disgruntled and opportunist elements in both camps.

His offer contemptuously refused, Burgevine next attempted to escape from Soochow, was apprehended, and put in some danger of losing his head, while his fellow foreigners had an increasingly difficult time. Gordon promptly tried to rescue him, and even wrote a formal letter to his captors:

To their Excellencies, Chung Wang, Moh Wang,

YOUR EXCELLENCIES,
    You must be already aware that I have on all occasions, when it lay in my power, been merciful to your soldiers when taken prisoners. . . . I now ask your Excellencies to consider the case of the Europeans in your service. In every army each soldier must be actuated with faithful feelings to fight well. A man made to fight against his will is not only a bad soldier, but he is a positive danger, causing anxiety to his leaders, and absorbing a large force to prevent his defection. If there are many Europeans left in Soochow, I would ask your Excellencies if it does not seem very much better to let these men quietly leave your service if they wish it; you would thereby get rid of a continual source of suspicion, gain the sympathy of the whole of the

foreign nations, and feel that your difficulties are all from without.

Your Excellencies may think that decapitation would soon settle the matter, but you would then be guilty of a crime which would bear its fruits sooner or later. . . . Your Excellencies may rely on what I say, that should you behead the Europeans who are with you, or retain them against their free will, you will eventually regret it. . . . Your Excellencies may depend you will not suffer by letting these men go; you need not fear their communicating information. I knew your force, men and guns, long ago, and, therefore, care not to get that information from them. . . . I write the above with my own hand, as I do not wish to entrust the matter to a linguist; and trusting that you will accede to my request, I conclude,

Your Excellencies' obedient servant,
C. G. GORDON
Major Commanding

With the letter went a present of a pony, but there does not seem to have been any response from the Wangs. Meanwhile Burgevine had the idea of re-establishing himself with the Wangs by capturing Gordon for them. For this purpose he confided in Jones, the American captain of the *Kajow*, who was an old friend and had lent his support to Burgevine's work with his ship. Jones drew the line against betraying a man who at some risk had tried to rescue him, and Burgevine resented his attitude so much that when, thanks to Gordon, the Wangs let him go, he took the first opportunity to draw a gun. Jones later deposed before the United States Consul: 'At noon I went to Burgevine who was lying asleep on board a 32-pounder gunboat, and asked him whether I should assist him to get ashore, as many of our officers and men were making remarks on the condition he was in. On his demanding the names of those who had made the remarks I declined giving them and shortly afterwards again attempted to remonstrate with him, in company with another officer. On my declining to give up names, Burgevine drew out his four-barrelled pistol, which he cocked and discharged at my head from a distance of about nine inches. The bullet entered my left cheek and passed upwards. It has not yet been extracted. I exclaimed, "You have shot your best friend!" His answer was, "I know I have, and I wish to God I had killed you!" '

Burgevine, far from hanging his head, wrote to a local paper, 'Captain Jones' account of the affair is substantially correct; and I feel great pleasure in bearing testimony to his veracity and candour whenever any affair with which he is personally acquainted is concerned'.

Chapter 4

HEADLESS KINGS

WITH Burgevine out of the way, Gordon in hot and enervating weather went ahead with his plan to cut off Soochow from the surrounding towns. But he was not yet clear of the net of treachery, even among his own officers. For instance, Captain Perry wrote an unwise letter to a pro-rebel. It contained intelligence about forthcoming operations; a spy's work made the more dangerous because Perry would have to take part in them. The fact gave Gordon an idea. Instead of having the young man executed, he was told that when the next forlorn hope required a leader, he would have the privilege of doing that job; to be forgiven if he survived, but in all probability to be shot by the enemy, instead of by a squad of his own troops.

Opportunity soon came. The rebel fire was accurate and heavy. Gordon crouched with his men in a ditch opposite the only breach in the town's walls. Beside him was Perry. Gordon told him that his time had come—to lead the charge. Perry did so. But even in such a case Gordon would not send any man where he himself would not go. So Gordon was beside him as he dashed forward. Perry managed to get ahead of his commander, and there received in the mouth a bullet which otherwise would have struck Gordon himself. Perry fell into the arms of the man he had betrayed for little reason and no effective reward. There he died. The charge had meanwhile succeeded. The town was won. Gordon's laconic comment is that Perry 'was such an owlet that it [the spying] made no difference'.

After heavy fighting for similar towns in the area, in most of which casualties were relatively low—until some of the Ever Victorious were caught in the cross-fire of their own artillery—Soochow was sealed off from reinforcement by land or water. The only communication still left open was by a track so rough and narrow that Gordon decided he could afford to ignore it. By this time General Ching's troops were

closely investing the city, but they left to the Ever Victorious
the dangerous task of capturing the stockades which protected
the outer earthworks, moat, and walls.

It was here that Gordon suffered his only unqualified
defeat. At two o'clock in the morning of the 27th of November
1863, he launched his first night attack. It failed to impress
the enemy, let alone dislodge him. The unique failure must
have pleased Ching, and perhaps also Li Hung Chang, as
much as victory would have done. For Ching had a blood-
brother among the chiefs of the defenders, a certain Lar
Wang, who was to become Gordon's favourite martyr.
Between them it was arranged that the North Gate, Lar's
particular charge, should be given up to Ching's troops on
condition that Ching would protect his 'brother' from the
vengeance of the other Wangs, and even try to safeguard his
troops. They were to wear white turbans so as to be recognised.

As professional soldiers, they would have given due credit
to Gordon for bringing them to this happy position of being
able to honour their blood-brotherhood in so pacific a fashion.
For Gordon it was who had so outfought the rebels, even at
odds of ten to one, that prudent persons, such as Lar, could
no longer see any future for the movement, which had come
so far from the original vision of the Heavenly King. They
might instead look forward to the day when, the war being
over, they would get rid of the Ever Victorious and its
honourable commander. Save in times of danger he was no
more acceptable to General Ching than to Lar Wang, who
were, after all, Chinese. They would not have been so foolish
as to try to attack on the 27th, for any Chinese would have
believed that the operation was foredoomed because there
was that night an eclipse of the moon. Not even the omens of
Heaven were appreciated by foreign devils.

In all probability the eclipse, and not any failure of plan,
was the cause of that unique defeat, though for an entirely
practical reason. Gordon had under-estimated the immense
asset of his personal command. At night his men could not
see him, and to be brave they needed the example of his
leadership, the sight of his magic wand, the sound of his voice.
They were even less inclined to take risks when the moon was
eaten out of the sky.

Ching could not keep the plot he was hatching with Lar secret from Li Hung Chang, and so from Gordon; though no doubt he would have preferred to do so. Gordon, therefore, took the initiative from him. It seemed that Soochow would fall without a shot fired, and so bring the campaign, and Gordon's service, to an end. For he had no intention of carrying on a moment longer than his duty to England required. It was at this juncture that Burgevine, that indefatigable opportunist, profited by the promise Gordon had made to preserve his liberty. This time it was the steamer *Firefly* that his men got away with, under the official noses of General Brown and the Inspector of Customs, both of whom were to have embarked in her at Shanghai. And so they would have done had she left as intended, but the General overruled Gordon's orders for her immediate return to Soochow in support. The mail had just come in and the General wished to peruse it before embarking, so the sailing hour was postponed and Burgevine's men had their chance. Burgevine was not present at the seizure of the ship, which was as powerful as the *Hyson*, Gordon's flagship; but he was captured while boarding a smaller ship, and this time kept under arrest.

Gordon was furious, for the *Firefly* would complicate matters considerably if she could come into action in time. The surrender of Soochow, therefore, became a matter of urgency. He gave a personal assurance to all the Wangs that if only they would yield they would be well treated, perhaps even be given commands in the Imperialist forces which would have ahead of them the job of finishing off the rebels in the south, where Tien Wang was still a rival Emperor. Just as this offer seemed about to produce results, there was another setback. Along that disregarded track Chung Wang, the most able military commander in the rebel cause, bearing the magical sword of the Heavenly King, entered the city and rallied its vacillating chiefs. Gordon attacked, and was beaten back behind his own stockades.

'Further than the eye could penetrate in the misty morning stretched the grizzled walls of Soochow, a city celebrated for ages in the history of China for its size, population, wealth and luxury, but now stripped of its magnificence. . . . To the right and left, mile after mile, rose the line of lofty wall and grey turret, while above all appeared not only the graceful pagodas, which have for ages been the boast of Soochow, and the dense foliage of secular trees—the invariable glory of Chinese cities—but also the shimmering roofs of newly decorated palaces confidently occupied by the vainglorious leaders of the rebellion. The proximity of the rebel line became apparent with surprising suddenness, for, following their usual custom, they greeted the rising sun with a simultaneous display of gaudy banners above the line of their entrenchments. The mud walls they had thrown up in advance, scarcely distinguishable before, were now marked out by thousands of flags of every colour from black to crimson, whilst behind them rose the jangling roll of gongs and the murmurs of an invisible multitude.' So wrote an English observer before Gordon had completed the investment, at a cost of thirteen officers and a hundred and fifty-four men, the heaviest losses of the campaign and an astonishing tribute, in that atmosphere of bad faith, to the battle-loyalty of his opportunist adventurers.

It seemed as though Soochow, like Nankin, might be able to hold out indefinitely; but the defenders had a different impression, so much so that even Chung Wang took his departure as secretly as he had come, having decided that he could not succeed in keeping Gordon out. He went to Nankin to report to the Tien Wang that Soochow would fall, and left behind, in the charge of a trusted friend, his ceremonial sword. This blade, consecrated by the 'False Emperor', was considered by the Taipings to be so august that he who wielded it could without guilt cut off the head of anyone in the Empire. Wrapped in dragon-embroidered yellow silk, it had been carried behind Chung Wang in battle; and so it would have been again but for a counter-revolution in the custodian's home town. While he was away the people rose against him and sacked his house where the sword was kept. To show where their feelings lay they sent the thing to Gordon, who might, if he had wished, have gained much 'face' thereby. But to display such a proof of superiority would have smacked of boastfulness, so he made no use of the trophy. Instead, he presented it, in due course, to the Duke of Cambridge.

So soon as Chung was clear of Soochow, the pacific Lar opened negotiations for surrender, only to be thwarted by Moh, the Captain of the City. For though each 'King' disposed of a separate force over which he alone had direct authority, necessity forced them to give an overriding authority to someone during the siege. In accord with his position, Moh Wang called a conference of all the rebel chiefs with the object of heartening them to continue resistance. As was usual, they met in a palace—his own, and began their deliberations only after a prayer meeting and a banquet. It was a dignified and impressive affair with robes of ceremony and all the mock-royal trappings which the Taipings affected.

After the meal they adjourned to the great hall, where Moh took the chief place on a dais at the head of a table. He made a speech, urging them to be fearless and strong, warning them that there were intending traitors among them. The scene must have had a macabre overtone of blasphemous comparison, for there was a potential Judas to Li Hung Chang's Pilate and Ching's High Priest. While Moh was yet speaking the Judas-Wang put off his robe, drew a dagger, and with it stabbed Moh nine times in the back. Moh died upon the steps of his throne. His body was dragged out into the courtyard where it was beheaded and otherwise mutilated. A message was promptly sent to General Ching to say that opposition to the plan of surrender was no longer to be feared.

That same night, the 4th of December, the gates were opened from within and Ching's troops made a token entry. The garrison were allowed to remain under arms. This being the case, Gordon was more than usually careful that the Ever Victorious did not get the chance to start looting; for that might have begun a fight which they would have been bound to lose. The troops for their part resented the prohibition more than ever, for Soochow was by far the richest place to fall, and it was they who had borne the brunt of the fighting. Now it looked as though the pickings would go to Ching's men, who had done little more than watch.

Gordon forced an interview with Li on the following day. He demanded for his men a bonus of two months' pay in lieu of loot and, when Li refused, told him that he would forthwith

F

resign. Li, after some hesitation, compromised to the extent of offering one month's pay, which Gordon had to accept, even though, on breaking the news to his men, he was almost faced with yet another mutiny. He, therefore, decided to march them off to Quinsan out of the way of temptation; but so hostile was the feeling, that Gordon himself had to stand guard—for once armed with a revolver—at the entrance to Li's tent while the Ever Victorious went by. Within, Li must have been hugging himself with his hands in his wide sleeves, for, with brother Santagen and ex-Wang Ching, he had contrived a surprise for Gordon—a demonstration of the superior and more subtle methods of the Chinese as compared with those of the barbarians.

That crisis past, Gordon went to meet the Wangs as they rode out to surrender. He found them cheerful and confident, an attitude which does not seem to have struck him as strange in the circumstances. Yet it was only to be accounted for by the fact that the person who had promised them life and liberty was he who had burned the Round Bright Garden. Such a man, unafraid even of the Emperor, could surely be relied upon to protect his ex-enemies from the vengeance of a Provincial Governor. Their confidence would have been increased by the banquet, with which they were to be regaled; for once they became Li's guests they would have the additional protection of the laws of hospitality—forgetting how little use these had been to Moh Wang! Seeing them ride off, Gordon felt well pleased. He wrote that they were 'in capital spirits' and, on the spur of the moment, asked Lar Wang to come with him on board a steamer.

It is nowhere suggested that Gordon had any specific reason for such an odd request, though it is hinted that he may have been afraid for Lar, as the one Wang who was his personal responsibility. But it seems likely that the real reason was to try to find out what were the terms of the deal which Lar had made privately with General Ching. If Lar refused to reveal all he knew, Gordon could easily have put pressure to bear on him, even with a blade on his neck. But Lar refused the invitation and rode away with the others to their honourable surrender.

The situation was rendered even more bizarre, and insult-

ing to Li Hung Chang, by Gordon's refusal to be present at
the ceremonial meal, which should have been in his honour.
That Li had only given him half the pay he had asked for was
a minor matter. After that incident he had constituted himself the Governor's personal bodyguard. It is conceivable that
he rated the affair as a mere social function on a par with a
London dinner-party; but he can hardly have expected the
manners-bound Mandarin to appreciate such a point. To the
Chinese view the refusal could only be a deliberate insult
which must inevitably weaken Gordon's influence, lose him
face and set his offended host free from any moral obligation
towards him. The oddest thing of all is that neither Gordon
nor the Wangs appear to have realised that, no matter what
the terms of surrender were, to offend a man like Li was extremely dangerous. In Gordon's presence there would have
been no breach of faith, for such would then have been contrary to the principles of good government; but in Gordon's
absence the Governor was by tradition almost an absolute
monarch—his word the law, his pleasure the right.

Careless of the insult he had offered his superior, disregard-
ing the obvious interpretation which would be put upon the
over-confident attitude of the Wangs, who had not even shorn
their long hair—the invariable sign for renunciation of the
rebel cause—Gordon calmly sought out Halliday Macartney
and put to him much the same invitation which Lar Wang
had received, that they two should go for a cruise on the lake.
The implication is that there must have been an important
reason for asking Lar because of the urgency of his business
with Macartney. In fact, it concerned his resignation, which
was bound to cause complications not only among the troops
of both sides but in official channels. He had no need to consider Li's reactions to such a step, but the command must be
handed over in good order or General Brown might make an
adverse report. Besides, with Gordon out of the saddle,
Soochow could soon become a rebel stronghold again. Then
other towns would follow, if only out of fear as to what might
happen to them if they did not. For, in spite of Gordon's local
victories, the enemy's main forces were still in being. Even in
North China their total effectives considerably outnumbered
those of the Imperialists and the Ever Victorious together.

Nor was their superiority only in numbers, as it had been at the beginning of the campaign. The Taipings were now better armed than ever before, and they were better led, both thanks to Europeans. Moreover, their formations included a hard core of battle-tried veterans who had learned much from tactical defeat at Gordon's hands.

Even in the immediate area of Soochow they could still call up a formidable army, and once the news of Gordon's departure became known, they would surely take advantage of the time-lag before a new commander could become effective. For that reason, and to justify himself as far as possible to the English authorities, Gordon needed, at once, two assurances. One he thought was already effective, the permanent, faithful 'change of heart' of the Wangs who were now surrendering. The other he needed from Macartney as his chosen successor, the only man who could at short notice be acceptable both to Li and to General Brown. The Minister would also have to approve, and so effectively that the appointment could if necessary be forced upon Li, who might well try to insist that he and not Gordon was the person to make it. Gordon was, after all, his employee and to him had given his resignation.

With adjurations to the uttermost secrecy, Gordon chugged into the middle of the Taiho lake. Not until then did he tell Macartney that he wished him to take over the Ever Victorious Army. Macartney said No. For the offer, whatever its motives—and they must have been good because Gordon never had a bad one in his life—would have put him in the impossible position of stepping over the heads of Gordon's own officers. He might have said much more, for, having far greater experience of China, it must have been obvious to Macartney that Gordon's attitude to Li could only lead to trouble. So, with considerable coolness between them, the two men put back to Soochow, where Gordon borrowed Macartney's horse to ride through the town in search of Moh Wang's body. Probably this was not only a sentimental journey, although Gordon seems to have had considerable respect for Moh. He may have wanted to give the corpse Christian burial, but it is more likely that, not believing the version of Moh's death which he had heard from Lar, he wished to check it with other accounts of what had occurred.

Meanwhile, beyond the creek, Li Hung Chang met his guests and spoke them fair, referring to honours which they would surely acquire in loyal service to the Emperor. But the uncouth Wangs remained too voluble, too boisterous, to be acceptable to Li's dignity. They behaved as though they counted on the foreigner's promise to save them from their own countrymen—a thought quite unacceptable to a man like Li, even without taking his desire for personal vengeance into account. He handed over his position as Master of Ceremonies to General Ching. Whether to Li's order or not, Ching preferred action to speech. His way with the proud prisoners was to admit executioners to the enclosure where the banquet should have been held. There fell the heads of the Wangs.

Meanwhile Gordon had reached Moh's house. It had been gutted. Looting was going on all over the town, not only out of natural exuberance but at Ching's order; which seems to have been singularly tactless in view of the number of rebels still under arms within the walls.

Gordon next sought Lar Wang's establishment. The master of it was out, being executed. His uncle was acting head of the house and was in a state of agitation for fear of what would happen to Lar's women if the looters broke in. No one yet knew that there had been any irregularity about the surrender. Gordon had time to burn until his own steamer should arrive and allow him to sail away into retirement, so he undertook to honour this claim upon his chivalry. It must have gone considerably against the grain to chaperone a hobble of Chinese women through the unquiet streets lined with very interested persons.

He took them to the uncle's house, and there suffered the ignominy of being detained. He was a prisoner all night, while the city seethed beyond the barred gates of the courtyard, in which three or four hundred rebel troops were bivouacked. Gordon had an almost equal chance of being killed by them or by the wild Imperialist looters. Towards dawn he got permission to send his interpreter to make contact with his bodyguard, for by this time rumour was busy about a plot. It was generally believed that Li had imprisoned the Wangs.

Not trusting to a verbal message, Gordon had written an order to his men which, had they received it, must have seemed to them crazy and dangerous. But they did not have to risk disobeying, for the interpreter was seized by Ching's guard at the gate, and, since they could not read English, the soldiers played safe by tearing the letter into pieces and putting the bearer away as a suspicious character—which, indeed, he was, to be coming out of the rebel-held town in the small hours with an incomprehensible message which he pretended was from the foreign Tsung-Ping. As if any Tsung-Ping, least of all Gordon, would be alone among the rebels on this night!

Not until the next morning, being Sunday, an ominous day for Gordon, did Lar's uncle begin to think of allowing Gordon himself to go outside the walls, and when eventually he did give his consent, it was with the condition that there should be an escort of long-hairs. Gordon accepted the escort only to be arrested, as his interpreter had been, on the charge of being in suspicious company. As he could speak no Chinese, and his escort would not have been believed anyway, it is hardly surprising that more than an hour passed before it began to dawn on his captors that their prey might really be the General. Playing safe, they let him go.

Over on the far side of the creek there was a crowd of people, and Gordon, who had managed to get into touch with at least some of his force—unless his bodyguard now consisted of a regiment, which is possible—sent one of his officers to see what was toward. This young man, Prince von Wittgenstein of Prussia, rowed across, and came back to report punctiliously that there were only some headless bodies lying on the grass.

Corpses had long been common enough, but Gordon had a presentiment that these represented far-reaching tragedy. He leaped into the boat and crossed the creek. The crowd parted before him, and there, in a puddled confusion of clotted blood, lay the headless bodies and the heads of the Wangs who had trusted the 'word of an Englishman'. No one had dared to touch them. Grotesque as they had fallen, the corpses had stiffened through the long night, their eyes fixed in an accusing stare.

Weeping, Gordon snatched up the head of Lar Wang and, with it hanging from his hand by its hair, went after Li. Some accounts say that he had a revolver in the other hand, but what Gordon intended was not to murder the Governor, only to depose him and, in due course, on authority from Pekin, have him beheaded. This meant that not only would Gordon be acting far beyond his authority, he would necessarily take over from Li that high official's civil and military powers. That he was prepared to do so is implied by his threat that if Li did not instantly resign, all the towns captured from the rebels would be given back to them—a course which would make Gordon's conduct equatable with Burgevine's. He would have betrayed not only his employers, the Chinese, but his own country which had lent him for the specific purpose of putting down the rebellion.

That in a normal state of mind he could ever have entertained such a notion is inconceivable. His action sprang from some deep level of the mind where live the opposites of conscious thoughts. This was an explosion brought about by the incompatibility of his ideas about duty and ethics with what he had to do, and with the people by whom he was surrounded. Out of the shadow, up from the devil, came the enemy which was more dangerous to him than the Taipings could ever be, those thoughts which can defeat the soul.

*   *   *

Anticipating trouble, Li had prudently absented himself from the neighbourhood. It is unlikely that he was disturbed by what had happened to the Wangs, who deserved to die ten times over in expiation of their many crimes. Besides, individual Wangs, particularly dead ones, were of no consequence to the crisis which was approaching. For the fall of Soochow had set in equipoise the whole force of the rebels against the Throne. Based upon Nankin, they might still put into the field perhaps a total of a hundred thousand men with an adequate reserve; while locally the balance of power was rendered the more delicate by the imminent risk of clashes between Imperialists and rebels. And the redoubtable Chung Wang, somewhere in the vicinity, was avid to avenge his peers.

Li had great responsibility. Not only was he the Governor, he was also the provincial General Officer Commanding, in relation to whom Gordon was only a tactical leader of mercenaries, however brilliant; whose resignation was of the same order of importance as the murder, or execution, of the Wangs. It might lead to some difficulties and even dangers, but could not affect either the final outcome of the war or the advancement which Li could confidently expect as the result of his success, to consolidate which was now his urgent task.

Meanwhile Gordon went fuming back to the city, and on the way met with General Ching. He tried to reason with Gordon, but was met with such passionate invective that he hurriedly withdrew, taking what comfort he could from the knowledge that it was Li and not himself upon whom the full force of the Englishman's fury was directed. For in the face of certain disapproval from Whitehall, Westminster, even Windsor—to say nothing of their representatives in China and the Chinese authorities themselves—Gordon was now determined not merely to force the Governor to resign but to put him under arrest.

At the very beginning of the campaign Sir Frederick Bruce had expressed an opinion that the Commander of the Ever Victorious would soon find himself in a position incompatible with his status as a gentleman and his duty as an officer. This was it. Gordon sat down and wrote out his demands, not omitting the threat to return to the rebels the towns taken from them. This letter he entrusted to Macartney, in spite of their recent failure to agree about the succession of command. Li, as Gordon also might have guessed, was at General Ching's headquarters. There Macartney handed over the letter and, when Li protested that he could not read it, refused to translate; because, he said, there were statements in it which, written in the heat of anger, he felt sure Gordon would not wish to repeat when his indignation had cooled.

'Then', said Li, 'if I cannot know what the letter contains, how should I presume to accept the letter itself?'

In handing the paper back to Macartney, Li demonstrated that even then he had no hard feelings for Gordon, whose forthright character he had learned to admire even though his manner was so very foreign. Had the letter been for-

warded to Pekin there can be no doubt but that the authorities would have had to act upon it, with the result that Gordon
might have had a black mark against him for the rest of his
career, if, indeed, it was not terminated. For no authority,
European or Oriental, can afford to tolerate threats of assault
by juniors upon properly constituted seniors. The gesture also
indicates how sure Li must have felt about the outcome of the
crisis. Had there been in his mind any need to acquire evidence to defend himself in high places against Gordon's accusations, he would again have had need of that letter, with
which to suggest that Gordon was not the kind of person who
deserved to be taken seriously.

Yet Macartney took him seriously enough to convince Li
that there was an immediate threat to his personal safety.
Whether the Governor understood Gordon's point of view is
doubtful, but he certainly appreciated that the real force
behind the explosion was not derived from the dead Wangs as
such but from the fear of personal dishonour. Governor Li,
therefore, asked Macartney to seek out Gordon at once, to
impress upon him that, in fact, he had no responsibility whatever for what had happened, which was entirely due to a
decision at a higher level of authority than his own. Once
convinced that he had no responsibility in the matter, which
in Li's view was certainly the case, there would be no reason
to try to vindicate himself by action against others. Li pointed
out to Macartney that when Gordon promised safety to the
Wangs he was doing so only within his competence. If,
because he was a foreigner, he had not realised this, they
must have done. They could not possibly have expected the
Provincial Governor to be bound by the word of one of his
employees.

Macartney, though not expecting reason to have much
effect, agreed to hasten to Quinsan; for he must have been
afraid of the consequences of any hostile act on Gordon's part.
The Imperialists might so much profit by the situation that
they could turn with impunity against all foreigners, and
drive them out of China on a new wave of patriotism. At all
costs, Gordon must be stopped. Having had no food all day,
Macartney set out by boat, the most rapid transport then
available. His rowers sweated but their passenger was chilled

to the marrow when the lights of Quinsan appeared. Soon he was hammering on the door of Gordon's house. He was admitted by a Chinese servant but refused audience. The General had left orders that on no account was he to be disturbed until morning; and the General's orders must be obeyed. So Macartney had to wait downstairs, drinking coffee and dozing, until the first light filtered weakly through the paper windows.

Then, in the chill, pale dawn he dared to go upstairs. He knocked on Gordon's door and, almost desperate to get the disagreeable interview over, walked in. The room was still full of shadows. Gordon, dejected, sat upon the bed, his feet on the bare floor and his head in his hands. Before Macartney could even say why he was there, perhaps before he was even recognised, Gordon leaned down and drew from under the bed a bulky object. Holding it out towards his visitor, he said in an awful voice, 'The head of Lar Wang, foully murdered'. Then he began to shudder with weeping. Macartney left the room.

In an hour Gordon came down, dapper as usual and apparently in complete command of himself. Macartney, who was waiting for him, begged for a private interview on business of the utmost urgency. Gordon said, 'You are not speaking for yourself. You come from the Governor.' And when Macartney admitted as much, he was told that anything there was to be said should be said over breakfast in the Mess. It was evident not only that Gordon was still determined on his dire course of action, but that because he was Li's messenger, Macartney had also come within the dark circle of his hatred.

Still, there was nothing to be done but accept the churlish invitation to breakfast with several other people, not all of them even officers of the Ever Victorious. Gordon ate in silence. Hungry as he was, it is doubtful if Macartney could eat at all. Gordon finished first and abruptly demanded Li's message, implying that to bear it at all was an act 'unbecoming to an officer and a gentleman', both of which Macartney certainly was. On hearing Li's explanation, Gordon dismissed it. He said he 'would have no mild counsels'. His original threat was to be carried out, and, since the Governor was so

obstinate, he would mobilise for that purpose the whole of the
Ever Victorious. He would forthwith attack the Imperialists
and take the Governor prisoner.

'Mild or not,' said Macartney finally, 'they are the only
ones which your Minister at Pekin and our Queen will approve.' The threat was a shrewd one, for, being in the Chinese
service, he was not responsible to the Minister as Gordon was.
One man only supported Macartney, the rest, in fear of
Gordon, kept silent; and Macartney realised that there was
nothing he could say which was not likely to be misinterpreted
to fit in with the picture Gordon had painted for himself. The
only thing to do was to get back to the Governor and warn
him. But would Gordon allow such a thing? He would be
more likely to regard the mere proposal as a new treachery.
Macartney slipped away—but not before Gordon quixotic-
ally offered him a place on one of the avenging steamers!
Macartney probably pleaded that he must get back to his
own command; at all events he was able to borrow a horse,
and a pair of spurs. In a few minutes the exhausted man was
on his way back to Li Hung Chang to warn him at all costs
to put himself beyond Gordon's reach.

So a new war became imminent on the very lines which
Burgevine had suggested. Once Gordon had committed his
men against the Imperialists he would be forced to recruit
reinforcements from both sides, and fight on until either he
won China or was killed. To give himself up, either to the
Chinese or to the English, would have been too difficult even
for Gordon. Though he would have stood serene before a
firing-squad, it is doubtful whether he could have faced disgrace.

Macartney had delivered his warning and the steamers
were half-way to Soochow before Gordon's mind began to
clear. Li meanwhile had found safety in an ingenious
oriental stratagem. Flight would invite disaster the equal of
that which Gordon was trying to bring about; and it would
lose much face. To stand and fight would also risk the loss
of all that had been gained,—and it was a great deal, in Li's
personal scales as well as those of the Empire. He therefore
ordered a ceremonial entry into Soochow, and himself headed
the procession, guarded by the triumphant troops of General

Ching and brother Santagen, who had every satisfaction in thus rubbing in to the citizens that, with the deaths of their leaders, they had now no hope in this world but in service to the Imperial Authority and the remote hope of its clemency. The gesture was masterly. At one stroke it exploited the initiative left by the execution of the Wangs, impressed the wavering citizens, made it quite impossible for Gordon to stage a successful kidnapping, and at the same time demonstrated to friend and enemy alike that not Gordon but Li Hung Chang was the hero of the hour.

Gordon meanwhile was himself trying to find a face-saving formula. Pride would not allow him to accept the advice he had been given. How could he make a fool of himself in front of his own men by admitting that he had planned an operation in a fit of temper and now wished to call it off? Like Li, he found an expedient which worked, though not so successfully as had the Governor's. With his Army in the background to lend significance to his intentions, he publicly denounced Li Hung Chang, accused him of broken faith and of murder, and swore that he would be brought to justice. Then he went off to Ching's headquarters, where, presumably from the piquet on duty, he obtained the decapitated body of Lar Wang and with it steamed back to Quinsan where it rejoined the head for burial.

At about this time he probably learned that Ching had been so upset by Gordon's vehement accusations that, to relieve his feelings, he had shot twenty of his own men who had been accused of looting. Considering that he had himself given the orders to loot, this was quite an achievement even under the code which passed for morality among ex-rebels. It must have made Gordon begin to wonder whether it was just to weigh the actions of Chinese in a balance appropriate to English officers. At all events he did not take any further direct action but, insisting upon his resignation from the Chinese service, handed over his command to General Brown; only to be ordered to remain at his post, though inactive, until further orders.

Meanwhile Li had emerged into the cool dignity of public life and placidly pursued his duties without apparently remembering that there had been any unpleasantness. In beautifully balanced characters he wrote a suitable despatch to Pekin, which called forth the following reply from the Inner Council of the Emperor:

'Li memorialises announcing that having led his forces to the attack of Soochow, he has retaken the city. The perusal of his report has afforded us joy and satisfaction indeed!

'Gordon, as Tsung-Ping of the province of Kiangsoo, in command of the auxiliary force, has displayed thorough strategy and skill, and has put forth the most distinguished exertions.

'We ordain that a medal of distinction of the highest class be conferred upon him, and, further, that he receives a donation of ten thousand *taels* in token of our approbation. Respect this!'

A private communication was also sent to the Governor:

'Li is enjoined to communicate our decree of approval and praise to Gordon for the great bravery and exertions which attended the recapture of Soochow. The donation of ten thousand *taels* is to be provided and sent to him by Li. Foreign nations already possess orders of merit under the name of "stars", let, therefore, the decoration of the first class, which we have conferred upon Gordon, be arranged in accordance with this system.'

Here was a handsome gesture on the part of a Government which, with its perpetual preoccupation with face, and its bitter recent experience of barbarians, could easily have forgotten to notice a relatively insignificant foreign officer who, under no matter what provocation, had threatened the life of a Provincial Governor and sworn to return to the rebels all that had been taken from them. Even Prince Kung was content. He summed up the entire episode by saying that if the Wangs had not been promptly beheaded the rebels within the city would have massacred the Imperialist forces to a man.

If the Chinese were satisfied, Official Channels were not, and while they seethed with activity Gordon was left to sulk at Quinsan, being allowed neither to resign nor to take part in the enquiry which at his insistence had been instituted at Pekin into the behaviour of Li Hung Chang. That the proceedings would never come to anything must at once have been obvious. Gordon's only means of relieving his feelings was to write his despatches, and to the papers, to demand Li's head, and to cast aspersions upon the character of Macartney.

Then one bright day there appeared an impressive procession at headquarters. Gordon, forewarned, met the leading Mandarin at the gate of the compound and there made him halt the column which carried the tokens of Imperial favour. The 10,000 *taels* of silver were in open boxes upon the heads of porters. The coin was covered by scarlet clothes, weighted with silver Sycee shoes. But this Arabian Nights' effect was secondary. The place of honour went to the Decree itself. Wrapped in sacred yellow silk and borne by a Mandarin of the highest rank, dressed in gorgeous robes of ceremony, it could not be halted by any man's order, and so was carried to a table in the hall of Gordon's house, where it was reverently deposited between two scarlet, lighted candles.

The Mandarin, whose name was Pow, then turned to Gordon and handed to him an English translation. Gordon, who already knew the content, took a pen and wrote on the back of it: 'Major Gordon receives the approbation of His Majesty the Emperor with every gratification, but regrets most sincerely that, owing to the circumstances which occurred since the capture of Soochow, he is unable to receive any mark of His Majesty the Emperor's recognition, and, therefore, respectfully begs His Majesty to receive his thanks for his intended kindness, and to allow him to decline the same.'

He signed it: C. H. Gordon, Major Commanding, and dated it the 1st of January 1864. Then he handed the paper back to Pow, who formally withdrew, leaving the original of the Decree between the altar-candles, to find its way eventually into the British Museum. Gordon accompanied him back to the gate where the rest of the procession was waiting. It was represented to Gordon that certain private gifts had a special claim upon him, battle flags captured from the rebels. There were four of them, two sent by Li Hung Chang, which he refused, the others by less important individuals, which he accepted. He then demanded that the procession return whence it came, and one account says that he hastened the departure of the porters, to their loss of dignity, by blows from his swagger pole, his 'magic wand'. 'If the sun had started from his sphere they would have been less frightened and amazed.' Aside from the great gift, he did accept a sum of money specifically offered for the comfort of the wounded, but he commented, 'I would have refused the 10,000 *taels* even if everything had gone well and there had been no trouble at Soochow'.

*   *   *

So Gordon was left alone again with his bitter thoughts and his idle, discontented troops, to each of whom a share of those 10,000 *taels* would have represented an acceptable bonus. He probably went through another 'dark night of the soul', a period of acute depression, in which he longed for the cloister and resolved yet more passionately to shun the world and take refuge in his private City of God, whose defences he must further strengthen. Yet he allowed no gloom in his letters:

'You will be glad to hear that we are all quietly back at Quinsan—not likely to move again for a very long time, if, in fact, we ever do. I have not time to give you any details of the fight at the East Gate or of the treachery at Soochow, and hope you will see the same in the papers. I have Lar Wang's son. He is a very sharp young fellow and very lively—about eighteen years old. His poor father was a very good Wang, and very far superior to any of the Imperialists I have met. You can have little idea of the regret I have for several reasons on account of the last affair. In the first place, if faith had been kept there would have been no more fighting, as every town would have given in; in the next we had accomplished the suppression of the rebellion with very little loss of life to rebels or Imperialists, and not much injury to the inhabitants, as our quick movements prevented the rebels from devastating the neighbouring villages; in the next, if I had not seen Lar Wang he would not have come over; and, in the next I fear that all my work has been thrown away. My only consolation is that everything is for the best. It is quite incomprehensible to me the reason which actuated the Governor; he must have known from previous acquaintance with me what a row would be produced, and of what a personal risk he ran, for when it happened my troops were not two hours' march from him.'

It is to be hoped that Gordon's correspondent did not, in seeking for details in the papers, hit upon a letter which appeared in *The Times* of the 29th January 1864: 'The *Carthage* has just come in from Shanghai. It appears that the rebel chiefs refused to surrender on the Governor's word that no unnecessary blood should be shed, whereon Gordon got the Governor's promise to himself, and gave his word, on which they capitulated. The Governor got in, had his troops concealed about, and, when Gordon was outside, commanded a wholesale massacre—men, women and children. Gordon heard of it, gathered a few men together, among the rest a Count or Prince Wittgenstein, and broke into the place; and the scenes there witnessed were so revolting that the Prince says they all fired and loaded and fired again on every Mandarin they met. Gordon is said to have shot 25 *buttons* (Mandarins) himself. . . .'

So much, presumably, for the Prince's imagination. The most revolting scene in Soochow was at the last supper of Moh Wang, but not far away there really was a massacre. For when Chung Wang heard of the tame submission of the city, he vented his fury upon those of the garrison who had fled. Two thousand of them were beheaded, a demonstration that the rebel power was as yet by no means broken.

Chapter 5

FAREWELL GLORY

NEITHER for Gordon nor for his disintegrating army did there seem at the beginning of 1864 to be an operational future. The headless Wangs of Soochow had accomplished more by death than in life. They had by their martyrdom eliminated their most effective enemy, corrupted his command, embarrassed his allies and deprived the Imperialists of the initiative. The title 'Ever Victorious Army' was now changed to 'Quinsan Force'.

For the first time since Gordon took command, the Taipings went over to the offensive. Their morale was ebullient, their troops, leaders and equipment better than ever before. And they were rank with lust for vengeance. Soon, in the north, the Imperialists could no longer even hold their ground, while the troops which should have constituted their strategic reserve congealed outside Nankin, that apparently impregnable 'Heavenly' capital, already besieged off and on for over thirteen years.

Burgevine was loose again. There were the usual rumours that he was plotting to go over to the rebels, this time in a novel way calculated to tip the scales decisively in their favour. Sir Frederick Bruce wrote to Gordon: 'Burgevine is a Southerner, the trading interests of America in China are Northern, and Burgevine attributes his treatment to the British authorities at Shanghai. It would not surprise me if he and the *Alabama* etc., were to make common cause with the insurgents, and then, you may depend upon it, they would directly attack the foreign settlements, either by steamers or by batteries, to prevent lorchas or armed vessels going up the Yangtze river. It might be easy for a force of these adventurers to raise the siege of Nankin, and then advance again on the province of Kiangsoo.'

Nor was the war in America the only preoccupation of diplomats. So tense was the international situation that in London there appeared an Order in Council requiring the immediate withdrawal of all British officers from the Chinese Service, the idea being to minimise commitments in the Far East and at the same time prevent repetition of such an embarrassing incident as the quarrel between Gordon and Li Hung Chang. This Order, which would take months to reach Pekin, must have been based upon Bruce's despatches, so it is the more remarkable to find him, in face of the present emergency, coming round to whole-hearted support of Gordon when the latter decided to take the field again.

General Brown, briefed by Bruce, and aware that the Dynasty hung by a hair, went so far as to pay a personal visit to Li, who had smoothly established himself in a Soochow palace. There the General requested, even demanded, an explanation of the affair of the late Wangs. The Governor blandly replied that the responsibility was entirely his own. And such was, in fact, the case. He was by Chinese custom answerable to no man, only to the Throne. He must have been tempted to adopt an English frankness and tell the General so, but for the fact that he was too Chinese a gentleman. The two parted with mutual respect.

Brown returned to Shanghai convinced that whatever the rights of the case, the situation was so threatening that Gordon must be induced to take the field again. Yet how was that to be brought about? At least by implication Li had accepted his resignation, while the only circumstance under which Gordon wished to see Li again was as his accuser in a court of law. At this juncture there intervened a certain Mr., later Sir, Robert Hart, who enjoyed the influential post of Comptroller of Imperial Customs at Shanghai and knew all the important people. It was he who, at that grim breakfast, had spoken in favour of Macartney's 'mild counsels' when Gordon was planning to attack Li. Bruce and Brown must have judged that if anyone could now make Gordon listen to reason it would be he, who had written: 'The destiny of China is, at the present moment, in the hands of Gordon more than any other man, and, if he be encouraged to act vigorously, the knotty question of Taipingdom versus "union in the cause of law and order" will be solved before the end of May, and quiet will at length be restored to this unfortunate and sorely-tried country'.

Accordingly, Hart journeyed to Quinsan and, after reminding Gordon that his duty was still to Queen Victoria
and her Minister, no matter what his relations with the
Chinese, he urged a return to active service. The argument,
to a man like Gordon, was conclusive. No personal consideration could ever be allowed to warp the rule of duty. He
agreed at once and went with Hart to meet the Governor in
his palace. There Gordon pressed his accusation for the last
time, and accepted Li's excuses, such as they were, embodied
in a public proclamation which read in part:

'On his arrival at the camp, the so-called Lar Wang had
not shaved his head, and his rebellious designs were patent to
view. He both refused to disband his men and insisted on
their being enrolled in the army, to the number of several tens
of battalions, and further urged the demand that the rank of
Brigadier-General, etc., should be obtained from the Throne
for his adherents, who were to be left at the head of their men
as garrison for Soochow. Not only was no sign of contrition
evinced, but, on the contrary, there was a design of preparing
the way for an eventual return to rebellion. Whilst his speech
was evasive and ambitious, his expression of countenance was
ferocious and bold in the extreme; and all this took place after
the surrender had been completed. The Governor could,
therefore, for his own safety, do no otherwise than guard
against a dangerous departure from the arranged conditions;
and these were all particulars with which General Gordon
was not acquainted. As regards the outset, when the Governor
agreed with General Gordon to accept the submission of
these men he had no conception that hesitation would take
place at the last moment; and with respect to subsequent occurrences, the signs of danger were disclosed in a single instant,
when, if no action could have been taken until after communicating with General Gordon, not only would it have
become too late, but all the advantages secured would have
been sacrificed. Supposing that the Governor had adhered
rigidly to his agreement, so that these few bandits had been
enabled to secure their own safety and resort to rebellious
practices, it was many tens of thousands who would have
suffered by the consequent misfortune; and the result would
have been far from what was contemplated when these men

were admitted to surrender. Fortunately, however, by a summary decision at the vital instant, by which these few bandits only were put to death and the mass of their followers scattered to the winds, benefit was secured to the same vast number of the people, whom to protect was the main object held in view.'

It may well have been the last sentence which decided Gordon to cease feuding, for he had entered upon his task not for the Imperialists, not for the Europeans even, but on behalf of the common people whose sufferings had so moved him while he was exploring the country round Tientsin in his first Chinese winter. At all events, he now agreed with Li and Hart that duty, taking precedence even above pride, required him to reconstitute his army and, finally to break the power of the Taipings.

Such a decision was not without risk. Gordon wrote:

Soochow, February 6th, 1864

MY DEAR SIR FREDERICK BRUCE,

In consequence of the danger which will arise by my inaction (with the force any longer in a state of uncertainty), I have arranged with the Governor to issue a proclamation, which he will send you, clearing me of any participation in the late execution of the Wangs, and I have determined to act immediately.

The reasons which actuate me are as follows:—

I know of a certainty that Burgevine meditates a return to the rebels; that there are upwards of 300 Europeans ready to join them, of no character, and that the Governor will not accept another British officer if I leave the service; and, therefore, the Government may have some foreigner put in, or else the force put under men of Ward's or Burgevine's stamp, of whose action at times we should never feel certain.

I am aware that I am open to very grave censure for the course I am about to pursue; but, in the absence of advice, and knowing as I do that the Pekin authorities will support the Governor in what he has done, I have made up my mind to run the risk. If I followed my own desire I should now leave, as I have escaped unscathed, and been wonderfully successful. But the rabble called the Quinsan Force is a dangerous body, and it will be my duty to see that it is dissolved as quickly as possible, and that while in the course of dissolution it should serve to benefit the Imperial Government.

I do not apprehend that the rebellion will last six months longer if I take the field. It may take six years if I leave, and the Government does not support the Imperialists. I propose to cut through the heart of the rebellion, and to divide it into two parts by the capture of Yesing and Liyang.

If the course I am about to pursue meets with your approval, I shall be glad to hear; but, if not, I shall expect to be well rebuked. However, I know that I am not actuated by personal considerations, but merely as I think will be most conducive to the interests of our Government.

The Governor does not want the force to move against Nankin, I imagine, as Tseng Kwo-fan has the wish to capture it himself.

The Governor, if he is to be believed, has some extenuating circumstances in his favour for his action, and, although I feel deeply on the subject, I think that we can scarcely expect the same discernment that we should from a European Governor.

This letter will relieve you of any responsibility on this matter; and thanking you very much for your kind letter, which I will answer shortly.

I am etc.

C. G. GORDON.

P.S.—If you would let the matter drop, and make me responsible for my action in the matter, I think it would be more conducive to our good relations with the Pekin Government than pressing them to punish and degrade the Governor.

The letter which Gordon referred to was by this time out of date, for its burden was to keep him from 'trying conclusions with the Chinese and to keep his force from deserting'. It must have been most unwelcome, and so he would have been all the more gratified to receive unqualified approval and support for his decision to go back to the war; even if at the same time he had to swallow a reprimand for tactlessness. Like most officials under whom Gordon served, Bruce's faith in his professional genius was qualified by uneasiness about his temperament. On receiving Gordon's decision he replied:

'I beg you to do nothing rash under the pressure of excitement, and, above all, to avoid publishing in the newspapers accounts of your differences with the Chinese authorities. We have supported this Government from motives of interest, not from sentiment; and as our interests remain the same, we must endeavour to get over our difficulties without taking any steps which would neutralise all the results of the policy we have hitherto pursued, and which you have carried out so successfully. In the resolution you have now come to you are acting wisely and rightly, and you may depend on my lightening your responsibility by giving you the most cordial official support. . . .

'The objects we ought to keep in view are to restore order in Kiangsoo and Chekiang, to cut off the insurgents from communication with filibusters, and to reduce gradually the disciplined corps so that it may not become a source of danger.'

*   *   *

Gordon's strategy was to cut the enemy's dumbbell-shaped force in two, which meant that he would have to operate, for the first time, out of touch with his base. This was more than merely inconvenient, it was unpopular—a sinister word in the context of near-mutiny. Thanks to his steamers he could still maintain adequate supplies of food for men and guns, but the men were uneasy at the prospect of being in enemy territory, with closely limited reserves and no line of retreat open.

So, through winter-bound country ravaged by years of warfare, the uneager column set off in sleet and snow, its morale as low as the temperature. Sixteen officers had been dismissed, and Gordon had himself shot a man on parade. Mutiny was as close as the hunger which stared at them all the way through the eyes of the wretched inhabitants. The first march should have brought them to billets for the night, but the town had been so destroyed that they had to push on to villages where at least some roofs remained to give an illusion of shelter from the consuming cold. Corpses lay about unburied, and were so disregarded through familiarity that sometimes they were trodden flat by passers-by. The dead were often hacked about in a characteristic way; and in the faces of those who yet survived was a wolfish gleam which turned even Gordon's horror-hardened stomach. 'No one',

he wrote, 'can eat a meal here without loathing.' Cannibalism
had become the rule.

In terms of personal shock to Gordon there was even worse
to come. An old woman, or a woman who appeared old, when
questioned about rebels in the district said that they had done
four foreigners to death. Gordon found the wreckage of their
bodies and enough of their clothes to identify them as the
crew of the *Firefly* which had run aground. They had been
tortured in reprisal for the Wangs of Soochow, an action which
suggests that, no matter what the facts might be, for the time
being the rebels blamed Gordon for what had happened. On
no other occasion throughout the war were Europeans subject
to gross cruelty.

In some localities the Taipings were themselves starving,
and at least one town surrendered for that reason. Yet, contrary to previous experience, even this had no effect upon the
main thrust which was coming up in rear of the Imperialists.
Prudence suggested retirement before he became cut off, but
Gordon pressed on, confident that if he could but complete
the operation as planned, then the threat to his rear would
collapse. He was probably influenced in his decision by the
fact that out of one hungry garrison which surrendered he
had been able to form a whole new regiment, equivalent to a
battalion, to add to his jittery but well-fed force. He would
have reasoned that in such a state of universal misery, a little
success anywhere would rapidly produce converts among the
enemy, the cheapest of all ways to win a war. Prisoners,
thanks to this idea, were as humanely treated as Sir Frederick
could have wished when he made Li Hung Chang agree to
obey the Western rules of warfare as a condition of Gordon's
return. Later on, when the Imperialists no longer needed
such recruits, there was another story.

But the campaign was no longer to be cheap, either for
Gordon or the Quinsan Force. They were becoming accident-
prone by repetition of hairbreadth escapes. Gordon's accident
occurred before the walls of Kintang. Twice his guns had
swept the breaches clear of the enemy. Twice the assault
had gone in only to fall back before fanatic defenders who
appeared as though from nowhere the instant that the guns
ceased fire for fear of hitting their own men. For a last attempt

Gordon changed his plan and, instead of making the approach by boat, led the storming party over a bridge. There he was hit. He went down calling to those near him to press on, and, though he could not move from the spot where he lay, and remained under fire, yet he continued to direct the action. Major Brown, the General's son, took Gordon's personal standard and went forward with it, hoping that the sight would reassure the troops, though the man with the magic wand had been proved at last to be no more bullet-proof than others. Brown took the flag right into the breach, and there victory was hanging in the balance of a *mêlée* when he in turn was hit. The men wavered and broke, bringing Brown back with them past where Gordon stayed, apparently bleeding to death, but allowing no one to touch him. At last Andrew Moffit, staunch friend and chief medical officer, came out to the bridge. When words failed to make any impression, he was not afraid to have Gordon manhandled back to his boat.

There it was found that if the spell of his 'charmed life' had failed, it was only by a little, for the wound was relatively minor. A lead musket-ball had gone through the fleshy part of the leg below the knee without breaking bone, cutting a major ligament, or introducing infected matter. Gordon was so contemptuous of it that he tried to get off the boat and take command again; but Moffit was too strong for him, and as the limb stiffened he knew that whatever orders he gave would not be from a standing position. His humiliating sense of frustration must have been still further increased by a well-meaning Imperial Decree which arrived a few days later at the yamen of his recent enemy, the Governor Li: 'We order Li Hung Chang to visit Gordon and inquire of him daily, so as to keep his mind at rest, requesting him to wait until he shall be perfectly restored to health and strength. Respect this!'

The idea of being told to rest—and by Li Hung Chang! It was worse even than being praised—though he may have been gratified when in due course he learned that Palmerston, Prime Minister and no supporter of the rôle of the Ever Victorious, had said in the House: 'Major Gordon, I am sorry to see by the last accounts, has sustained a check and has been wounded—I hope not severely. He is a most able and distinguished officer and one who has performed great services for the Imperial Government.'

Those services were by no means at an end. The news that their great enemy, who for so long had seemed to enjoy Heavenly—or Infernal—protection, had been struck down, went through the rebels like wine. They arrogantly proclaimed that they would soon attack Shanghai and then move on Pekin. Already Fushan, Gordon's first conquest, had again fallen to them, and it was common belief that the only thing left to stop them was the sea. Such is the price to be paid for the myth of the hero, that when he whose name held the enemy in awe, whose presence on the battlefield was almost the equivalent of a wreath of victory, is shown to be only mortal after all, the pendulum of morale swings to the other extreme.

Of the three thousand men with which he had reopened the campaign, Gordon was now sure enough of only a thousand, six hundred of whom had but recently come over from the rebels. The rest must be given time to recover at least some of the Ever Victorious spirit. How could they have such a respite unless the enemy were distracted by some gesture? Accordingly Gordon determined that he would at once make a water-borne reconnaissance deep into enemy territory, with the object of confirming his suppositions about their strength, lines of communication and principal dispositions. Though he still could not put his foot to the ground he sailed away, while the rest of his force went back to Quinsan. Colonel Chesney wrote: 'Never, surely, did commander show more confidence in his own resources than this wounded man, pushing forward along the creeks in his flotilla (for he was unable to walk or ride) with a few hundred troops, part of whom had been in arms against him a few days before, into the heart of the district occupied by unknown thousands of Taipings'.

Gordon's resources were inadequate. He must have realised this, for, when his *mystique* allowed him to see clearly, none knew better where boldness becomes rashness and courage folly. In all probability, therefore, he undertook this perilous expedition as an act of faith. He may even have accepted his wound as a hint that he had been too much concerned with worldly matters, and ought to offer himself as a hostage to fate according to the common delusion that God demands the discard of prudence as the price of intervention.

The Quinsan Force was dangerously divided. Artillery and headquarters were water-borne while the two infantry regiments, one of them consisting entirely of the ex-rebels, moved overland. The objective, another walled town, was to be assaulted according to the usual formula, by which the infantry first cover the establishment of gun positions. When the walls have been breached, a storming party goes in under covering fire of grape-shot from the guns. Cooperation at all stages is essential. This time there was none. Reconnaissance is essential. This time it was so inadequate that the boats were led up a creek with banks so high that while they prevented the guns from bearing on the enemy, the boats were exposed to fire from above and from both sides. With the greatest difficulty they were extricated from this predicament with its threat that Gordon might be taken prisoner; by which time contact with the infantry had been lost. Against precedent and common sense these had made their approach-march by separate routes under commanders of equal rank, who, careless of the well-tested recipe for walled towns, went into the attack without artillery support. They were soundly put back by the defenders of intact walls, who then made a sortie and, although largely without firearms, inflicted a defeat which prevented the two regiments from joining up again. Into the gap then poured some rebel cavalry which had been kept in concealment. Retreat became rout, and for three miles the pursuit was kept up, until it was checked by the surprising competence of the camp piquet. Gordon's act of faith had failed.

Now there was no choice for the sick commander. He withdrew the remnant of his force and waited for his wound to heal enough to allow him to get about on foot. Meanwhile the Imperialist troops had been scoring some minor successes and Li Hung Chang had himself taken the field, spurred into activity by the fall of Fushan and the threat to Chanzu. Their momentum was increased by the good service of a Franco-Chinese force, organised on the same lines as Gordon's, and under the command of Captain d'Aiguebelle. In cooperation with General Ching they took Hangchow. This signal and surprising success wrested the initiative from the rebels and opened the way for the final stage of the operations as originally conceived by Gordon. Ching, however, had been shot in the head.

It might be expected that the death of the man who had given the orders to the executioners at Soochow, who had fired upon Gordon's flag, and who had begun his war on the wrong side, would have passed almost without comment. Yet, on hearing of it, Gordon wept. He begged Li for Ching's snake-flags to take back to England as a reminder of him. Even after returning home he could be so moved by Ching's portrait, 'shown him by a near relative', that he became speechless with emotion.

No doubt Ching was brave in life. In dying he was magnificent. According to the Chinese code he appears to have been an honourable man; and yet in Gordon's eyes had been quite otherwise, particularly in the Soochow affair over which he was far from repentant, saying, of the men he had beheaded, 'Their crimes have been outrageous; their punishment should be proportionately severe'. It is probable, therefore, that Gordon's sorrow was due largely to the manner of Ching's end. Obsessed by the idea of, even the longing for, death, Gordon must often have imagined his last hour; so that on hearing how the uncouth Ching had behaved in the shadow of eternity he might well have thought, 'There, by the grace of God, die I'.

It is said that Ching asked for a yellow riding-jacket, no doubt an award of honour, though not so august as that which Gordon was to receive from the Emperor. Struggling into it, he forced his mind into clarity for the last time and, in spite of the bullet in his head, dictated a message to Li on a plan to complete the destruction of the Taipings. With his last strength he raised himself up, bowed in the direction of the Imperial Palace, and so died.

*   *   *

Eleven days after receiving his wound Gordon was out of bed, and by the 6th of April was again on active duty, explosive with the pressure of frustration, yet with a new caution. He did not even spurn tactical cooperation with Li's troops, no doubt feeling that while the Quinsan Force might acquit itself well in company, it could hardly be expected to do so on an independent mission so soon after defeat. Li disposed upwards of seven thousand men and was as determined as was Gordon to bring the campaign to a close as quickly as possible. Their partnership brought an early success, which was immediately followed by the execution of two captured Wangs, against which Gordon offered no protest.

This is hardly likely to have been due to any fear of Li, but rather to the terrible local conditions which rendered acts normally reprehensible part of the nightmare of destitution, starvation, treachery and cruelty.

An officer wrote: 'Hundreds of gaunt, starving wretches, with hardly any other means of sustenance than human flesh, and the few scraps of refuse they can pick up from the Imperialist troops, wander hopelessly about, more dead than alive, amid the ruins of their villages. The living are too weak to bury the dead, and the latter lie about on the ground in every stage of decomposition, tainting the air and horrifying the beholder.' That the two executed Wangs had been guilty of stealing and hoarding rice, would surely have been their death-warrant at Gordon's own hand, without the help of Li Hung Chang, whose cynical expediency had been in no way modified either by the death of Ching or by Gordon's new friendliness. Indeed, it is possible that the Governor was already planning to eliminate the Englishman 'by accident' so that he would not survive the final victory to dim the lustre of the Commander-in-Chief.

Opportunity presented itself one night when Gordon was engaged in the siting of a siege battery, protected on both flanks and in the rear by Imperialist piquets. When the work was almost completed these fired into the gun position, killing the second in command, and giving another lease to the myth of Gordon's charmed life. For the fire which came from his allies was echoed by the enemy, an almost all-round concentration. There was thus hardly any cover, and yet, perhaps due to the darkness, he escaped. Whatever his suspicions, Gordon treated the whole incident as a mistake and continued to cooperate with Li, who was not slow to let him down on another occasion which should have caused his death. This time the situation called for a combined assault by Li's troops and the Quinsan Force, now almost up to strength again. When the critical moment came, the Imperialists were mysteriously absent, so that the whole of the enemy's fire was concentrated upon Gordon, as usual leading his men. With nineteen officers wounded the Quinsan Force withdrew, and Gordon refused to renew the assault. While reorganising he planned a final thrust with Li, in which, for once, his own troops were to remain in reserve.

When this came to be executed, though the Imperialists fought well, the rebels upset all calculations by the desperation of their defence. The besieging forces withdrew, to attempt to take the city by guile. Li in this cause had great banners painted, on which bold characters promised safety and food to any who would desert. The response was encouraging, but the city, Chunchufu, still held out. Then Gordon got into touch with treacherous elements within the walls, much as he had done at Soochow. Letters passed, of which the following is an extract:

'Our party are on guard during the fifth watch and will assist you, our cry being "Death to the rebels!" Should you not come, hoist one lamp to the East Gate. No future time for your attack need be fixed, as we can be guided by your signals. We are talked about as traitors, and, should anything be proved against us, two thousand of us would lose our lives. Our movements will be regulated by what is going on outside the city; and after the place falls we shall collect at the East Gate and await Your Excellency. You must have no misgivings about our sincerity. May heaven and earth conspire against us if we are found to be liars! Pray keep our communications quiet, lest anyone coming into the city betray us.'

But the lesson of Soochow had not been lost on the rebels, and Cock-eye, who was in command, discovered the plot. To impress the attackers he had the consequent executions carried out upon the walls. So there was no alternative but another assault. This time the Imperialists again took the leading part, as much because of Li's desire for face as because of Gordon's determination not to be involved in another tactical 'accident'. Yet in the event it was Gordon who won the day, for, when Li could make no more headway against defenders reduced to dropping stinkpots, bags of powder and fire-balls, the battered, venal, worn-out Quinsan Force decisively intervened, as splendid a tribute to their individual courage as to the heart of their inspired leader.

What other man in such circumstances would have thrown in everything he had to wrest victory out of his old enemy's imminent defeat? What other man would have led the assault in person? This was Gordon's finest Chinese hour, and Fate, as though making amends for the bullet she had allowed to rip through his leg, set the final act upon a peak of drama. The guns ceased their uproar as the assault-wave left cover and silently advanced towards the crumbled wall. In front of them jogged a thin, limping, uniformed figure, wearing the breeches and boots of a field officer and waving a short stick. They slowed down, clambering over débris and the dead to gain a gap, which the guns, by a searing jet of canister and grape, had just cleared of every sign of life. As the smoke drifted away, the attackers instinctively checked. They saw the gaping muzzle of a big gun trained upon them point-blank. A man was in the act of touching it off. This was the thirty-two-pounder which had been taken out of the *Firefly* and it was capable of wiping out in a single blast both Gordon and his men. But no flash came; no report. The 'magic wand' had called down another miracle—or the Taipings had failed to keep their powder dry.

Gordon moved forward; the rest followed. The town was won and Cock-eye captured, to suffer summary decapitation. Still with no protest from Gordon, there followed a large number of executions, and it may be that, judging by a letter he wrote the day before, being the 9th of May, they were no surprise to him:

'I shall, of course, make myself quite sure that the rebels are quashed before I break up the Force, as otherwise I should incur great responsibility, but on these subjects I act for myself and judge for myself; this I have found to be the best way of getting on. I shall not leave things in a mess, I hope, but I think if I am spared I shall be home for Christmas. The losses I have sustained in this campaign have been no joke;

out of 100 officers I have 48 killed and wounded, and out of 3500 men nearly 1000 killed and wounded; but I have the satisfaction of knowing that, as far as mortal can see, six months will see the end of this rebellion, while, if I had continued inactive, it might have lingered on for six years. Do not think that I am ill-tempered, but I do not care one jot about my promotion or what people may say. I know I shall leave China as poor as when I entered it, but with the knowledge that through my weak instrumentality upwards of eighty to one hundred thousand lives have been spared. I want no further satisfaction than this. The rebels of Chanchufu are the "originals" of the rebellion, and though there may be some innocent, still the mass of them are deserving the fate that awaits them. If you could see the horrible cruelties they have everywhere perpetrated, you would say with me that it is impossible to intercede.

'They are the runaways of Soochow, Quinsan, Taitsan, Woosieh, Yesing and many other towns; they cut off the heads of the unfortunate country people at the rate of 30 to 40 per diem for attempting to run away.'

All his letters home are like this, dry, almost professional. To unbend on paper was with him even rarer than to unbend in conversation. When the final assault had, by such a very narrow margin succeeded, he wrote, only an hour or two later:

My dear Mother,
Chanchufu was carried by assault by the Quinsan Force and the Imperialists at 2 P.M. this day, with little loss. I go back to Quinsan on May 13, and shall not again take the field. The rebels are now done; they have only Tayan and Nankin, and the former will probably fall in a day or two, and Nankin in about two months. I am happy to say I got off safe.
Your affectionate son,
C. G. Gordon

*   *   *

Brevet Lieutenant-Colonel Gordon, who in fifteen months had saved an Empire to the admiration of friends and enemies alike, returned to Quinsan to find an order removing him, with all other British officers, from the Chinese Service. The mills of Whitehall grind exceeding small. This was the belated result of his own complaint about Governor Li. Had the order reached Pekin before Gordon recovered from his wound, the Taiping rebellion would have dragged on for years; perhaps at last succeeded in sweeping the Manchus off the Dragon Throne and the men from Europe back into the sea. Thanks to the delay, the news was now welcome, and not only to Gordon, who made haste to disband the Quinsan Force before it dissolved, or even went south to the relief of Nankin. To leave it in being, but without work to do, would be asking for trouble. There would certainly be no more fighting, not only because of the withdrawal of British officers, but also because the Imperialists would lose face by having to share with foreigners their final victory.

In spite of all their differences and the hard things they had said about one another, Governor Li and Gordon again became firm friends, a development assisted by the former's unwonted generosity in the matter of bounty, each man receiving enough to pay his passage home and something over, while a wounded officer benefited by as much as £900. Gordon even unbent to the extent of accepting an invitation to breakfast at Li's palace. There he met Halliday Macartney, with whom he had gone on feuding because of his rôle as Li's messenger. He wrote after the meeting:

Shanghai, July 5, 1864

MY DEAR MACARTNEY,

It is with much regret that I perceive in the last Blue Book on Chinese affairs a Report from me to General Brown on the occurrences at Soochow, which report contains an injurious remark on your conduct.

I am extremely sorry that I ever penned that remark, as I believe you went out of your way on that occasion wholly on the same public grounds which led to my taking the field myself, and I can only excuse my having done so by recollecting the angry feelings with which I was actuated at that time.

It will be my duty to rectify this error in other quarters, and in the meantime I beg you to make what use you think fit of this letter.

Yours truly,

C. G. GORDON

He had also written home: 'The only man I have seen worth anything is the Governor of Kiangsoo, Li, who is stigmatised by Osborne as unprincipled, etc., etc. That the execution of the Wangs at Soochow was a breach of faith there is no doubt, but there were many reasons to exculpate the Governor for his action, which is not at all a bad act in the eyes of the Chinese. In my opinion Li Hung Chang is the best man in the Empire, has correct ideas of his position, and, for a Chinaman, most liberal tendencies.'

History was to show the correctness of this judgement, and to tinge it with cynicism. For Li, who, thanks to Gordon, was the least anti-European of men of power in China, was later cast as the big bogy-man of the 'Yellow Peril'; chiefly, it seems, because he learned well from Gordon, and would not brook, when he came to viceregal power, that China should again risk civil war through an insufficiency of modern armed force. Nor was his appearance in accord with the popular idea of a diplomatic Fu Manchu, the 'inscrutable oriental' plotting the downfall of the West before a flood of little yellow men with magazine rifles: 'A wondrously tall, beneficent-looking stranger from another world he seemed,—glorious in his blue robes, dignified in his gait and bearing, and beaming with courtly smiles of appreciation at all he saw. For distinction of appearance it would be hard to think of any man of this or the last generation to approach Li Hung Chang. It was not that he gave you the impression of great achievement or personal power, but his mien conveyed a sense of personal dignity as of some demi-god self-sufficient and detached, yet suave and condescending to struggling mortals.'

That was written by his biographer, Bland, who saw him entering the House of Commons, admittedly some years later, but the quality must have been there all the time.

* * *

The Force disbanded, how could Gordon bear to be idle? Yet what was there to do until he could leave China? In the south an army of Imperialists was tunnelling under the gigantic walls of Nankin and periodically exploding quantities of gunpowder with inadequate effect. Within, the 'Heavenly King' still kept his queer Court ritual. It was

H

natural for Gordon to wish to be present at the end of the siege, even if he could only do so in the capacity of an observer and guest of the commander-in-chief, Tseng Kwo-fan.

In contrast to operations in the north, here things were done on a grand scale. The complex earthworks of the besiegers, arranged in depth, stretched for twenty or thirty miles around the great city of the Porcelain Tower. Saps by the dozens fell in or were blown up, yet it was still believed that an assault would prove too costly. Starvation would be cheaper. Then, perhaps in honour of their distinguished visitor, the Chinese blew their biggest mine, packing some forty thousand pounds of gunpowder. A twenty-foot gap appeared in the wall and sixty thousand impatient troops prepared to enter the city.

While his fanatics fought to the last under Chung Wang, who with his bodyguard cut his way through to a brief freedom, Tien Wang set about his ascension with characteristic efficiency. He had already got rid of all the enemies in his power, usually by flaying alive or pounding to death. Now he hanged all his wives as a perverted compliment to their attractiveness, and drafted a suitable proclamation. The text does not appear to have survived, but of it Gordon's friend and biographer, Egmont Hake, wrote: 'He wished to be remembered by posterity as inspired by Heaven—as the Heavenly King. He scouted the suggestion that one so great as himself should fly: he had received, he said, the command of God and Jesus to come down upon earth and rule it. "I am the sole Lord of ten thousand nations," he cried out, "what should I fear?" He told how he held the empire, the hills and the streams with an iron grasp.'

It is a pity his ravings did not reach those English zealots who still preferred to see his hell-bent career as a crusade. In China he was not mourned when, having delivered this last testament, the False Emperor sucked gold leaf into his lungs and so, pseudo-imperially, expired.

Then Gordon returned to Shanghai, where he received with a good grace various eulogistic tributes; but he could not be induced to go to Pekin, where Chinese and Europeans alike were eager to do him honour. Instead, he took the first opportunity to get back to work—teaching British drill to Chinese. He owed this unromantic post to the anxieties of the merchants, who were naturally insistent to have a disciplined and well-armed corps at their disposal now that the Quinsan Force had disintegrated. The immediate future might seem secure, but they remembered the days when Taiping tide had lapped at the thirty-mile perimeter. Next time there would be no Gordon, nor even a Ward.

So it was 'on the square' that the hero's days were spent while he awaited permission and a passage home, in time, as he had forecast, for Christmas. He wrote to his mother saying that ' "the individual" is coming home', a contemptuous contrast to the Very Important Officer which had long been his rôle, and which, when he was not gloomy, he thoroughly enjoyed. He added that she must be careful not to let anyone know, for he would tolerate no visitors, particularly ex-comrades in arms. They would 'be worse than the waits'.

The fact is probably that he did not want to go home at all. There were plenty of people who wished him to stay, and would surely have rewarded him handsomely for doing so, not only in money but in power; for, quite apart from the commercial interests which had little faith in exclusively Chinese protection, Prince Kung and Sir Frederick Bruce were both anxious to keep him, at least until peace was consolidated. Chinese officials, however, were jealous. They preferred to have him out of the way while they set what was after all their own house in order. At home politicians and the War Office feared that such an erratic and independent person might somehow involve the country in further incidents and unwelcome commitments; while cranks cried out for his recall because of the alleged atrocities committed by his 'heathen' troops against the 'Christian' rebels. Whatever the basis for the stories which circulated, at least Gordon himself was not guilty, as the following record from a rebel source shows:

'Well are we accustomed to the ruffianly conduct of many of the low scoundrels who disgrace the name of Englishman, and whom we know to be capable of any atrocity, we do not imagine that the great leader of an army would ever consent to the perpetration of murders so horrible. Yet never did the plains of China blush with blood more unrighteously spilled than on the day succeeding the capture of Quinsan, when the disorganised Hua contingent satiated itself with outrage. No, not even in the ancient days, when the men of Han fought valiantly with Mongol and Manchu, not even in the sanguinary but glorious days of Chu, did undisciplined and semi-barbarous troops equal the atrocities of the English drilled army. I have heard that Gordon grieved bitterly over the cruelties he could not prevent, and that his heart burned when he thought that in your happy and prosperous country beyond the Western Ocean these horrors would be ascribed to him. It may gratify him to think that even amongst those who would willingly be his friends, but are forced to be his enemies, he does not receive the blame of the events he could not control. . . .

'Often have I seen the deadly musket struck from the hand of a dastardly Englishman (tempted by love of loot to join our ranks) when he attempted from his place of safety to kill Gordon, who ever rashly exposed himself. This has been the act of a chief, yea, of the Shield King himself. How then can one be accused of blind hatred, even to our enemies?'

Gordon himself came to the conclusion that it would have been better if Europe had left China alone—a far cry this from his early missionary zeal, his conviction that only Europe was civilised and that it was her duty to confer her culture upon other nations willy-nilly. So, while Li Hung Chang was settling like a noble bird to feather a higher nest, and Chung Wang was writing his life before being beheaded, Gordon went on drilling, waiting for his ship and examining his conscience. In spite of his own claim to have saved so many lives, it is clear that he was by no means satisfied with himself: 'I have sent my journal (of 1863) home. I do not want the same published, as I think if my proceedings sink into oblivion it would be better for everyone, and my reason for this is that it is a very contested point whether we ought to have interfered or not, on which point I am perfectly satisfied that it was the proper and humane course to pursue; but I still do not expect people who do not know much about it to concur in the same.'

The Chinese took quite the opposite view about letting his 'proceedings sink into oblivion'. There came a decree written with the Vermilion Pencil: 'We command that Gordon be rewarded with a yellow riding-jacket to be worn on his person, and a peacock's feather to be carried on his cap; also that there be bestowed upon him four suits of the uniform proper to his rank of Ti-Tu, in token of our favour and desire to do him honour. Respect this!' Evidently the British Minister, officially as well as personally, shared their view, as the following despatch to the Foreign Secretary, Lord John Russell, shows: 'I enclose translation of a despatch from Prince Kung, containing the decree published by the Emperor, acknowledging the services of Lieutenant-Colonel Gordon, Royal Engineers, and requesting that Her Majesty's Government be pleased to recognise them. This step has been spontaneously taken.

'Lieutenant-Colonel Gordon well deserves Her Majesty's favour, for, independently of the skill and courage he has shown, his disinterestedness has elevated our national character in the eyes of the Chinese. Not only has he refused any pecuniary reward, but he has spent more than his pay in contributing to the comfort of the officers who served under him, and in assuaging the distress of the starving population whom he relieved from the yoke of their oppressors. Indeed, the feeling that impelled him to resume operations after the fall of Soochow was one of the purest humanity. He sought to save the people of the districts that had been recovered from a repetition of the misery entailed upon them by the civil war.'

The business community were not slow to add their praises in the form of an illuminated address which read in part:

'Your career during the last two years of your residence in the East has been, so far as we know, without a parallel in the history of the intercourse of foreign nations with China; and, without entering at all upon the political bearings of the great question with which your name must ever remain so intimately connected, we feel that we should be alike wanting towards you and towards ourselves were we to pass by this opportunity without expressing our appreciation and admiration of the line of conduct which you personally have pursued.

'In a position of unequalled difficulty, and surrounded by complications of every possible nature, you have succeeded in offering to the eyes of the Chinese nation, no less by your loyal, and, throughout, disinterested line of action, than by your conspicuous gallantry and talent for organisation and command, the example of a foreign officer serving the Government of this country with honourable fidelity and undeviating self-respect. . . .

'Once more wishing you a prosperous voyage and a long career of usefulness and success. . . .'

This address was signed by over fifty firms of which the first four were: Jardine Matheson & Co., Dent & Co., Russell & Co. and Smith Kennedy & Co.

All this was dwarfed, in terms of ceremony but not of sincerity, by a procession which arrived one morning at Gordon's barracks. This made the presentation of the 10,000 *taels* a second-rate performance, for the mission with which they were entrusted was, as near as maybe, the investiture of Gordon with the two highest 'orders' in China, as it might be to the Garter and the Bath, together with his appointment as Field-Marshal.

Hundreds of Mandarins processed in ceremonial robes to the accompaniment of gongs, fireworks, a multitude of incense-burners and a file of state porters carrying a sequence of finely wrought chests, each covered with white linen bearing the vermilion dragon. The chests were carried into a big mess-tent which had been prepared for the purpose. Outside, the Chinese ranged some artillery with which they fired a series of salutes while, for five hours, Gordon endured his ceremonial robing and re-robing according to the time-honoured ritual of the Yellow Riding-Jacket and the Peacock's Feather. He seems to have taken it all in good part, though his smile is described as cynical—probably 'contemptuous' would be more accurate. Once he showed anger.

At each display of the new garments of nobility, attendants kow-towed, beating their heads on the earth and backing away. One of them fell into a shallow pit full of water which the officers had been accustomed to use as an improvised wine-cooler and had evidently been overlooked when the tent was being prepared. Gordon glared at those who showed traces of amusement, and then overcome, for once, by a sense of the ludicrous, saved what might have been an awkward situation by smiling. The unfortunate Mandarin was restored with brandy in champagne.

His 'trousseau', as the French account of Biovès has it, included silk shirts, robes, jackets, hats, caps, fans, girdles, jade thumb-rings, shoes, boots. Each chest contained one complete 'outfit'. Each 'outfit' had to be ceremonially donned, to the accompaniment of gun-fire, the braying of copper horns and the beating of gongs. A more embarrassing business for a man of Gordon's temperament could hardly have been contrived. His only consolation must have been that he had at least succeeded in avoiding once again a money present, this time in excess of the 10,000 *taels* which before he had so peremptorily refused. For the sake of comparison, a responsible letter to *The Times* suggested that his services had been worth 20 millions of *taels*, in which context the total cost of the campaign appears cheap at £200,000, and Burgevine, 'alive or dead', expensive at 3000 *taels*, offered by Governor Li at the time of the seizure of the *Firefly*.

With the departure of the Emperor's emissaries, Gordon went back to his drill and his unquiet conscience. The days must have seemed long before he could say good-bye, for he undertook to complete the survey which had been interrupted, in its final stages, by his appointment to the Ever Victorious Army. Even when there dawned his last day in China he would make no change in his usual routine, and at evening slipped away from his friends to shut himself in his cabin on board the *Hyson*, which was to take him on the first stage of his journey. So he escaped a European send-off, but for a mile and a half the steamer paddled between banks lined with Chinese who had not forgotten their usual noise-making apparatus. The din resembled that of battle. Darkness had fallen. The course of the canal was outlined by thousands of paper lanterns carried by sad, simple people. Their deliverer was leaving them. What would they have thought had they known that behind the *Hyson* trailed a bundle consisting of a brand-new suit and a billycock hat? How could they have understood that their hero regarded their gratitude as something of an insult, and, far from feeling proud of his achievement on their behalf, wished it to be forgotten as soon as possible?

In his own eyes he was far from being a fine bird, and so fine feathers were not only inappropriate, they were sinful.

The suit, presumably the only one he possessed, must have caused raised eyebrows in the saloon of the P. & O. liner on which he voyaged home. It would have made him conspicuous, the very thing he so much wished to avoid, perhaps. Gordon was proud of his humility.

Chapter 6

FAITH AND FORTS

GORDON'S home, at 5 Rockstone Place, Southampton, was ruled by his ailing father, administered by his doting mother and kept up to a heavy spiritual collar by the unsmiling eldest sister, Augusta. The *ménage* was snug and smug. It offered to the returning hero little more than a call upon his filial piety. Yet he avoided contact with wider-minded people; still less, and largely for fear of a matrimonial risk, would he attend any mixed gathering.

Soon even the early morning prayers began to pall, and long religious discussions lost their power to bring him peace. He was by now an addicted smoker, but the kitchen was the one room in the house where his cigarettes were permitted, presumably only when the cook had gone to bed. He had good reason to display even more than his usual irascibility, for he had acquired a terse, almost belligerent manner with equals and superiors; though he kept his forbearance for juniors, and his saintliness for circumstances beyond the unavoidable clash of domestic or professional temperament. Yet at home he does not appear to have resented being treated as an infant prodigy rather than a veteran warrior. He acted, he says, as 'A.D.C.' to his mother, going out with her in the carriage and assisting with shopping, which took up, with its inevitable gossip, much of her time. Though he did so dutifully, she can hardly have been under the illusion that he liked it, and must have thought him boorish to resent even the mildest social occasion, such as a musical evening. He had no ear for music, and no interest in any subject for conversation outside his two professions—of arms and of faith—neither of which was suitable for the drawing-room. So the family, with perhaps an occasional intimate guest, had to sit mum in the evening unless they were able to draw him out. He would then talk volubly and at length, perhaps exaggerating speech as he exaggerated silence. Hake says: 'As Gordon stood every evening for three or four hours descanting on the things he had seen, now pointing to the map before him to explain a position, now raising his voice in sudden anger at defeat, or dropping it with victory in mercy for the fallen, the company was spell-bound and amazed'.

Reassured by such signs that he might be thawing out, his mother on one occasion did not trouble to conceal from him, as he entered the room, a map she was showing to some friends. It was one he had drawn while at The Shop. He blew across the room like a black squall, snatched the map, tore it to fragments and threw them in the fireplace. That later on he rescued the pieces and painstakingly pasted them together again would not have reassured her. The war, she must have realised, had done something in him too deep for her to reach, too deep for any woman, or any man. A later, somewhat similar incident confirmed her opinion. When a well-meaning Minister wished to allow a wider circle to benefit from the journal which Gordon had lent him, he had it set up by a local printer. The infuriated officer, finding the good man out when he called to protest, drove on to the press. There, not content with burning the journal, he had the type destroyed. Later still, fearful that a writer engaged upon an account of the Taiping Rebellion might be praising him, he insisted on tearing up 'sheet after sheet' in front of the wretched author, who was his guest at the time.

His father fell ill and died, an event which profoundly affected this battle-hardened son for whom he had had such a distant regard. Soon Gordon found that he could no longer bear the home life for which he had yearned while abroad; and so, with only eight months elapsed out of his two years' leave, he applied for immediate employment, making the condition that he should not be posted ahead of officers of equal seniority who had not had opportunity for foreign service.

In the ordinary way, unless the Army Council had some real reason for keeping him back, he should have been given a further spell of active service abroad. No doubt he counted upon it, if only because at home, in spite of his hermit's life, he was a public figure dodging the limelight which tried to follow him. Already *The Times* had published the following letter, sequel to an earlier one:

'It has already been pointed out that Colonel Gordon's being an engineer, no less than his peculiarly retiring character, has kept him from the employment for which his genius seemed to indicate him, and which less exploits than his might fairly have claimed. But there is probably another reason for this apparent neglect, of which I have only become aware since writing to you last week. A gentleman, himself in the public service and well acquainted with China, happening to identify at a guess the writer of *The Times* letter, has just communicated to me the following account of matters intimately connected with the fall of the Taipings, and our share in it which I take the liberty of introducing in his own words to your readers' notice. He states:

' "Being at Shanghai in the summer of 1864, I met the late Sir Frederick Bruce, our minister, on his way to England. He told me that the very day before he left Pekin he was astonished at receiving a personal visit from Prince Kung, the then Regent of China, who had some days before come to say good-bye to him. The Prince said, 'You will be astonished to see me again, but I felt I could not allow you to leave without coming to see you about Gordon. We do not know what to do. He will not receive money from us, and we have already given him every honour which is in the power of the Emperor to bestow; but as these can be of little value in his eyes, I have brought you this letter, and ask you to give it to the Queen of England, that she may bestow on him some reward which would be more valuable in his eyes.' Sir Frederick showed me a translation of Prince Kung's letter. I only remember that it was couched in the most charming terms, and that it pleaded Gordon's services as to what he had done to 'promote kindly intercourse between the two nations', while fully acknowledging the immense services he had rendered to China. I went", adds my informant, "to Pekin in the autumn of that year, where Gordon had been officially invited; but his dislike of being made a hero prevented his going. Had he done so, he would have been received with almost royal honours."

'Now, sir, receiving as I have done this narrative from a man of honour, who speaks earnestly and in good faith, and coupling it with the well-known fact that when Colonel Gordon presented himself at the War Office some months later, the Minister seemed hardly to have heard his name, and to know nothing whatever of his successes, may it not be true— as a weekly contemporary of yours seems to suggest—that the letter of Prince Kung never reached its destination at all; indeed, never got beyond the pigeon-holes of the Foreign Office? At least, in the interest of historical truth, I would hope that some active-minded member of Parliament may not think it too late to draw attention to the subject, and to seek the production of the missing despatch, the absence of which possibly has excused that extraordinary neglect of a great soldier with which the War Office have been charged.'

The writer of the letter got no satisfaction. He might have realised at the time that such publicity would be no more acceptable to Gordon himself than to the War Office, where in all probability there was a feeling that, because of the relatively small force under his command, the tributes of the Chinese had been excessive. There may even have been an idea that the 'inscrutable Oriental' had been trying to foist this cuckoo into the Army nest; for it could hardly have been appreciated at the Horse Guards, then the fount of military dogma, that it was largely because the Ever Victorious had been small that it could be both mobile and hard-hitting; the sharp end of a wedge for victory. Gordon had found a war of attrition. He made it a war of mobility, and so demonstrated the limitations of Crimean tactics. As to the magnitude of the attrition, the population of China dropped during two decades (1842–1862), most of which was covered by the wastage of the rebellion, by a hundred and fifty millions.

But for all that, there was still a vociferous body of critics which had been ably represented by Mr. Forster in the House of Commons: 'Our operations in China are a species of buccaneering. . . . We had a good deal to do with the anarchy now prevailing in China. . . . The end of the policy would throw another China war on our hands and oblige us to effect the conquest of that country.'

Nor had the rumour about Gordon's own responsibilities been scotched. His campaign was represented in some quarters as a wicked drive to impose our will upon China by violence for the sake of trade. Atrocity stories still circulated, for instance, that at the fall of Soochow thirty thousand people had been massacred, behind all of which was the calmer, but longer, view that whatever his personal integrity, Gordon had been the chosen instrument of an ignoble policy which had brought not only him but all Europeans into disrespect. A corrective to such ideas was contained in a Memorial which about this time Li Hung Chang addressed to the Dragon Throne, and though it could not then have been available in England it is too important to omit in the present context:

'In the course of time foreigners came to China, opened various marts and conveyed their merchandise everywhere. They traded at as many as five ports, and all with no other object than that of making the wealth of China contribute to their own. A little consideration shows that those who ventured to come to this country must have placed their reliance upon something to have rendered them so fearless; and there is not the slightest reason why that which they confided in should not also become a source of confidence to China. . . .

'The Memorialist has had several years' experience in conducting business with foreigners and is thoroughly familiar with their character. He has found that, no matter what they are engaged in, they act honourably, without deceit or falsehood. But although it is possible to acquire a general knowledge of their mode of action in the conduct of their own affairs, yet there is no means of becoming thoroughly acquainted with the details of the motives of their conduct. Their bearing, however, in military matters affords clear evidence of their straightforwardness. There is an instance of the Englishman, Gordon, late commander-in-chief at Soochow, who, having organised three thousand troops of the Ever Victorious Army, took the field against the rebels. Subsequently, at the capture of Soochow, the Memorialist himself observed that officer personally leading in advance of his troops with a courage and *sangfroid* worthy of all praise.'

It is noteworthy that Li does not regard Christianity as the source of the foreigner's merits, though he did give it considerable study and concluded that it might have a limited application within the Empire. Instinctively he came to recognise that the real source of integrity is in the individual character, which, contrary to popular belief, can be clothed, but not moulded, by custom and by creed. Even without Li's opinion, the Horse Guards had more to take into consideration than Gordon's reputation and record in the public eye. From his personal contacts with important people they knew of his embarrassing impetuosity, his conviction contrary to the yet unchallenged idea of the superiority of white skin over coloured, his honesty often pushed to the point of downright rudeness and his indifference to rewards or punishments where matters of conscience were involved. The snubs which he administered to people who, with the best of motives, wished to assist his career, might have turned the scale against his re-employment except in some situation where it was virtually impossible to display initiative.

In all probability his request to go back to duty before even half his leave was up was an embarrassment to the Adjutant-General. It must certainly have been a shock also to his mother and Augusta, who, without even drawing upon the religious bond, might reasonably have expected that following his father's death he would stay with them for some considerable time.

Gordon's own mind may well have been troubled about his duty towards his home, and yet he had every reason to believe himself free of responsibility because Augusta was so clearly capable of looking after the house, her mother and everyone within reach. Less easy to explain to himself was why, after pining for a period of retreat and contemplation, he should so soon, in his own phrase, 'hail the tram of the world'. The answer in a single word was 'boredom', but he would not have seen the issue in such simplicity. It is more likely that he blamed himself for failure to settle down to the contemplative life, for being in need of the constant stimulus of duty and physical activity.

Looking back from this remove in time, it is permissible to take the explanation a stage further. Gordon wrote to Augusta, 'Talk of two natures in one. I have a hundred, and they none think alike and all want to rule.' Yes, they all wanted to *rule*. Rulership was his passion, government his business; and if it began with self-government the fact remains that he was a man divided, even at war, within himself. From that intolerable state there is only one effective escape—

into such action as forces a temporary and superficial integration of personality. When a country is divided, it seeks a common enemy. When a sane man is divided, he seeks an integrating occupation; but, unless he be a gross materialist, mere physical, or even intellectual, activity will be insufficient. Man functions on many levels. At least three were involved in Gordon's treatment of his internal strife. First came sheer muscular effort. He could never stroll, even when by striding he would arrive too soon. Then there was the virtual blackout imposed upon his intellectual life by insistence that all essential truth is written in the Bible; so that not only is speculation unnecessary, it is highly undesirable. One needs only to wonder, not to think. Finally, he took his divided nature to the great unifying principle, religion, believing that, united with the Father by the Son, he must be united in himself. The means he chose were necessarily those of government. His erring aspects of personality must be drilled and dragooned into conformity with orders from Above. The result was an attempted imitation of Christ which made him miserable. For love, though he offered it in all sincerity, he knew not except under sterile conditions. Consequently, he was tied and bound, not so much by the chain of his sins as by a tow-rope. With it he toiled to drag his life along the narrow canal of his principles towards its confluence with the mystical River of Life. It never seemed to occur to him that the River might be reached before the body died.

To call forth ever greater effort, he continually reminded himself how unworthy he was, and yet also that he had something few others could boast, an intimation of immortality. Therefore, most people seemed to him shallow and trivial, a judgement dangerously close to contempt. Was that why he cut himself off, as far as possible, from all contacts except those which seemed spiritually and emotionally, but not physically, safe? Whatever the motive, when, having failed to adjust himself to home life, he went back to duty, Gordon set about the impossible task of loving God and Man but not people, not *individuals*. He loved his neighbourhood, but did he really love his neighbour? Deprived of normal social contacts though surrounded by the sick, poor, sad and bad, his over-developed conscience treated his body like a prisoner, and shut up his mind with the Bible, making hard labour out of the service which should be perfect freedom.

*   *   *

His new appointment was Officer Commanding Royal Engineers at Gravesend. His particular responsibility was the supervision of the building of five forts intended to protect the capital by denying the river to the enemy. To anyone else with his record it would have seemed an insult, for he was at the time the most experienced officer in the British Army on the subject of fixed defences, their capabilities and limitations. Not for nothing had he fought in the last two years quite twenty sieges against towns which were, tactically speaking, forts. Yet Gordon appeared to welcome the idea of being the mere foreman of works sited and designed without consulting him. Perhaps he hoped to make a new kind of reputation, as distinguished in its way as that of 'Chinese' Gordon, but not in the world's terms. He would fight actions just as hard, just as perilous as any against the Taipings, but they would be 'in the spirit'.

His headquarters was a rambling eighteenth-century house overlooking the Thames. It had originally been compact but, being promoted to be the seat of a senior officer, had recently been added to. The effect was confusing. From the original stone-built pair of gables there extended an exuberance of pitched roofs, each with its complement of sash windows set in clapboards. To complete the haphazard effect was a lean-to greenhouse, painted white. The garden had a fine, sloping lawn from which the Thames shipping could be seen with a pleasing sense of privilege; and there was a sufficiency of cultivation for the exacting demands of a contemporary Colonel's lady. Such was his command post, from which he would direct his war against 'principalities and powers' and establish a line of communication, not to a military or diplomatic superior, but to the source of Moravian orthodoxy, which, as near as it can be defined, seemed to be his theological inspiration.

For this he had plenty of time. Not even he could spin out military duty for more than six hours a day, though he did his best to make those hours as strenuous as possible, driving himself and his subordinates, most of whom were civilians, as though in war. Yet not only did he know that the forts would not be immediately required; he realised that their construction was a tactical error based upon a strategic misconception. They would be useless if the test came, and represented not a deterrent but an invitation to invasion. Yet their cost amounted to twelve million pounds.

Though he protested, he did not go so far as to threaten resignation. After all, the site of the forts was not his responsibility, so his conscience was not involved except in the details of construction. He pursued the work-schedules with fanatical vigour. For a man obsessed with the idea of eternity he was strangely time-bound—'Another five minutes gone and this not done yet, my men! We shall never have them again.'

Even so, the work took more than the six years he held the appointment. By then the faults in the plan were beginning to be appreciated. Of the five forts, the three south of the estuary could be sealed off by an enemy who thought of flooding the area, so turning them into ineffective islands of resistance. The two northern ones could be by-passed, leaving them open from the rear to fire from commanding ground which would render them untenable.

Once installed at Fort House, he set about creating as near a monastic routine as could be contrived without benefit of community. He rose early enough to spend a full hour at his devotions, accepted a minimal breakfast from his sorely-tried housekeeper, the 'Giantess'. Exactly at eight o'clock he went out to his official boat. This had been a two-oared affair, solidly built. It was not fast enough for Gordon, who exchanged it for a light four-oared gig. This, manned by elderly Thames Watermen, he used as though it were under fire, driving his rowers until, by the time they reached their destination, they were 'seriously distressed'. Gordon would leap ashore and almost run from place to place, while junior officers, foremen and contractors puffed after him. This went on until two o'clock in the afternoon. He would not tolerate a mid-morning break.

Such is Wrotham's record, its theme that Gordon's life was dominated by his favourite phrase to the boatmen, 'A little faster, boys, a little faster!' Yet it is only proper to add that with it all there is no suggestion that Gordon was unkind or even inconsiderate. If he drove people hard it was only because he was convinced that it was good for them. Back at Fort House, the front door of which was permanently open because he believed that no one in need should be turned away, he took his meal out of the drawer of one of the four deal tables which were his principal items of furniture. That is not to say he foraged, the Giantess had to lay his place in it, neat and tidy, knife and fork. The object was that if anyone, meaning anyone seeking help—for he would not tolerate a social call—came in, he could shut the drawer, brush the crumbs off his considerable moustache, and never betray the fact that he could not manage to live without eating. He did his best though, giving away all the vegetables his garden still grew, in spite of the fact that much of it had been turned into allotments. The gardener was an infirm old man who drew his pay largely for the privilege of snoozing in the potting-shed, from which he could peer out to see who was taking advantage of the Colonel's gift of a key to the garden door. In fine weather there would usually be several old people in chairs on the lawn.

He seems to have lived largely on bread, tea and salt beef, this last a concession to the beggar-boys, his 'Kings' or 'Wangs', some of whom he usually had staying with him. When a neighbour dared to remark that his solitary meal looked unappetising and was obviously insufficient, he took the stale remnant of a loaf and crammed it into the slop basin. He then added the contents of the teapot, remarking that when the mess was cool enough it would be all he needed. Half an hour after a meal, he demanded, does it matter what has been eaten?

Consequently his appearance at this time was almost frail. 'He was rather under average height, of slight proportions, and with little of the military bearing in his carriage, so that one would hardly have imagined that this kindly-looking, un-assuming gentleman was already one of the most distinguished officers in Her Majesty's service. . . . The great charm of his countenance was the clear blue eye which seemed to possess magic power over all who came within its influence. It read you through and through, it made it impossible for you to tell him anything but the truth, it invited your confidence, it kindled with compassion at every story of distress, and it sparkled with good humour at anything really funny or witty. From its glance you knew at once that, at any risk, he would keep his promise, that you might trust him with anything and everything, and that he would stand by you if all other friends deserted you.'

Another account says: 'When he entered I was, for the moment, disappointed. I had heard and read much about "Chinese" Gordon and had formed in my own mind an ideal of the man who had done such wonders. . . . But in the very quiet and unassuming man, with a manner that seemed almost nervous, I could trace nothing of my idea. In a very few minutes, however, I began to know him; and during the three years of our intercourse I grew to appreciate the power of the man. . . . I never knew a man who lived so near to God. He literally looked not at the seen but the unseen, and "endured as seeing Him who is invisible".'

All boys were 'royalty' to Gordon. They came to him through the Ragged School Union, the local Missionary and by the increasing number of local people who knew him personally. So heavy did his self-imposed burden become that he had to buy suits by the dozen and boots by the gross. What was left of his pay went to maintain his pensioners, including one of his boatmen, many of whom continued to receive their weekly money long after he left Gravesend and even until his death.

The resident boys, whom at need he washed under the pump in the back-yard, whose clothes he patched, whose ignorance he taught, and for whom he found jobs, usually prevented him from entertaining more conventional guests, though on one occasion Augusta paid a visit. She was not welcome: 'My sister comes, D.V., next Monday, and the place is to become a hermitage. I cannot help it. She likes it, so I shall tell my friends I am in New Zealand till she goes.'

This may have been due less to a cooling of his fraternal feeling for her than to a fact of which she would have been certain to disapprove. In a neighbour, Mrs. Freese, he had found the only woman friend of his life. She was a wife and mother, who first met him with the extraordinary advantage that she did not know who he was. Near neighbours, they shared charitable and religious interests for months before her husband enquired Gordon's opinion on the policy with regard to China. He was told, 'I am the man who put down the rebellion!'

Since he could not afford a horse, Gordon's only recreation was walking in what was then the open country round about. Even this had to serve a serious purpose—to distribute tracts. These he would leave in the most unlikely places, following, as nearly as possible with printed 'seed', the parable of the sower. Upon the margins of the paths, in the good ground of the fields, his tracts would fall. Occasionally one would be balanced on the top rail of a stile, prevented from blowing away by a suitable stone, which further pointed the moral of the heading, 'Beware that thou stumblest not'. He even used to fling out of the window of his railway carriage bundles of tracts and small books. They do not seem to have injured any-one working on the line.

On one occasion, having missed the last through train from London, he tramped from Woolwich, where he could easily have found a bed, to Gravesend: 'I walked down the 16 miles in 4¼ hours and got here at 5.15 A.M. This is pleasure—the last eight miles in the rain. However, I liked it, it is so quiet, and in passing the villages you see lights up where there is sickness and death, sorrow and crying. The weary workers at the factories wending their way at an early hour to hard labour. How any one of us can think this world a happy one is a wonder with so much sorrow.'

The social conscience to which this letter is witness was highly developed, but, just as his mysticism was too wide for a religious sect, so his sense of humanity was too generalised to allow him to fit into any political pigeon-hole. While he realised, with an intensity rare in his time, the human suffer-ing entailed by the new slavery in factories and mines, he neither vilified the rich nor glorified the poor. The character of a man was more important than his social status, the remedy for abuse of riches and privilege the same as that for sin. To take away from the rich and give to the poor would be only a commercial transaction. Gordon was not interested in commercial transactions as such, for he realised that they can never solve a human problem.

'We do not find Him taking the part of the poor against the rich individually,' he wrote to Augusta, 'yet, to hear of the work in a coal-mine, however well told, could not give us a particle of an idea of what the work there really is. To know that truly we must work not a year there, but a lifetime, to know the bitterness of that labour, of hard masters, of heat and cold and dirt in the delicate fibres of the skin, of the sorrows of those around us bereaved by sudden catastrophes.'

What is now called the redistribution of wealth seemed to him to be much less important than the substitution of a concept of service for the struggle for gain. So he took no part in the growing agitation for better working conditions. In any case, his social effort was always personal rather than collective; no doubt, on the reasonable assumption that if each did his duty to his neighbour there would be little need for the clammy charity of impersonal organisations.

* * *

Apart from his work he had no interest in anything but religion, and in few people except those to whom he could do good. He would not receive but only give, the dubious moral of his naïve theology based upon a rigid dualism according to which all that is of the world and the flesh is sinful without exception; so the only proper attitude is one of resignation to the belief that death will give not only relief, but *pro rata* compensation: the more suffering now, the more bliss hereafter. Those who do not suffer ought to, and the proper business of life is the contemplation of death. No wonder he made a practice of visiting the dying, being sent for 'in preference to the clergy'. He could tell them how fortunate they were.

When Christmas came round he wrote to Augusta: 'I must write and wish you a happy Xmas. I will not say many of them, for our joy is in our Lord, and we cannot wish many years will pass before He comes to deliver us from our contemptible bodies and infirmities.'

In another year he put off his Christmas leave to nurse one of his boys, Bob Weston, through a 'putrid fever', presumably typhoid. He then wrote, though not to Augusta, showing that his secret hope was that he might contract the disease and die of it. Any risk was apt to bring the same thought, as when his gig got into difficulties in the Thames. He had no use for this life except in terms of salvation through suffering.

From such a viewpoint death readily becomes an obsession and the observer must needs turn his back upon the most innocent joys. Gordon took this to such an extreme that he had no use for flowers. As he wrote to Augusta, 'The flesh you inhabit is "as grass, its glory is the flower of the grass; the grass withereth and the flower thereof fadeth, but the Lord endureth for ever" (I Peter i, 24, 25)'. He preferred, he said, the 'human face divine'. As with flowers, so with domestic animals: he had no use for them. After all, they had no souls. He wrote, 'Man that is in honour and understandeth not is like the beasts that perish (Psalm xlix, 12)'. Years later he was surprised to discover that camels feel fatigue and thirst.

Yet in spite of the knot he had tied himself in by intellectual contortions for the justification of an intuitive faith, he remained essentially kind where others would have become sadistic, broad where others would have become narrow. An officer wrote that he was 'the nearest approach to Jesus Christ of any man who ever lived'. No accumulation of negatives cancels a spiritual positive. To appreciate such a man, a cynical attitude is no better than the clinical one which would dismiss what he thought was *angina pectoris* as that 'false angina' which is often the product of emotional distress. The symptoms, even in his own day, were eventually referred to the liver. Neither the cynic nor the doctor ought to judge, they can only analyse and diagnose. If in their terms Gordon appears to have been a schizoid escapist, inventing devils to scare himself into being good, and enemies to turn his weakness into strength; imagining pleasure in the next world to compensate for pains in this one (he hoped that Heaven would have cities for him to govern)—theirs is still a superficial and misleading observation. It is almost as inadequate as the Freudian *reductio ad absurdum* that his character and achievement are explicable solely in terms of repressed, sublimated and projected libido.

There is an element of truth in such an analysis, but if it were more than trivial, Gordon would have developed accordingly. He would have become an impractical idealist, or a patient, or both. He did neither, because he clung to a rock of personal integrity amid the treacherous currents of his ideas; and for all his 'false angina' he was so healthy that he wore out and outlived many strong men with whom he worked. So it may be assumed that the character evinced by the way he wrote and spoke about religion was only a relatively superficial aspect of the whole man. He seems to have sensed this himself, reiterating that mere words, whether written or spoken, are no substitute for spiritual experience. That he had such experience is probable if not certain. In spite of his mental and physical symptoms he became stronger, not weaker, because their roots went up through the darkness into the light. As do all mystics, he stumbled over the interpretation of the reality which he intuited and felt rather than thought and believed. There is a vast difference between the two. And so it is legitimate to take the view that Gordon was already too big to be put into one category or another. He was not either a genius or a lunatic. He was not either deluded or illuminated. He was not either a success or a failure. In each case he was both. There are few indeed of whom so much can be said, who have known what it is to be 'in the spirit' and by comparison have seen the world's light as darkness. These succeed, if at all, not in the world's terms. To them physical defeat may be spiritual victory and *vice versa*. Whatever their calling, theirs is fundamentally the selfless service of tormenting light.

Gordon's own phrase for his illumination was 'the indwelling'. It is the cardinal fact of his experience and must have preceded the development of his theology, though there is no record of a climacteric ecstasy. Instead, the impression is of the gradual growth of a childlike, sometimes childish, faith, which has sometimes been misunderstood either as the whole of Gordon's mystery or as a mere aberration. The facts are against either of these facile judgements. His was the experience which, if it be equated, as is usual in the West, with the mystical birth of Christ, 'brings not peace but a sword'. The blade divides the chosen sacrifice not only in his personal relationships, dramatised as 'he who hateth not father or mother for my sake cannot be my disciple', but in himself.

Only when direct light shines is darkness localised as shadow. Before that happens in the mind, there is a sense of wholeness, however illusory. But when illumination occurs, the subject feels that he is being cut in pieces, and while he strives to 'pull himself together' he may be driven into illness. Realising this trend, he works desperately hard to understand what is happening and to project the conflict onto some exterior, or apparently exterior, concept such as God. To the psychologist there is no choice: he must contain or project his conflict if he is to integrate his personality. To the priest also there is no choice: he must confess his sins and seek wholeness by absolution, or else be damned. Whatever the chosen method, if it is to be effective it must be based upon the recognition that there are many orders of reality, many kinds of experience, and that it is asking for trouble to try to describe experience of one order in terms of another. Yet this is almost invariably what the independent mystic feels he must try to do, with the result that he frequently comes between his reader and the light. It is in such a context that, for instance, the following extracts out of Gordon's letters to Augusta, from Gravesend, should be taken:

'The world is a vast prison-house; we are under hard keepers, with hard rules, in cells solitary and lonely, looking for a release. What have we not to put up with from our masters? By the waters of earthly joy and plenty to the world's inhabitants (our flesh), but by the waters of lonely afflictions to our souls, we sit down and weep when we remember our home, from which death, like a narrow stream, divides us. Yea, we hang our harps upon the willows in the midst thereof, for they that oppress us require of us mirth, saying, "Sing us one of the songs of Zion" (Psalm cxxxvii). How, oh how, shall we sing the song of the Lamb in a strange land, in the (to us) waste, howling wilderness, in the land of strangers? Oh, for that home where "the wicked cease from troubling, and the weary be at rest" (Job iii, 17); where the good fight will have been fought, the dusty course finished, and the crown of life given; when our eyes will behold the only One who ever knew our sorrows and trials, and who has been with us in them all, soothing and comforting our weary souls!'

This letter is not exceptional but typical, not only in content but in style. He wrote to Augusta as an instructor in her own subject, text-work, but not as a fellow mystic: 'I feel my remark about getting time by rising at 6 A.M. was hard on you. Peace is a fruit of the Spirit and is obtained only by the indwelling of the Spirit; therefore the more we realise the truth of God's indwelling, the more this peace will be produced—this realisation is the gift of God. The indwelling of the Spirit makes the Christian faith different from all other religions. Meditate much on the fruit of the Spirit (Gal. v, 22, 23) and with God's blessing you will soon have done with dark times, which all arise from our thinking good of ourselves, or rather in our thinking we are improving.

'It is just as God manifests Himself to us, so we shall walk. It is through crosses that we live; let us have few crosses and we shall starve and be cold, let us have plenty of crosses and we shall thrive. We must feed on our own flesh, and, as we feed on it, we shall grow in proportion.'

Yet it is in no man's power utterly to control his moods by his mind, and even this dismal creed could not rob Gordon of laughter nor prevent him from communicating to people something of the inner optimism on which his pessimism had been grafted by pitiful necessity. Perhaps had he been more orthodox he would have escaped the worst of the dark days. But he, as one of Nietzsche's 'self-rolling wheels', had not the comfort of a community. There was no sense of 'belonging' to any of the churches at which he was a regular worshipper, for his creed was wide enough to include them all, and he held most parsons to be milk-and-water people. For all his preoccupation with texts, they seemed to him to lack evangelical force; which is hardly surprising since so few can speak from personal experience. In comparison, Gordon was an eye-witness, and somehow he managed to convey that impression: 'God's indwelling in us is the key to all the mysteries and apparent contradictions in the Scriptures; study them boldly and humbly. As long as you do not realise this truth of the dwelling of God in us, the Bible is a sealed book. It is sure and certain, whether you feel it or not.'

* * *

To Mrs. Freese, genial, middle-aged, middle-class, with a congenial husband and an adolescent daughter, Gordon appeared boyish; yet his eyes, she said, held an expression as though he were a thousand years old. What began as a common interest in missions and social welfare soon became friendship. She understood his shyness, and was the only person, including his family and particularly Augusta, with whom he seems to have been spontaneous. When he forgot for the moment about the ills of the world and its burden of sin, he could be gay and even witty, talking with youthful animation about trivial things. Usually he required solemnity, with long silences between remarks upon some grave matter.

To win his uncritical confidence seems to have been equivalent to gentling a timid animal. Even after Gordon had formed the habit of dropping in to see the Freese family, he could flare up or walk off on the slightest provocation. For instance, if he were asked to stay after he had intimated that he ought to be gone, or if any question were asked about his exploits, he would either subside into morose silence, or fling out of the house. To ask him to dinner would have been a great offence. He would say, 'Ask the poor and sick; don't ask me who have enough'.

It was hardly true, for he never ate what is now known as a 'balanced diet' and what he did have was minimal. Yet when Mrs. Freese ventured to protest at some particularly frugal drawer-full, he flared: 'Madam, I would not stand that even from my own mother!' Nor was it any easier when they called at Fort House. On one occasion, having passed through the 'ever open door', they heard him in full retreat to the cellar. Like a good Nannie, Mrs. Freese refused to be put off, and firmly sat herself down to wait for him to get tired of the dark and the damp. After all, he left the door open for the specific purpose of having visitors. But his patience in the cellar outlasted hers in the drawing-room. She and her husband had to go away again without seeing him.

Naturally perhaps, there was not the least tender sentiment in this relationship. As for the daughter, Ada, she seems to have been ignored, perhaps because on one occasion she so far forgot herself as to be pert to the solemn officer with the moustache and the queer, pale eyes. She was leaning on the Freese garden gate, which Gordon frequently used on a short cut. When he asked her to let him pass, she told him, teasing,

that he had better go round the long way. He told her
mother. The incident may possibly have had some bearing on
another which otherwise seems pointless. He had acquired a
camera and promised to take a photograph of the Freese
family. But, contrary to his own code, he not only failed to do
so; he sold or gave away the camera, 'as a snare keeping him
from God'. At about the same time he fought a losing battle
against his one indulgence, cigarettes. It took a fortnight for
him to confess, 'It's beaten me', and he regarded the outcome
as a serious spiritual defeat.

Yet Mrs. Freese remains the only person who ever seems to
have had a warm friendship with Gordon, certainly the only
woman. In the light of it he at last began to see through the
cheerless, sterile, proprietorial piety of Augusta, whose mysticism was as negative as her sex. It was her influence which
had given him such a fear of women and of marriage, in spite
of the scriptural commendation of the 'honourable estate'.
For Augusta was jealous even of her sisters, who consequently
had little chance to see their distinguished brother after they
were married. Gordon did not spend much time at her cheerless house, for there were always poor people to be visited, or a
class to take at the Ragged School or Sunday School. The
Infirmary and the Workhouse were on his list for regular
visits, and down on the estuary there was always the chance
of more 'royalty' to be rescued: the homeless, the workless,
the despairing and the incorrigible. There were no factories in
Gravesend but, together with Tilbury just across the river, it
was a considerable port and had a fishing fleet. So there was
no difficulty about getting recruits for his company of kings.
As he said of another place, 'there are boys worth millions
running about here'. And he did not mean their value to any
man but to the country.

Nor was he woolly-minded when it came to dealing with
them. Perhaps one reason why he specialised in boys was just
that they had to be handled briskly: there was almost certainly no motive more sinister than an emotional charity. If
he made them sing Victorian hymns, he also rammed into
their not over-willing heads, the hairs of which he himself cut,
elements of the practical knowledge they needed in order to
get jobs aboard ship, which was their usual destiny. Of course

he had losers, but he was not the man to mind that. Jesus did not complain when the healed patient failed to say thank you. The most that he would do when a boy deserted or otherwise misbehaved past reclamation, was to remove from the wall-map which showed where each of them was, the flag representing the culprit.

In spite of every effort, however, even Gordon could not contrive an unvarying routine. On one occasion a senior officer bearing the same name insisted on coming to stay. His unwilling host had to borrow wine from Mrs. Freese. Sir William Gordon was at that time General Officer Commanding Scotland, and the purpose of his visit was to offer his clan-kinsman the post of A.D.C.; no doubt feeling, as did many others, that someone ought to rescue him from the *oubliette* into which the War Office had dropped him. Strangely, Gordon accepted, only to repent of it almost immediately as a sin of complaint against his lot. One must never, in his code, seek to improve one's condition. So strongly did he feel about it that he begged Sir William to release him from his promise, which was done at the cost of another promise, to go up to Scotland and stay in return for the Gravesend visit. Gordon evaded this until Sir William, suffering from a severe attack of hypochondria, summoned him as though to the deathbed. This Gordon could not deny, but he could, and did, refuse to be made Sir William's legatee, saying that he would accept only a silver tea service, in order to have something with which his executor could pay for his funeral when the time came, that his body need not in that event be a burden to others.

This was no mere figure of speech. He actively disliked money, could not manage it, and was nearly always on the edge of having none at all. This was in spite of the obvious 'temptation' to use the rewards, which could so easily have come his way, to further the many charities to which he was committed. As it was, he gave away even the medal specially struck for him in China. And before sending it to the Lancashire Relief Fund he erased the inscription. It must have been large, for even so it realised £10. He had visited Manchester and reported: 'The poor scuttlers here, male and female, fill me with sorrow. . . . It does so painfully affect me, and I do trust will make me think less of self and more of these poor people.'

At first it is difficult to understand why, having taken the trouble to go to Manchester and interest himself in the Cotton Famine, Gordon did not take the one step which would have made his interest effective, namely, lending his name to an appeal for the unemployed. Yet, from his attitude to charity in general it is evident that he would not have regarded anything but a personal gift as meritorious. God required him to give what he had, not to make other people give. Soliciting on behalf of charity would have seemed not only to be putting himself forward, but to be contrary to his faith that God worked through each individual and not by multitudes, by qualities not by quantities. Gordon's appeal, when scattering tracts or handing a 'screw o' tea' to an old woman, a 'bit o' baccy' to an old man, was personal. He would not have it otherwise, and so made no representations to official quarters, launched no appeal through the Press.

He had a special interest in the Cotton Famine because it had a bearing on Sir Hope Grant's campaign in China. Though the loss of the American market, owing to the Civil War, was the main cause of the trouble, the need to find secondary markets was significant. China was an obvious choice. Nor was the 'export drive', as it would now be called, a mere commercial device. Distress in 1863 had reached such a point that no less than three-quarters of a million pounds were contributed through relief organisations to the unemployed, who, as the *Annual Register* primly puts it, 'were reduced to eleemosynary subsistence'.

Yet his interests were wide, far wider. Distress always moved him, and he was as much perturbed by the Irish peasant's want as by the hard conditions of the English miner, the Chinese coolie or the fishermen of the Danube. His heart-felt charity, as with his heart-felt religion, had that touch of universality which is the mark of the genuine mystic and is conspicuously lacking in those of thought-out piety. Gordon, in fine, was different from other people. In spite of his unimpressive appearance, anyone talking with him soon realised that he was a man apart, taking the springs of his effort and belief from a source within himself and not from the common wells of dogma, whether religious, political or military. As such he was inevitably suspect, and with some reason. For to those whose task is government, the very unpredictability of such a man is a grave handicap to his employment. Under discipline he would always be a non-conformist, at any moment capable of challenging his superiors at the bidding of an inner voice. In an independent command he could not be relied upon to carry out a set policy because, as events modified his ideas, he was in duty bound, according to his private code, to exceed, abrogate or modify his instructions to meet what he considered to be the ethical issue of the moment.

No wonder the men in power looked at him with mixed awe and anxiety, torn between recognition of his inspired integrity and fear of where it might lead their cherished schemes when his conscience came into conflict with their expediency. So the Gravesend appointment was probably as well fitted for him as any, especially at this time, when he needed not months but years in which to build into his character the bitter lessons learned in China. No doubt the War Office thought that in the end he would settle down in the reliable if rigid mould of the Regular Officer. He would then be safe for employment more suited to his record. But he himself would not have seen it that way. He always knew that he was being led, by the pillar of cloud in the day and of fire at night, to some sufficient Golgotha.

* * *

During his tour of duty at Gravesend there was only one appointment which he coveted, apart from the despised job of A.D.C. It involved his posting to an expedition from India to Abyssinia under Sir Charles Napier, who reasonably insisted on drawing all his officers from within his own Bombay Command. Even so, Gordon thought he ought to have been chosen, and said as much in what he hoped would prove to be the right quarter. When nothing came of it, he was so disappointed that for a whole day he shut himself up in Fort House and would speak to no one. The incident, trivial in itself, serves to show that even when he was apparently engaged wholeheartedly upon the Way of the Cross, he remained human enough, even ordinary enough, to be bored and sulky.

Yet when the chance came to go to Paris as a judge of some engineering at an exhibition, far from welcoming the break, he could only complain of the worldly preoccupations of his companions, make a few patronising comments upon French architectural style, and add that though there were some wonderful things in the show, 'You will soon see greater and greater wonders, such as the human eye hath not seen nor ear heard'.

At last the War Office concluded that his period of exile should end, and, perhaps as a reward for inconspicuous behaviour, he was offered a plum sinecure, particularly so considering that his regimental rank was still only that of Captain. The appointment, however, was diplomatic rather than military, and it involved survey work; so that the choice of Gordon was entirely proper and the pay, at £2000 a year, not inappropriate; though it has been represented less as a tribute to the worth of the Commissioner than as compensation to him for the social and domestic deficiencies of his situation. His post was at the Roumanian town of Galatz, some sixty miles from the mouths of the Danube, the international control of whose manifold waterways had already caused friction.

With the end of September 1871 Gordon packed up, a very thorough process, for instead of putting his possessions in store he gave them away until all he had left was a brass fender. This he carried round to Mrs. Freese to present it to her. The ceremonial robes from China went to Augusta, the battle-flags of the Taipings to the Ragged School. It was evidently his intention to sever all connection with the past.

Then, as the day of departure became imminent, he admitted to a feeling of loneliness at leaving the familiar place and virtually his only friends. So much did he feel parting from the Freeses that he begged them to accompany him as far as Dover, which they did. He then tried to persuade them to cross the Channel with him. Mrs. Freese, pleading that she was a bad sailor—and so was Gordon—would not; but her husband did. During the crossing the mental fog around Gordon began to lift as, after six years, he felt again the clean wind of adventure. He even admitted that he enjoyed travel, but added quickly that it 'made him feel carnal'.

One way or another he managed to balance carnality against the opposite desire to return to his friends. He even resurrected the old gibe against social life. 'How I like England when out of it', he wrote. Arrived at Galatz, he soon found himself a prey to one of his worst enemies, idleness; for there was little official business, no social life that he would countenance, and no way through the barrier of language which kept him from the 'Russian laddies', whose excitement he notes when their fathers caught sturgeon. In practice the high-sounding title of Commissioner became an empty one. There was little international responsibility, and the expected survey work gave place to the supervision of dredging operations.

He even pocketed his pride to the extent of asking Mr. Freese to come out to him, inventing a secretarial post so that he should have both an excuse and something to do. He was to bring with him one of the Gravesend boys, a 'tractable' one, who would be paid £3 a month. This plan, which would hardly have found favour with the War Office, fell through; fortunately for Gordon's subsequent career. Freese was a sick man, and no suitable boy could be found who was willing. So Gordon had to take refuge, as usual when life was particularly difficult, in his peculiar fatalism, concisely expressed in a conundrum of his own: 'Would you wish anything different from what it is? If so, you would wish it different from what God does.'

When summer came again, he had opportunity to break the monotony on business and then to take some leave. His congenial task was to visit and report on the war cemeteries in the Crimea. They were much neglected. He also noted that the Russians were in process of making Sebastopol a first-class fortress again, and were preparing to reoccupy their territory lost as the result of the Black Sea Treaty. When entertaining Gordon, and the officer who accompanied him on the gunboat, the Russians were entirely correct, but that was all. Gordon must have had a feeling that the great sacrifices of the Crimean war might prove to have been in vain.

On the way home, Fate arranged a 'casual' meeting with the Prime Minister of Egypt. Gordon, as was conventional, had called on the British Embassy in Constantinople. Nubar Pasha happened to be there, and those two unlike men took

an instant liking to one another. From that day Gordon, to a
very large extent, was to be delivered out of the hand of the
War Office, if not out of the reach of Westminster. He
promptly went to Cairo, where in short order Nubar's cau-
tious enquiry as to whether Gordon knew of an officer suitable to succeed to an important post, became a definite offer to
him, provided that he could get his release from Whitehall.

Nubar was in some difficulty to find a successor to the retiring Governor of Equatoria, southernmost province of the
Egyptian dominions and one having no effective boundary
in that direction, unless it might be the source of the Nile. The
appointment was not one for the usual run of administrators,
for the whole of the Sudan, together with the no-man's-land
to the south, was in a state of near chaos, riddled with corruption, largely directed by officials who had more interest
in the maintenance of the slave-trade—in the organisation
of which Englishmen had played a major part—than in the
equitable government of the vast territory. The situation
was rendered the more complex by the peculiar international
situation of Egypt as a Turkish vassal under the direct influence of European creditors, particularly England and France,
operating through Jewish banking houses. It was in fact just
the kind of melting-pot into which Gordon would naturally
plunge. Nubar, subject to official confirmation, gave him the
chance before he started for home; where he found that his
youngest brother was dead and that his mother had entered
what was to prove her last illness.

Depression settled upon him. He reviewed those who
would surely oppose his appointment and persuaded himself
that he would not be unduly downcast if he were not allowed
to take it up: 'Against me will be Baker and his adherents,
Pce. of Wales, etc., Geographical Society, the Anti-Slavery
Society, and all those who think they ought to have been
chosen for the post'. Sir Samuel Baker was the retiring
Governor, a rich and sporting gentleman. He had been
adopted by the Khedive Ismail, second Turkish Viceroy of
Egypt, at the instance of the Prince of Wales, less as an administrator than as an explorer. English society's interest in
the slave-trade was the primary reason for the adventure and
so Baker might have been expected to approve of Gordon as

K

his successor, but Gordon was contemplating a dead-end.
First Gravesend, then Galatz, then home; and all equally
dull! Where was the responsibility, the adventure, which his
soul, in spite of every effort to stop it, insisted upon craving?

There was war brewing in Ashanti, on the Gold Coast.
Public clamour began for him to be sent out there. 'Letters
were written to the papers in which his exploits were revived,
and leading articles appeared in *The Times* and elsewhere, in
which the Government was urged to employ the services of
the matchless soldier, who had been told off to fritter away
his genius as Vice-Consul on the Danube. . . .' But, 'The
voice of the press and the voice of the public died away in an
echo of the old strain that in this country to be an engineer is
to be unfit for staff employ'.

After contemplating royal mortality at the funeral of
Napoleon III, Gordon seemed to be aware that he was standing upon a threshold of destiny. That he left behind him a
mother who, paralysed, could no longer recognise him, would
have set the final seal upon his determination to seek in
foreign service the kind of life, denied him by his own
country, to which he believed himself peculiarly well fitted.
For the effect of the refusal of adequate re-employment in the
Army had gone deeper than any previous disappointment.
He knew well that, whatever might have been said about the
Abyssinian campaign, he was well qualified to command in
Ashanti. He must have reflected, on being left out of even a
subordinate position, that there could be no more active
future for him in the service of England. He had been able to
accept Gravesend as another station on his *via dolorosa*. Galatz
he had tolerated with difficulty, being deprived of the solace
of his social and religious work. His dreary leave, capped by
the realisation that he was considered too eccentric for responsible employment, had been purgatory. And so, when he
received a telegram from Cairo confirming Nubar's offer of
the Governorship, even he could not conceal his eagerness.

Yet, while waiting for the decision, he indulged in his usual
lonely walks and contemplation of the saddest aspects of life
he could imagine. Even sheep at pasture only reminded him
that in a sense they were all sacrifices. 'The good shepherd
was he who gave most sheep to the butcher.'

Chapter 7

OF SLAVERY

SINCE about 1590 when Elizabethan Hawkins took the first cargo of 'black ivory' to the plantations of the West, fifty millions of slaves had been exported from Africa, and as yet, when Gordon came to Cairo in February 1874, the traffic to Islam was hardly affected by the abolition of 1834. It is true that the European owners of slave-stations had recently pulled out, but only after selling their interests to men even less scrupulous than themselves.

Of such was Zebehr of Bahr Gazal, 'The Black Khedive', lord of thirty stations. He affected royal state, kept a pair of lions in leash, and melted twenty-five thousand silver dollars to make bullets for use against enemies protected by magic. He was a tall, aquiline Arab, with more than a notion of war-like discipline. His army could readily become a threat to Egypt. 'Smart, dapper-looking fellows,' Gordon was to write, 'like antelopes, fierce, unsparing, the terror of Central Africa.' In comparison the Egyptian troops and their Turkish levies were of no account. Many conscripts were sent southwards in fetters, the criminal scum of an international sink. So the main motive behind the Khedive Ismail's desire to stop the slave-trade was to ruin Zebehr. The effect of such a stroke would be far-reaching. It would convince the world that Egypt, in spite of its importance to her economy and social structure, was seriously concerned to put down the abominable traffic. The consequent improvement in relations with the West would stimulate the demand for Egyptian cotton, and so assist the exchequer, now in desperate straits.

The Egyptian National Debt had been begun by Ismail's predecessor, his uncle Saïd Pasha, who had contracted with England, Austria, France and Germany to pay Egypt's share in the expenses of the construction of the Suez Canal by supplying forced labour. When the workers failed to arrive, the Powers demanded the cost of the work, and, failing to get any satisfaction from Saïd, appointed Napoleon III to arbitrate between their claim for compensation and Saïd's counter-claim that it was the Powers themselves who had, by making slavery an international crime, prevented him from supplying the *corvée* for which they had asked. As might have been expected, Napoleon found for the plaintiffs and mulcted the defendant so heavily that Egypt began the accelerating process of coming under European rather than Turkish domination. For the money could not be found either in Egypt or Turkey, and Saïd had to borrow £3,293,000 towards the 'compensation' figure of nearly three and a half millions. The money, or rather £2,640,000 of it, was advanced by Messrs. Frühling and Goschen, leaving a margin of £653,000 for which Saïd was technically liable both as to interest and capital, though in fact he had not received it.

On similar lines Ismail had increased the debt until now, according to Gordon, he was paying thirty-five per cent on some of his loans and 'would gladly sign his name to twenty millions if he could get sixteen. . . . The Jew has taken a terrible vengeance upon the land of his captivity.' For Gordon regarded the financial policy of the Powers, acting through international bankers, as an unethical effort to achieve dominance over Egyptian affairs. In his view it was wrong because, instead of helping the people, it still further increased their wretchedness owing to the taxes they must bear to pay interest on the loans. Gordon never shrank morally or physically from the task of setting in order the houses of people too backward or barbarous to do it themselves. To help and not to hinder was the task of Empire and its justification. Only when that principle was honoured, and appreciated by both governors and governed, could the two grow together in friendship, the alternative to which was ever-increasing coercion, which, no matter how strong or ruthless the imperial power, could only temporarily succeed. In its failure it must wound the Empire and, for the people, put back the clock of progress towards heaven on earth.

At the same time Gordon must have realised how cogent were the strategic arguments for a docile Egypt. Behind the bankers were bayonets, and they would be mobilised, on the pretext of the pressing creditor, at the slightest sign of Cairene independence. For commercially the Suez Canal was already

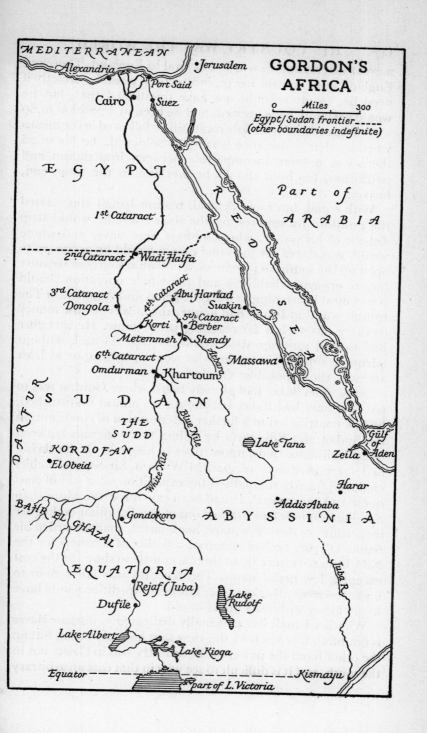

GORDON'S
AFRICA

0 ____ Miles ____ 300

Egypt/Sudan frontier - - - - -
(other boundaries indefinite)

MEDITERRANEAN
Alexandria
• Jerusalem
Port Said
Cairo
• Suez

E G Y P T

Part of
A R A B I A

1st Cataract

2nd Cataract   Wadi Halfa

3rd Cataract
Dongola   4th Cataract
                 Abu Hamad
                 Suakin
        Korti   5th Cataract
     Metemmeh   Berber
                 Shendy
6th Cataract   Massawa
Omdurman   Khartoum

R E D   S E A

D A R F U R

S U D A N

THE
SUDD

Blue Nile

KORDOFAN   Lake Tana
• El Obeid   Gulf
                                        of
                                        Aden
                                  Zeila

BAHR EL
GHAZAL   Harar
      White Nile
                    • Addis Ababa
     • Gondokoro   A B Y S S I N I A

E Q U A T O R I A   Juba R.
      Rejaf (Juba)
                        Lake
                        Rudolf
   Dufile

Lake Albert
              Lake Kioga
Equator ─────────────────────── Kismayu
              part of L.Victoria

a great success and in war it was vital to England. Therefore England must control Egypt, indirectly if possible, directly if need be. Gordon would not have questioned that, but he would certainly have insisted, had he been in a position to do so, that his ethical principle must still be followed in the means whereby that dominance was to be achieved. To his mind there was nothing incompatible between imperialism and patriotism, for both should be working to the same end, heaven.

With equal, but more cynical, realism Ismail appreciated the position. By suppressing the slave-trade he would strip Zebehr of his power, whose soldiers were slaves and whose wealth was slaves. At the same time it would be necessary to open up the southern provinces, a potential source of treasure but at present a liability; and the whole operation should prove most heartening to the Europeans and Americans. The trouble was that Ismail had neither the means nor the money to carry out such a far-reaching programme. He therefore had to find someone who would attempt the task without adequate support, someone who would perform, or at least attempt, the impossible: Gordon.

Sir Samuel Baker had already failed where Gordon was to try. Not only had Baker left the slavers almost undisturbed, he had contributed to a further deterioration of conditions in the Sudan and Equatoria by failing to distinguish between quasi-legitimate raids, upon tribes in league with the slaves, and mere predatory *razzias*. M'William, Sir Samuel's chief engineer, frankly stigmatised the expedition as 'a war of conquest and aggression'. It had been expensive too. More than a million pounds had drained out of the Egyptian exchequer on account of the big, square, hook-nosed, spade-bearded Sir Samuel. True, he had acquired a flotilla of steamers for the Nile, but apart from them there was little to show for the cost except a few useful maps. The Khedive was not a man to make the same mistake twice. The next expedition would have to get along without a grant-in-aid.

Whether Ismail was personally dedicated to liberate slaves is doubtful. Gordon took the view that he was sincere, but on the other hand the power of the industry was in Cairo, not in the south, and it is difficult to see why in that case an arbitrary

Viceroy, who was quite capable of having people 'put away' without process of law, boggled at direct action. To send Gordon to try to clean the business from the other end of tenuous communications should have been unduly optimistic; as optimistic as was Gordon himself when he left England. The 'doles' had gone. He now saw his appointment in terms of the divine mercy, his rôle as relevant to the vision of the thirty-fifth chapter of the book of the prophet Isaiah. He sent a post-card to Mrs. Freese, decorated with a sketch showing the sun's rays like a path of gold in which, under a solitary palm, stands a human figure. Underneath is written the biblical reference, of which the keynote is this: 'The wilderness and the solitary place shall be glad; and the desert shall rejoice and blossom as the rose'.

Gordon did not go to Africa on Her Majesty's Service. He did not go, primarily, to serve the Khedive or even to abolish slavery. He went to continue the work he had begun in China and confirmed at Gravesend, the service of mankind. All other considerations were as secondary as money, for which he cared only negatively, to avoid it as much as possible.

He arrived in Cairo at midnight, with starlight in his pale eyes and an immense impatience to be away on his Master's business. Suspicious officials would not hurry. They wanted to have this new broom in their own yard for a while, to observe it carefully. Gordon gave them only fifteen days. In that time he succeeded in collecting his staff and making most of the arrangements necessary for three or more years of exile in hostile territory. He had cut his salary from £10,000 to £2000, obtained a reputation for eccentric other-worldliness, pledged personal friendship to Ismail, but seen through the hypocrisy in his *entourage*. He had also confirmed his own view about the slave-trade, one which differed considerably from the woolly humanitarianism fashionable in England.

He saw slavery in Islam as a patriarchal system of which the slave was an integral and protected part. The owner of a valuable beast looks after it, and though at this time the North African market-price for a slave was only twenty or thirty dollars, it was sufficient. Those who had been driven over the desert were usually weak and sick, which may have accounted for a bargain rate. One of the effects of chasing the slavers had been to increase the suffering of the slaves—as Gordon would soon see in circumstances which echoed the horrors he had seen in China. Meanwhile the unction of the smooth men of affairs nauseated him, and only the Khedive's famous charm held him to an appearance of conformity. Ismail, whatever his faults, had a presence which impressed all who entered it, even Gordon. And yet he had little in the way of physical assets. He was fat, and one eyelid permanently drooped. Yet he had dignity, and those to whom he spoke found themselves convinced against cherished opinions. It is to this almost magical influence that Gordon's acquiescence in his instructions should be attributed; for it was not only to pacify a province that he was being sent to the far south. Ismail wanted to see the Crescent fly upon the Great Lakes. He wanted to annex what is now Uganda and then was the kingdom of M'Tesa, to be, like Pharaoh, an emperor in Africa. In this Gordon loyally served him—·even at the cost of what was left of his popularity at Westminster.

Gordon was equally content to undertake his mission with a minimum of resources, travelling as light as possible and recruiting what force he could from local material. This was in marked contrast to Sir Samuel, who had lived in relative luxury protected by regular troops. He had been accompanied by his wife, who caused something of a shock-wave in society when she was reported as wearing bloomers among the naked savages of Equatoria.

At his right and ruling hand, Gordon chose an Egyptian out of a Cairo gaol, where a murder charge was hanging over him. His name was Abu Saud, and he was a slaver; but he so impressed Gordon as an efficient thief-catching thief, that the charges against him were dropped and he took his place with the rest:

Chaillé-Long, American, Lieutenant-Colonel in the Egyptian Army.
William Campbell, American.
Frederick Russell, British.
William Anson, British, a nephew of Gordon's.
Romulus Gessi, Italian, brought from the Danube.
Auguste Linant de Bellefonde, French.
Witt, German, a botanist who paid his own expenses.

Josef Menges | German, naturalists who acted as
Friedrich Bohndorff | Gordon's personal servants.

Such an omelette can hardly be made without breaking
men, even in a climate less deadly than Equatoria's. Tragedy,
however, was still in the wings. The present act was more
like *opéra bouffe*, and unconvincing at least to Gordon, who
would not adopt Egyptian uniform, and chose to wear instead
plain Engineer undress, with fez. So clothed, he and Chaillé-
Long—the rest were to follow with the stores—were seen off
at the Cairo station with every evidence of the Khedive's best
respects. Gold braid flashed in the sun. Salutes, bowing and
hand-shaking were elaborate and prolonged. Gordon fretted,
thinking that he should have insisted on his original proposal
that, despite Ismail's contention that the dignity of Egypt
demanded a state journey, he ought to have travelled as a
private person. The special train was to convey him to Suez,
where a chartered steamer was waiting to take him to Suakin.
Thence he would ride, with an escort of two hundred
Egyptian cavalry, over the hot hills and down into the desert
at Berber on the Nile. There should be waiting one of the
handy paddle-wheelers that Sir Samuel had left behind. In
it he would complete the long river journey to Khartoum,
and thence, largely on foot, to his very own capital city,
Gondokoro.

At last the engine began to pull. The platform and civilisation slipped behind. The desert closed in. Gordon's vision
must have been bright before him as the clean sand began to
slide past and the smell of the city no longer dominated the
stuffy carriage.

Civilisation left behind? Not yet! Ahead of the special
another train was standing on the single track, its engine de-
railed. There was an interminable delay while matters of precedence were argued. At length, abandoning the special as
such, the new Governor-General was able to get on, his
coach hitched ignominiously to the back of the common train.
Even then there was no clear run. Out of the desert rode a
gesticulating cavalcade. Robbers? No, Monsieur de Lesseps,
builder of the Canal, and his two beautiful daughters. They
had missed their way. What more natural, in those days, than
that they should stop a train? And having done so, how could

the shy Governor-General refuse to be polite? He had to sit talking seriously to de Lesseps, while Chaillé-Long, a good-looking bachelor and something of a lady-killer, did his best with the two girls.

At last Suez appeared, and the steamer. Gordon felt himself in control. The way this access of authority affected him was to produce a fury of effort. What other man would have been in the least anxious to gain the sickness-ridden, danger-charged isolation which would be for some years his life and work? Yet Gordon not only pressed on, he did so to such purpose that he brought down by three whole days, nine from twelve, the record for the hard, mountainous ride between Suakin and Berber. His escort were exhausted, men and beasts, by the time they saw the sheen of the Nile; but not Gordon. Without pause he would have pushed on, but had to delay to receive official hospitality from the local governor.

Free of Berber, Gordon forced the steamer at her best pace against the current. The Nile was low but the ship would not have more than five or six knots, for the big paddles were driven by less than thirty horse-power and the iron hull was far from streamlined. He reached Khartoum at dawn on the 13th of March 1874, and promptly produced a copy of the *Pall Mall Gazette* dated the 13th of February. He was proud of the coincidence of dates because he had proved that Khartoum was now only a month from London. No man as yet had been so fast.

Ayub Pasha, the Circassian, Paris-educated Governor-General of the Sudan, then occupying the Palace, was particularly anxious to make a good impression. It would be a grave blow to him if this Englishman were so foolish as to try to interfere with established institutions, such as beating tax-defaulters with a raw-hide thong, or, when the slave-season opened, flushing black ivory from its forest retreats. Accordingly Gordon put on full-dress uniform, complete with medals, C.B. and sword. In it he inspected an infantry battalion, a battery of artillery, and a band which with difficulty convinced him that they were playing 'God Save the Queen': not that he had the least ear for music. After the inspection came a rest, then entertainment of a different sort, calculated to do more than any number of parades to make the new

man conform to the situation in which he found himself.
There was a banquet at the Palace, a lavish banquet. Gordon
realised that he could not refuse, and so politely sat through
it. All seemed to be going well towards mutual confidence
between these administrators, who between them held peace
and war, slavery and emancipation, for an area larger than all
Europe, in excess of a million square miles. It should have
been a moment for proud, elegant and comfortable relaxa-
tion. The young Engineer Captain had become a Provincial
Governor, at least in theory the ruler of a huge territory,
surely chosen by Providence for high destiny in a worthy
cause. He would soon be tasting his first sip of authority on
the grand scale. Even now he sat at the right hand of a man
who held more personal power than the Prime Minister of
England, but this man was his superior officer. . . . Five
hundred Dinka and Shilluk tribesmen, wearing white tunics,
came thumping their bare feet in a barbaric rhythm moni-
ored by drums. In frenetic unison they danced, proud, fierce,
virile and undisciplined. The new Excellency began to fret.
He was afraid such lack of decorum might lead to something
worse and soon his fears were justified. The drums ceased, the
warriors departed. In the following silence a sinuous line of
dancing-girls wound into the arena. Shrill music of a kind
which would have found no favour at all at No. 5 Rockstone
Place, began their dance in almost complete nakedness.
Shocked, and perhaps offended because his host imagined
that such entertainment would be acceptable, Gordon got up
and walked out.

For the first of many, many times, that night he must have
stood alone to bend his uncompromising faith over the great
river. For him the Nile was more than a geographical feature
or the mere symbol of a unique historical continuity. He
thought there was something mystical about her, as though
she too were a divine instrument. Perhaps he even felt kinship
with her stream of life as millennia before the Pharaohs had
claimed it, and for the same reason: they too believed themselves to be God's channel for the living water. There under
the beckoning stars, between such tawdry banks, ran Time
itself; for the Nile must, according to the chronology in the
margin of his Bible, have been there 'in the beginning': the

first chapter of Genesis at the ninth verse. Was not the worl
created in four thousand and four B.C. precisely? The riv
and the desert, even the stars, could not be older, but the
were as old. That silver-bronze streak was sliding by und
the moon when Adam and Eve were still in Eden. Tho
palm-fronds rustled in the evening wind when Thothme
Lord of the Two Lands, set his stele beyond Babylon. Th
desert lounged inert when Israel, led by Moses, straggle
through the first phase of the diaspora.

More practical considerations obtruded. After the offen
to his host, it was more than ever necessary to push on. Th
route would have appalled another man. Three hundre
miles or so of bare, flat plain would give place to the *sudd*, th
aquatic wilderness where islands float and firm ground is
random as the weed. There primitive natives pick their wa
in a febrile miasma more suitable for snakes. The desolatio
of deserts can be sublime, a frightening immensity where ma
strains away from earth because the sky is pulling out his sou
But the desolation of the *sudd* is sinister. All that belong the
are creeping things, the real rulers of a wilderness in whic
higher animals, particularly man, are only interlopers.

The original plan had been to go by river until furth
progress was barred by floating debris, thence to procee
on foot round the two-hundred-and-fifty-mile width of th
swamps. Lately, however, a long, laborious effort to clear
waterway had at last succeeded. For months an army
natives had, with a flotilla of boats under military comman
been cutting and pulling at the vegetation which blocked th
main stream. It had seemed, when Gordon left Cairo, th
they would never succeed, but by the time he arrived
Khartoum the river had yielded. A flush of water, une
pected at this time of low Nile, had cleared a floating islan
out of the way, and, gathering force, hurled the mass again
the next resistance. It too had given way, and so like a wate
avalanche rushed on, to the horror of those who watched. F
among the furious tangles of the trees, grass and shrubs, can
tumbling companies of crocodiles, hippos and snakes, powe
less against the current. So far the new channel had remaine
clear. In 'Steamer 9' Gordon could travel, with somethir
approaching comfort, as far as the frontier of Ayub's dominio

and thence in his own *Bordein*, an imposing paddle-boat with high stove-pipe funnel and a navigating bridge. After that? No man yet knew if the river came from Lake Albert, Lake Victoria, or had a still secret source. The only maps were Baker's, the only ally God.

*   *   *

One thousand two hundred miles of desert lay between him and Cairo, a thousand miles of grass, marsh and forest between him and Gondokoro. Beyond that again lay more and more and more miles, while the interminable inanity of Africa sweated towards the sea. The steamer reached Gondokoro in twenty-eight days of effort during which Gordon became more and more impatient. He would take off his trousers and get into the river to help pull the boat clear of a sandbank. Someone had told him that crocodiles do not attack if one keeps moving. He caused mortal offence to the Egyptian captain by slapping his face. The offence? He would not get on. The excuse? There was no wood for the boiler, and by Long's account that was true. Long relates how he himself had to go out foraging for fuel, waist-deep in the sludge. Such incidents were not a good augury for the future, and that they took place when most of the staff and all the heavy baggage had not yet caught up; when the first enthusiasm of the expedition was still undimmed; when the climate had as yet not debilitated and infuriated the men, was worse.

To crown the unnecessary race from Cairo with a fitting anti-climax, Gondokoro, capital of Equatoria, formal headquarters of Sir Samuel Baker, turned out to be 'in the last degree squalid'. It consisted of a huddle of dirty huts surrounded by a defensive stockade beyond which the miserable handful of men who made up the garrison hardly dared to go. Nor was there any alternative, for the only other Egyptian post in the whole territory was not even on the river. Between them, the two posts disposed some five hundred men, of whom Gordon wrote, 'I have never in the course of my life seen such wretched creatures dignified by the name of soldiers'. The officers, he said, were 'brave as hares'. They hardly dared to leave shelter, for the local tribes had become bold enough to make it a serious risk to do so. They had even discovered that

the troops were so incompetent with firearms that a man
with a shield and spear was usually at an advantage. 'They
are terrified of the natives and interested only in their slave-
wives.'

Not that Gordon disapproved of slave-wives. Later he
found it so practical a method of disposal for liberated
damsels that on one occasion two hundred and fifty brides
together entered the holy estate, their names, for purposes of
the ceremony, being the French numerals up to Deux Cent
Cinquante. The wedding dresses consisted of fresh leaves.

So hopeless did the situation at Gondokoro appear, that
Gordon promptly went north again, back to Khartoum.
There he would think of something. There he *must* think of
something, for already, without adequate reconnaissance, he
had issued his first decree. It had not been calculated to open
tactfully the impending struggle, and yet was now clearly impossible to enforce. Its premature promulgation already put
Gordon in an embarrassing position in relation to what little
government there was—Ayub in fact. The decree, issued in
Khartoum, read:

> By reason of the authority of the Governor of the Pro-
> vinces of the Equatorial Lakes, with which His Highness
> the Khedive has invested me, and the irregularities which
> until now have been committed, it is henceforth decreed
>   1. That the traffic in ivory is the monopoly of the
>   Government.
>   2. No person may enter these Provinces without a
>   'teskere' from the Governor-General of the Soudan
>   which 'teskere' being available only after it shall have
>   received the *visa* of the competent authority at Gondo-
>   koro or elsewhere.
>   3. No person may recruit or organise armed bands with-
>   in those Provinces.
>   4. The importation of firearms and gunpowder is pro-
>   hibited.
>   5. Whosoever shall disobey this decree will be punished
>   with all the rigour of the military laws.

Ayub, with a guilty conscience about paragraphs one, three
and four, quaked at Gordon's quick return from Gondokoro,
but was relieved to hear that the erratic Englishman claimed
to have done so in order to collect his heavy baggage and

meet his staff, still making their way southwards. It is doubtful if Ayub believed such a story. How much more likely that
Gordon had already realised that the régime in Khartoum
offended against both the spirit and the letter of the new
decree? Only the fact that technically Equatoria was now
separate from the Sudan administration protected Ayub.
Even then, he must have reflected that Gordon was probably
in secret correspondence with the Khedive. He was no longer
safe. The Khedive was an unpredictable man, knowing more
than one supposed, for instance about the *razzias* which went
forth from Khartoum, and the ivory, both white and black,
which found its way through the province to the Red Sea, or,
with appalling hardships, to the slave-states of North Africa.

Gordon's decree could not be enforced even in Equatoria,
but its principles struck at the root of the oligarchy which was
the only real ruler south of Cairo. Its wealth was ivory, its
strength private armies analagous to those of twelfth-century
English barons. Ayub had only one course open to him. He
became again the effusive host, and Gordon was invited to
inspect the hospital, take the salute at a review and generally
appear as the favourite friend of His Excellency Ismail Ayub
Pasha, Governor-General of the Sudan.

Gordon seems to have sensed this. He probably thought of
Ayub as a nominee of Nubar's concerning whom he had
written home: 'I think the Khedive is quite innocent, or
nearly so, but Nubar is the chief man. . . . There has been a
mutual disappointment. Nubar thought he had a rash fellow
to deal with, who could be persuaded to cut a dash etc., and
found that he had one of the real Gordon race; this latter
thought he had the real thing, and found it a sham, and felt
like a Gordon that had been humbugged.'

To demonstrate that he was not impressed, still less
deceived or intimidated, Gordon informed Long that he
proposed to obey convention and return the Governor's hospitality. Long protested that they had no means to do so and
would be excused on that account. Gordon persisted in his
idea. Long pointed out that they had in fact just twelve tin
mugs, twelve tin plates, one Arab cook. Gordon still would
have it, and Long in misery went to confide in Ayub, to ask
what could be done to avoid an unfortunate incident.

When he returned to the house they were using he found Gordon in his shirt-sleeves in the kitchen. He was slopping a white mixture into pans. 'Tapioca puddings,' he said, 'forty of them! How's that?' Lieutenant-Colonel Chaillé-Long, something of a dandy, and French enough to take such matters seriously, was speechless. He dashed back to Ayub.

After a shocked silence, Ayub sighed. What threats and orders would hardly have achieved, the dreadful prospect of tapioca accomplished painlessly. He invited Long to accompany him to the magazine, and there, concealed among kegs of powder, cases of small-arms ammunition and racks of rifles, was a series of packing-cases. When the first was opened, Long was profuse in his thanks. And with reason, for that evening he was able to lead Gordon to as perfect a table as could be set in Paris. There were cloths of the finest damask, china from Sèvres, glass from Bohemia. In the kitchen Ayub's Turkish chef was at work with a trained staff and, in improvised coolers, bottles and bottles of Veuve Cliquot were waiting.

For once Gordon had to accept the rôle of host to a table of luxury, and the evening, it seems, passed off as a great success—without dancing-girls. This may partly have been due to the fact that many of the guests had never tasted champagne before and were unaware, to begin with, of its stimulating quality. At the right moment Ayub confided to Gordon that in no sense had the convention of hospitality been broken, for the table was by rights his own, the stuff having been left behind by Sir Samuel, and prudently put away for his successor.

*   *   *

After collecting his staff and baggage on a river journey north, and making the tedious return past Khartoum to Gondokoro, Gordon took over Baker's old bodyguard, appropriately enough known as the Forty Thieves, and set about as big a single-handed task as any man has attempted. To carry out the order concerning King M'Tesa he had to lose Long, who took the Khedive's secret into the tropical wilderness. To carry out the order concerning the slavers, he had to destroy the perverted economic system of the area, and to do that he must recruit his own forces out of nothing, train them and use them to staff a series of new posts, each within a day's march of the next, from Khartoum to the Lakes. He even recruited some cannibals from the interior. Whatever Ayub and his cronies wanted to do, they would no longer find it a paying proposition to send *razzias* into Equatoria.

The condition of the local population, what was left of it, was comparable to that of the Chinese under the Taipings, and the climate was infinitely more unhealthy, if not as uncomfortable, as the cold of a Chinese winter. As the Taipings spread desolation so did the slave-raiders. According to Baker a whole district which had been intensely cultivated 'like a vast garden' in a few years returned to wilderness. The remnant of local natives had also to contend with raids by the garrisons, both for slaves and for cattle, since their scanty and irregular pay came often in terms of gin, and soldiers will eat.

One wet evening with a hot wind blowing, Gordon, from the door of his beehive hut, saw what appeared to be a skeletal old woman staggering up from the water's edge in the quick shadows of sundown. She was so weak that she had to halt when a gust blew against her, to stumble in the following calm. Gordon ordered that she be given shelter and something to eat. He did not sleep that night because of a thin wailing quite close by. In the morning he found that his orders had been ignored. The woman was lying in a puddle. She was apparently dead. Concealed in a patch of grass near her was a year-old child.

In blazing anger Gordon took the woman to a hut with a fire in it. He gave her brandy and hoped that she would die. Starvation had gone a long way with her. She was only sixteen. He wrote to Augusta grimly, as to someone who could not understand what life is really like. 'Your black sister' he called the dying woman, but added that notwithstanding the suffering which was so aggressively obvious, one day she would meet Augusta and tell her that it was all in conformity with the divine mercy.

He was horrified that the slaves he liberated were so apathetic. They had sometimes been a year and more on the road. Privation, pain, sickness, brutality and exhaustion left them like *zombies*, who, when the slave-sticks were taken from their galled necks, could only stand and stare, dumb with

L

misery beyond expression. Such wreckage could not find its way home, if home remained. It could not be left where it was because the local natives would kill it. Sometimes the slaver was only too glad to have done with it because it would never have reached the market alive.

Gordon sometimes bought a slave himself, usually a boy. One, who accompanied him for months, was a little Shilluk, 'all legs', who had sold himself for a handful of millet. Sometimes even purchase was no use, as when a mother exchanged her child for a cow, and preferred the bargain to the money Gordon offered to pay on her behalf. She did not believe in money. Until Gordon's arrival coin had been almost unknown. Even the soldiers relied on theft and barter. Gordon tried to change all that. He brought 'a boat-load' of silver dollars from the treasure of Khartoum, and ignored the protests of Ayub. With these he established salaries and discharged the accounts of the administration. For the rest he tried to introduce copper piastres, but it was hard work.

'Up to the present time the habit has been to give the chief of a tribe some beads or calico, and he makes his men bring wood or do any work required. Now I want first to break through the feudal system of the chiefs; the only way to do this is to let their subjects see that they can stand on their own feet—that is, gain something for themselves independently of the chiefs. Before I began the system which I hope to establish, the chief would keep the mass of the things given to him, and give only a few to his subjects. I began by paying each man who worked some beads. Next day I gave each man who worked half a piastre (one penny) in copper, and offered to sell him beads to that amount. . . .

'Today I made a first-rate affair. A chief brought a tusk, and wanted two bells for cows to wear round their necks in exchange. I said, "No, I will give you two dollars for the tusk." He said, "Yes," so I gave him two dollars. "Now," I said, "I will sell you two bells for a dollar each." '

Gordon created law and order almost unaided, for no man would do more for him than he must, some going to extraordinary lengths to deceive him; as the commandant of a new post who for six months wrote as though from there when he was forty miles away in a more comfortable locality. Yet the subtle power of this new leader, which had made him in China an object of superstition, overcame distance. Even out of that isolation his personal influence began to work like the proverbial leaven. The steamer-service which he established began to run to schedule. The posts he set up, though kept with minimum garrisons not only because there were no reserves but also because Gordon believed it kept them alert to be constantly in fear of attack, began to earn the confidence of the natives, among whom Gordon strode as though he were immune to fatigue. Everywhere he went abuse was checked; justice, hitherto a poor relative of tyranny, became a power greater than the slavers, and mercy, long dead, came to life again.

The physical strain, the effort of getting through a day's work, or a day's march, was enough to undermine any constitution borne by man, even Gordon's. Sick, he carried on, sustained by his own momentum and his own theories about the cause of disease, which might even be mental, a concept in advance of his time: 'I have been so cross since I wrote to you —and why? The reason is that I was made ill by the utter feebleness of my staff.'

Malaria, commonly thought to be due to marsh mist, for which the specific was coffee, by Gordon was associated with food, though he insisted upon everyone taking quinine; unfortunately not as a regular dose but only when they felt ill. There was thus no malarial prophylactic in a place where the mosquitoes were so offensive that on the march men did not have their arms ready to fire in case of ambush because of their perpetual preoccupation with insects. Life was bearable by day only away from the bush. The minute night fell a general retreat took place under nets, where, in torrid heat, one had to remain until dawn.

Apart from coffee, the principal specific was alcohol, which was widely believed to render the water safe to drink. Among drugs, Gordon put his faith in Warburg's Tincture and Chlorodyne B.P., the former a shot-gun prescription based upon aloes, a powerful purge, with some fifteen other drugs of no consequence. The latter, oddly enough, was its pharmacological opposite. In addition to its use in diarrhoea, chlorodyne, containing a morphine derivative, chloroform and ether, can be a pleasant comforter, giving rise to mild intoxication. Gordon, however, claimed that fifteen drops, half the usual dose, 'set him up', a significant moderation in the light of the accusations which have been made against him for drinking brandy to excess. To have done so would have been inconsistent with his character and imprudent under the conditions imposed by the climate. That he managed to remain active at all is remarkable. He certainly could not have done so had he abused his body with alcohol or any other poison.

Each day was dragged out in a state of painful fatigue, yet not only did this wiry man organise his command almost single-handed under nearly impossible conditions; when his staff began to fall sick he nursed them at night while he still worked in the day. Eventually they were all laid low, and he gave up all other cares to paddle about in the mud which by now had invaded the huts. They were, he said wryly, 'in the hands of one of the best doctors I know (myself)'. But he had not the means to save them, and Witt followed Willy Anson into a waterlogged grave. Eventually all the rest had to be invalided, save one prosaic German who prudently decided to go home. Gordon was left with the venomous hypocrite Abu Saud, who was contriving a mutiny on the lines of what used to happen in the Ever Victorious Army. Gordon suspected that something was amiss, but he had no proof. It was some months before he could feel sufficiently confident to write a letter banishing the traitor northward and threatening further penalties if he did not behave himself. Then, alone again, as he had been when things were worst in China, he could sit and write to Augusta that he took comfort from considering even more unpleasant experiences, such as a picnic, a visit to the Crystal Palace or a masked ball. Such diversions were 'utterly melancholy', presumably because through such suffering as that there would be no salvation.

Convinced that his health depended upon constant activity, Gordon abandoned his miserable 'capital' and set up a new headquarters on virgin ground, higher and further from the pestilential stream. Here, realising that even he could not continue to be both an administrator and a nurse, he issued orders that he was not to be visited except on duty and particularly not by the sick. Here the convalescents joined him from Khartoum, and here Chaillé-Long, his mission to M'Tesa completed, was offered at dawn the hospitality of Gordon's brandy, Bible and quinine. It was following this meeting that Long reported Gordon as retreating to his tent for days on end, with a hatchet and a red flag at the door to warn everyone that he was on no account to be disturbed. Long implies that the retreat was bibulous, when, if it happened at all, it was most likely to be biblical. Gordon may well have spent days in his tent alone. He was a 'God-intoxicated' man, and that state is not always elegant or desirable, but the chances are much against him being intoxicated with eau-de-vie, and there appears to be no record, his life long, of any such occasion.

Emaciated and fevered, Long was hardly at that time a clear-headed judge. His mission had taken him through unknown country and a series of theatrically dangerous encounters. But M'Tesa had accepted the proposition of becoming a vassal of the Khedive's, and Gordon naïvely wrote home to suggest that England would not be eager to see Egypt 'debouch on the sea'. It proved an understatement. No doubt M'Tesa thought little of his pledge, for he was an accomplished if crude diplomatist, believing only in force as the final arbiter, yet glad to play off a Protestant missionary against an Ulema of Islam. Long had arranged with an eye to effect his arrival at the Court. These people had never before seen a horse and so Long made a showy ride of his approach. He produced consternation rather than admiration, for the crowd thought he was a centaur, which became 'dislocated' when he dismounted. Then, being led into the audience hall, it was his turn to be dismayed. At a nod from the King, thirty subjects, chosen at random by his bodyguard of executioners, had their heads bashed in. M'Tesa politely explained that rough methods were the only effective ones for a people such as his. Long then produced his presents, a mirror, five foot by three, which must have been an awkward load; a musical box which played *Il Trovatore*; and an electrical machine which he so regulated that while others were writhing on the ground unable to let go of the innocent-looking terminals, he himself remained uninfluenced. The King was delighted, to the extent of presenting Long with several women, including his own daughter, aged eight. Long had married off the other girls to men of his escort, but the Princess was another matter. What was he to do with her? The problem was not one for which Gordon, of all people, could have had a ready answer, but eventually it was solved by sending Long back to Cairo on sick leave with instructions to take the girl with him and arrange for her education. There would be much to learn, and she began on the way northward, being appointed 'waiter-boy' on the boat which carried Chaillé-Long, from whose old clothes, in white drill, were made the first fabric garments she had ever worn.

*   *   *

The way was now open for Gordon to carry out the next stage of the Khedival dream, the annexation of the two great lakes, Victoria Nyanza and Albert. Soon the line of posts and the administration which he had created would have to stand without him. He must disappear into the unknown.

Feverishly he made his preparations, and as usual they seemed to be hindered by fate. His assistants went sick. Material did not arrive or the wrong stuff was sent. In work-parties there never seemed to be a single man who could deal with emergency. Of two young Engineer subalterns sent out from England, one had to be evacuated with fever, the other with a huge swelling on his neck. He hardly regretted their departure, for, as he himself admits, he was not easy to live with. Chippindall, who lasted the longer of the two, wrote to the other: 'Sometimes I think I shall have a row with Gordon; for though he has such a lot of anxiety and worry, he has no right to nag and worry you in return for it. Oh! and how he bores me night after night about the levels and the distances! I should not mind if he would make one good night of it and settle it, but every night to discuss whether Baker's levels are right; whether the distance is this or that; then, if you give an opinion, to be nailed at once, and your reasons asked and worried out, till out of sheer fag you agree to any proposition he likes to put forward.'

The young officers irritated their C.O. just as much, partly out of inexperience, but chiefly, it may be supposed, because they took life no more seriously than they had to. Gordon lived each day as though it were his last, but youth lives each

day as though the series is infinite. So Gordon was alone
again, the more so because he had received no reply from the
Khedive to his secret proposal for the consolidation of the new
dominions. This called for an expedition to be sent to the
East Coast. A party was then to strike north over what have
become the 'white highlands' and join up with his own party
moving south. Technically this ought to make Egypt the ruler
of everything from the Indian Ocean to the Mediterranean
along the line, on either side as wide as could be enforced,
from Cairo to Mombaz Bay (Mombasa).

Gordon's task was perilous, for, out of touch with reinforcements, he had entered a country where the natives told him
frankly: 'We do not want your cloth or your beads. We do
not want to meet your chief. We want you to go away.' And
they had proved their point by killing off a reconnaissance
party under Linant de Bellefonde. Gordon felt guilty about
his death because he had given the unfortunate man a red
shirt which made him unduly conspicuous.

If Gordon felt guilty about the shirt, he had other and more
weighty reasons for an uneasy conscience. He felt an intruder
and sympathised with the natives who reiterated, 'This land is
ours, you shall not have it, neither its bread nor its flocks'.
Then, in retaliation for their hostile acts, he became a leader
of cattle-raids, and, as if that were not bad enough, on one
occasion the cattle did not belong to the hostile tribe at all
but to a friendly one. He could understand Baker's difficulties
now, and to them add others with which it is doubtful if
Baker was ever concerned. To aggravate his guilty conscience
there was the primitive magic by which he was surrounded, a
permeation of superstition which would not give the Christian
mystic any choice but to allow that when, for instance, he had
prayed for a success, it was denied not because of some in-
advertence on God's part but because the prayers of the poor
ignorant heathen, even though they knew not Christ, had
been heard before his own. Prayer was, as ever, his constant
resource. It accompanied the passage of the rapids. It preceded every dangerous sortie. Yet he was aware all the time
that here among the black men was a kind of religion which
he could neither grapple with nor ignore. He did more than
share Livingstone's belief that the native untouched by civilisa-

tion is an honest, happy, if idle character, requiring no police or even any apparent code of law to keep his community in harmony. Gordon saw them as equals in the sight of his God and had grave misgivings about the rôle he was playing as the means by which 'civilisation' was catching up with their almost paradisal state of ignorance.

'If *we* conquered the country, we would at least in some measure benefit the conquered; but here I cannot say I see the least chance of the country being improved or the people benefited; the civilisers are so backward themselves that they cannot be expected to civilise others.'

In any case he began to see civilisation as a very doubtful benefit to people who in some ways seemed nearer to God than the gentlemen of the West. To take further examples from his letters: 'I asked a sheikh if he had ever seen strangers or white people. He said, "Why ask such a question? All men are the same." No country presents such a field to a philosopher as this country does with its dense population quite innocent of the least civilisation. I should say that they are singularly free from vice; their wars are generally very harmless and seldom cause bloodshed.'

'Man is a very fine-looking animal when in a natural state. The grace with which these natives walk and run is remarkable; and they look very grand when in their picturesque groups and satin skins. . . . The ladies strut like turkeys with their long tails.'

He could not even take refuge in that humour which is based upon the instantaneous recognition of one's own superiority. If the local women wore tails, the habit raised no smile to Gordon's lips; for above them those queer eyes were too busy, too tired, and too concentrated on a vision.

Approaching the equator, the country and the climate became ever more impossible, until he entered a tract where there was almost continuous rain, and saw, with increasing misgiving, ridges of high ground, forest-clad, which still hid the secrets of the river between him and the lakes. His foreboding was justified: 'October 17. IT IS ALL OVER! I started from Dufile this morning and, keeping on the higher level to avoid the wet edges of the river, came on it about five miles from here. I fancied for some time I had heard a voice like thunder, which increased as we approached the river. At last we stood above it on a rocky bank covered with vegetation, which descended abruptly to the stream, and there it was appalling to look at, far less to think of getting anything up or down except in splinters. . . . I bore it well, and for all you could see it might have been a picnic party to the Fola Falls; but it is rather sad, and will give me a mint of trouble and delay.'

'Trouble and delay' involved getting a message back to Gessi to tell him that a steamer must be moved overland in pieces and reassembled above the falls. Seven hundred men would be needed, and where were they to be found among the inert or hostile natives? And how was such a loaded porterage to move, the iron burdens boring into men's backs? The grass was six feet high, a sea of grass through which it was as much as one man, unladen, could force his way. The grass must be burned. But how? Even if the steamer's disintegrated carcase were to arrive where the river became navigable again, what chance was there that she could successfully be put together? And even then, what barriers still remained before the lakes which Baker had discovered? Gordon appeared to forget the odds against him, and, if he showed any sign of strain at all, it was in a general disenchantment with everyone and everything from the Khedive downwards. Even the Royal Geographical Society shared in the mood, for he feared that if he were to be, in spite of everything that Nature could do, the God-fated ravisher of the virgin lake, then they would confer upon him a gold medal. So seriously did he take this threat, that when by superhuman effort the little iron boat puffed around Lake Albert, it was Gessi alone who stood on her foredeck and knew the full heart of that immense accomplishment. Gordon was somewhere behind, plunging with methodical desperation through the sodden forest and mapping, mapping, until, in his own words, he was 'nearly dead'. 'I never had such fatigue. What misery! And what for? To map that river for 8 or 10 miles I have to walk in pouring rain through jungle some eighteen miles.' As for the climate, 'The moment the sun goes down, a cold damp arises which enters one's very bones. There is not an interval of 5 minutes from the setting of the sun and the rising of the dreadful damp, and you feel the danger, as it were at once.'

Nor was climate the only enemy. Lightning nearly killed him in his tent. A snake fell on him as he rested under a tree, and a scorpion stung him three times on the hand. He had frequent adventures with dangerous animals, and even suffered from a poisonous kind of wild fig. Africa is a hard teacher and teaches only by experience.

He almost envied the natives, though they said 'We want no Turks here', and he called them 'a lazy, unenterprising, happy lot'. Not even their gods seemed to worry them, and as for Empire, it had no meaning at all. Imagine, they could not even distinguish between an Englishman and a Turk, but thought all visitors unwelcome because of the slave-trade—which was all they knew of foreigners. And they were inured to the climate, even to the mosquitoes.

From Lake Albert the voyage into Nyanza might seem by comparison no great thing, but it involved the navigation of over a hundred miles of unknown waterway, jinking through dense forest, barred by nine rapids and hazardous with papyrus islands, before reaching Lake Kioga. From there ran a further sixty miles of waterway, believed to be navigable. Gordon would surely have attempted it, if not with the steamer then with some lighter craft. Gessi had circumnavigated Lake Albert, and found it to be much smaller than Baker had supposed, but through that simple gesture it was now by etiquette Egyptian, whatever M'Tesa—or England—might say. To do the same for Nyanza, that vast inland sea of fresh water, was equally part of the private dream which Gordon shared with the Khedive and Chaillé-Long.

Rumour came to camp. M'Tesa, it was said, had disarmed and made prisoner the Egyptian detachment, a hundred and sixty strong, which had been sent to his capital, ostensibly as a gesture of good will. Perhaps the black despot had tired of his toys. Perhaps he had quarrelled with one or another of the missionaries who were working on him. Gordon had suspected them of being 'more secular than spiritual' and M'Tesa was no easy man to deceive. The explanation was not important, what mattered was that something serious had happened to change M'Tesa from a kind if unconventional host to Long, to an enemy confident enough to disarm the soldiers of his overlord. Gordon was in no position to take further risks. His few fighting men were unreliable and tired out. M'Tesa controlled a wide strip of territory across the escape-route northwards, on which, less than a decade before, Baker had been seriously embarrassed. Even Gordon could make no other decision than to retire.

In bitter exhaustion he turned northwards, forcing his men so fast that they passed through hostile areas before the natives had time to take concerted action. In that climate, in that country, with no route to follow and no stores but what they could carry, his column in one day traversed thirty-five miles. Such a march is not only against time, heat and distance, but against such previously trivial things as boots and breeches which from ordinary discomfort can become acutely painful. Gordon marched in high boots of the Hessian order, drill trousers tucked into them and a collared jacket over his shirt. Even so, *jiggas* must have gone under his toe-nails, leeches found the flesh under his shirt.

Such subsidiary trials in the aggregate are so hard to bear that after a time comes an overwhelming sense that nothing could be worse than further effort. Sweat, which pours down the body and through the clothes, forms a sticky, salty crust and attracts the horse-fly and the tsetse. Boots, however well fitting, chafe sodden feet. Metal carried, such as a gun-barrel, becomes so hot that it will burn the skin of the forearm, and thirst becomes such an obsession that even drinking does not give relief. 'Pour the Nile down your throat and it will not assuage your thirst. The immense amount of perspiration exhausts the body, so that it is hours, even after drinking ever so much water, before it re-acquires its balance by absorption.'

Under such conditions it is easy to suffer mild hallucinations. An ant-hill seems like an animal or a human enemy. Mirages appear on sandy patches among the grass. It is easy to think of danger, and gradually the habit of checking that everyone is in sight becomes an obsession. So does the amount of water, for there is no safe water but what is carried, and that has to be rationed. Where are the bags to be refilled? Will the hole be dry? To all this Gordon had to add the difficult but sanity-saving effort of calculation. He could not allow his mind to stray from the perpetual problems of distance and direction, having with him only Baker's maps and his own, knowing certainly that if the speed of the retreat slackened it would be to invite attack: 'Marched fifteen miles. The enemy kept on drumming and blowing horns all yester-day afternoon around us. Having the account of Baker's re-treat before me I was far from comfortable; for here I was with, at the outside, one hundred soldiers of whom thirty are scarcely over sixteen years old. However, I thank God—not in words but heartfully—we got through safely.'

Small wonder that when he reached his advanced base at Dufile, early in November 1875, he was mentally, morally and physically depleted. He regarded his accomplishments as negligible, and saw no future success in any direction. It was nine months since he had written to the Khedive his secret suggestion for an expedition to Mombaz Bay, and the absence of a reply could only mean that Ismail, his friend, had lost faith, or even had gone over to the side of the slavers. Perhaps Cairo had hoped that he would never return from Equatoria, for if they had wished him to succeed in the annexation of the Lakes and M'Tesa's dominations, they should have given him better material to work with. The cowardice and inefficiency of his insufficient troops disgusted Gordon the martinet as much as the corruption and sloth of the Egyptian administra-tion irritated Gordon the governor. While over all lay the squalid misery of the people whom he had hoped to deliver, still trapped in the hungry desert which he had so much hoped he would cause 'to blossom as the rose'. Even his refuge in faith was no longer impregnable. He missed the eucharistic 'eating' and the sense of divine guidance was hard to regain. To fill his bitter cup he received a telegraphed message from Cairo conferring upon him, for his excellent achievement in gaining M'Tesa's submission, an Egyptian Order of the first class. It was bad enough to receive a deserved reward, but to receive one which was so palpably an empty sign—that was too much. Gordon came to the conclusion that his position was hopeless.

This appreciation of the situation was dramatised into a decision by the arrival, on the 15th of the month, of a delayed postbag. In it there was only a cool, formal letter from Ismail, containing no reference to the scheme for Mombaz Bay and no such phrases of personal friendship as Gordon had become accustomed to. Forthwith he decided that he would serve Egypt no more, and immediately gave orders for his body-guard to be ready to move northwards the following morning. He then wrote out three telegrams to be sent as soon as opportunity presented itself to transmit them. They contained his formal resignation to the proper quarters, Egyptian and British. They were never despatched.

At the bottom of the mail-bag there was a fat packet with the Khedival seal and a superscription to the effect that it should be placed in Gordon's hands by a certain official, who, it transpired, had been ambushed and killed. The killers had not bothered with his baggage, and when the remains were collected, so was the packet—by someone who could not read. So it had been put in with the rest of the mail when the next steamer went south.

The packet contained the Khedive's warmest prose and enclosed an account of how he had acted upon Gordon's suggestion for the Mombaz Bay expedition. As he read, Gordon's depression lifted. Not only was Ismail still his friend, the expedition had actually been sent! Chaillé-Long, who had been recuperating at Plombières, was in charge. He had sailed under sealed orders not to be opened until five hundred miles south of Suez. Good, Ismail realised the importance of secrecy! Gordon tore up the three telegrams, cancelled the orders to move. He settled down to gain new strength, and confidence with which to continue his purgatorial task.

Even so, he would not undertake the overland expedition to join up with Chaillé-Long. He knew that to attempt to do so now would be sheer folly, and so he told Cairo. It was as well that he did so.

On the day before he had reached the Fola Falls, the expedition under Long had hauled down the Zanzibari flag on an old coastal fort, raised the Crescent and Stars in its place, and lustily cheered the Khedive for his new dominion. The fort, however, was at the mouth of the Juba river, three hundred miles north of Mombaz. Thereafter Long and his considerable force—he had thirteen hundred men, some horses and a camel detachment—occupied a strong position and awaited orders. Reinforcements they received, and a steam launch which the Khedive had ordered to be taken from his new Nile yacht, but no orders. The reason Long gave was that he, the Khedive and Gordon would soon feel 'Lord Derby's sharp stick'. He proved right. The Foreign Secretary of England could hardly countenance such play-acting— though it was hardly more, owing to the incapacity of Egypt to produce sufficient forces to follow up her dream of empire. Both Gordon and the Khedive received marks black enough to break them, and meanwhile the Sultan of Zanzibar, confident that such high-handed gestures would not go unpunished, was so civil as to send to Long's encampment a ship-load of all that he needed to keep himself and his command in good fettle. The accompanying letter read:

To the Commander of the Egyptians at Kismayu.

MY BROTHER,
I send you the coal you desire, also fruit. The latter may serve to keep you in good health, the former to take you away from my country. Go, and peace be with you.
BURGASCH-BIN-SAID

And go they did, in due course recalled by the Khedive on representations from the British Consul-General. It was probably not until he reached Cairo again that Long realised he had been sent to the wrong place. Kismayu was too far northward to be a base from which to join up with Gordon moving south from the Lakes, nor would the permanent communications which Gordon had envisaged—including the line of the railway much as it now exists—be practicable on that route. Had he not decided, quite independently, not to undertake such an expedition, he must inevitably have driven down through what is now Kenya to the coast, the empty coast from which he might never have returned. The Fates still had him between their feline paws.

*   *   *

For the rest of his sojourn in that pestilential country Gordon concentrated on the duller aspects of his great responsibility, invoking his original vision in the service of the common people. It was plodding work, but not without danger, for he made many enemies and the Khedival arm was hardly long enough to reach so far, either to save him or avenge him.

Yet he was preserved from ambush and treachery as from sickness and accident. His old fear-proof fatalism displayed itself in action when, as often happened, a slave-gang's escort showed fight. It is recorded that on one occasion at least he stopped, while under fire in the open, to light a cigarette.

There were solid results of his administration by now. Money was in fairly honest circulation. The people, even the most wretched, began to know that they had, at least in the eyes of the new Governor, certain inalienable rights. Their response showed in the spread of peace and the reduction of hunger, in readiness to inform against slavers, in willingness to work. Where, hardly two years before, only well-armed parties could move in relative safety, a man with a stick might now stroll. Where there had been the desolation of isolation for garrisons, who therefore tended to become as bad as the slavers they were supposed to put down, well-knit posts sat neatly behind their zaribas, each a day's march from its neighbours up and down the Nile. While on the river, which had until recently been passable only occasionally, when luck favoured a particular boat, steamers up to one hundred and eight tons burden were moving to schedule between Khartoum and Gondokoro. Thence, if with more difficulty, communications were maintained through Rejaf, Bedden, Kerri, Moogie and Labore to Dufile.

He laboured through the greater part of 1876, but increasingly it became evident that for his health, as for the future of his dominion, he should return to Cairo and thence to England. He does not seem to have been seriously ill, but he was debilitated and very tired. He does not seem to have been seriously perturbed by the repercussions of the abortive expedition by Long. But there was a great need to try to convince the Khedive that the slave-trade would never be stamped out until he personally took action against corrupt officials at the top, particularly against Ayub Pasha, Governor-General of the Sudan.

With a clear conscience, therefore, and still in hope of accomplishing more, Gordon sailed northwards. He would confide all his hopes and his fears, his evidence and his suspicions to the Khedive, who would be delighted to hear that Equatoria was now paying its way. Then he would take ship for

England, recover his health and come back to the task. On the way, however, he changed his mind about confiding in the Khedive, whom he believed to have betrayed a friend, a favourite even, the Financial Minister, Sadyk. When Gordon was last in Cairo, Sadyk's good sense and great fortune had been a power behind the throne. As Gordon was returning northwards his boat was just too late to meet one on which Sadyk was a prisoner. The story was that the Khedive had lured his Minister on some trivial matter to the saloon of a Nile boat, where he had left him 'for a few moments'. The Khedive never came back. Sadyk was never let out. Nor did he receive any explanation for the action of his liege-lord. The boat's windows were boarded over and she sailed south. Sadyk, desperate, tried to set fire to the saloon, but failed. He was never again seen alive.

Gordon determined that he would no longer serve a man capable of such an unchristian action, and so, on arrival in Cairo, he resigned the Egyptian service. Even then Ismail's charm so worked upon him that he was induced to give what amounted to a promise that if he were asked to do so he would return. But whatever the form of words, it is clear he believed that, happily, he would not see Ismail, or his dominions, again. He had been away, as he wrote, 'three years without a Sunday'. He had done more than even he could have expected, and had succeeded perhaps too well against the slavers in that he had alarmed the Cairene plutocracy who were associated with the trade. Yet no amount of unpopularity would have made Gordon give up. Had he still believed in his mission, in his Old Testament vision, he would have been eager to return. If Gordon had changed Africa, Africa had changed Gordon, and in a way which China had not begun to do.

Under Li Hung Chang he had learned respect for the philosophy of non-Christians, but his faith in the missionary imperialism of the West, with its blessings of Trade and Progress, was if anything strengthened by his experience of the muddles into which foreigners fall when left to themselves. On leaving China he still believed in the capacity, and duty, of the civilised to seek out, clothe, educate, organise and proselytise the poor, benighted heathen.

Now he saw the slave-trade as the work of the 'civilised', and the corruption of state policy and finance he saw in terms of the perversion of ideals for which civilisation ought to stand. He had found the naked savage happier than most civilised people. In China and in England the mystic had seen the kingdoms of the world and the glory of them. In Equatorial Africa he had seen *through* them.

Chapter 8

OF MASTERY

ON Christmas Eve, 1876, Gordon, tired and ill, arrived in England to find the same sort of reception which had greeted him on his return from China. He was again the popular hero, and hated the rôle more than ever. So he refused even the mildest social engagements and snubbed eminent men who would have lauded him. He went into isolation at Rockstone Place, now presided over by Augusta. He had promised himself oysters for luncheon, the only time he ever seems to have looked forward to a meal, and his intention was to stay in bed till noon. But it is doubtful whether Augusta would have permitted either such luxury—though oysters were not so expensive—or such laxity, which would mean missing morning prayers. While his horizons had widened beyond her comprehension, hers had grown narrower. And she still insisted that he smoke only in the kitchen. It is to be hoped that Cook and Mary had no objection, for their desire to leave had been a theme of his sister's letters which had annoyed him while he was wrestling with mortal problems in Equatoria.

Under the circumstances it is hardly likely that soul-talks brought the same solace which they used to do. Even at Gravesend he was too big for a sect, now he was too wide for the Church. His dedication had so altered his character that he no longer belonged exclusively to any country, or race, or creed; and yet he remained in bondage to his own daemon, so kind to others, so cruel to himself. There is an appalling loneliness in such a situation, a sense of desolation which only madmen and the mystic know. It drove him to further prodigies of effort, too seldom warmed by the intense companionship of ecstasy:

> Danger no refuge holds, and war no peace
> For him who hears love sing and never cease. . . .
> The sad, he lonely, the insatiable,
> To these Old Night shall all her mystery tell;

God's bell has claimed them by the little cry
Of their sad hearts that may not live nor die.

Yeats' description fits Gordon. Within a week the self-despising hero felt again the beckoning of the Pillar, that finger of God which he had invented along with the Doles, the Archers and Agag—his moods of depression, temptation and pride. Popular outcry, supported by the thundering *Times*, would have made him the Governor of Bulgaria, but the authorities were not at all likely to approve a post where he could so easily embarrass the Government. He himself favoured service under the Sultan of Turkey or of Zanzibar. For the latter he may still have hoped to garner those East African territories which, had his plan succeeded from Equatoria, might by now have been Egyptian.

As for Turkey, it is doubtful if a patriotic Englishman would have cared for such a post. According to the *Illustrated London News* leader for the first week of the new year, Turkey brought to the international scene only 'bankruptcy and moral worthlessness', and it was generally expected that the Ottoman Empire in Europe would soon fall—to Russia. For which reason, to work in Bulgaria would hardly have been a better choice, for she was allied with that recent enemy of England in the Crimea, an enemy whose expansion was again making Whitehall feel uneasy.

In fact, Gordon's alternatives to idleness appeared to be those least calculated to gratify the Adjutant-General and the Foreign Office. The only person to whom he might have appealed was the Prince of Wales, whom he had unjustly suspected of being an enemy. Instead, Royal Edward had followed with interest the Equatoria adventure and approved of Gordon personally upon making his acquaintance. He alone would not have been awed by the jacks-in-office, but unfortunately he was on his way to India for a State visit. So in spite of a compulsion to press on in any direction save that of Egypt, Gordon seemed as much becalmed as the Ancient Mariner and was almost as haunted as though he had slain an albatross.

Formally to confirm the resignation which he had given verbally to the Khedive, he cabled to the Honourable H. C.

Vivian, the new British Consul-General at Cairo. Egypt was sealed out of his future. Yet on the 17th of January a telegram arrived:

> My dear Gordon,
>
>   I was astonished yesterday to hear from Monsieur Vivian of a despatch you had sent to him saying that you would not come back, particularly as I recall our understanding at the Abdin Palace about completing the work which we had begun together. So I must attribute your telegram to the entirely natural sentiments which affect you now that you are back home among your friends; but, my dear Gordon Pasha, I am unable to believe that a gentleman like Gordon could go back upon a solemn promise, and so I await your return.
>
> Your affectionate
> Ismail

Gordon was trapped. Whether or not there had been a 'solemn promise', if the Khedive believed in it, then Gordon was bound by that belief. In despair he went so far as to try to pull strings, putting his plea in person to the Commander-in-Chief, the Duke of Cambridge. They already knew one another, and the Duke had a personal admiration for Gordon; but he held that there was no alternative but to comply with the Khedive's wishes, no doubt reflecting that it would be safer to have Gordon out there under his own command.

The judgement of the C.-in-C. could not, however, alter Gordon's feelings. Though the Pillar pointed to Egypt, he was still determined not to go. There was still one way out, to impose a condition on his re-employment which the Khedive could not meet. But what condition? It must not be too outrageous, yet near enough to set him free for ever from that fated land. He telegraphed, therefore, to say that while he would by no means break his word, he could keep it with honour only if he was given authority over the whole of the Sudan. The request was preposterous enough, for Ayub Pasha was firmly entrenched at Khartoum, and around him were ranked powerful social and commercial interests which even Ismail would hardly dare to challenge.

But Gordon had underestimated the straits to which the finances of Egypt had been reduced by the pressure of the money-lenders and extravagance of the Government. The Khedive was reputed to have overspent his income by seven millions a year for thirteen years. This had created a huge debt on which the lowest rate of interest was twelve per cent. So acute had the position become while Gordon was still in Equatoria that even cure by conquest had been tried. The idea was to annex Abyssinia, still reputed to be rich. The means were to be the Egyptian Army together with the Turkish Irregulars known, and despised, as *bashi-bazouks*. The money to pay this force in cash had been found by Mr. Disraeli, all unknowing; for the English sovereigns which he had paid for the Khedive's share in the Canal, nearly four millions of them, had recently flowed into the empty treasure-vaults of Cairo.

The campaign should have been a walk-over, no matter what the discipline of the invading forces, for the Abyssinians were still mostly tribal warriors without firearms, while their enemies had Remington rifles and an up-to-date military organisation. The conclusion proved so far from foregone that the invaders were decisively routed, leaving so much treasure on the field that the victorious tribesmen would not believe that it was real, and after the battle were willing to trade a handful of gold coin for eighteen Maria Teresa silver dollars. So the result of Ismail's desperate throw was only to stir up a hostile Abyssinia on the flank of his new commitments in the Sudan, and still further to worsen the state of his finances.

At all costs he had now to become so popular with the Western Powers, particularly with England, that he would be protected from bankruptcy. And so he became, whether sincerely or not, the loudest anti-slavery voice outside Europe and the United States. If he could in the popular mind be associated with the end of that odious traffic, it was likely that none of the idealistic democracies dare be hard on him. So, at almost any price, Gordon was essential to his plan. The victim-hero did not yet realise this, and the night before he sailed for Egypt he said he expected to be back within six weeks. Before then he received, in Cairo, a personal letter which left little more to be said. It reads, in translation:

Abdin Palace
February 17, 1877

MY DEAR GORDON PASHA,

In appreciation of your integrity of character and the great services which you have rendered to my government, I have decided to unite in one great Governor-Generalship, all the Sudan, Darfur, and the Equatorial Provinces; and to confide in you the important task of their administration.

Since the territories are very extensive, it will be necessary for good administration that you have under your orders three deputies, one for the Sudan proper and the Equatorial Provinces, the other for Darfur, and the third for the Red Sea littoral and the eastern Sudan.

Should you think any changes necessary you should give me your observations.

The Government-General of the Sudan is completely independent of the Finance Ministry.

I would draw your attention to two points, the suppression of slavery and the improvement of means of communication.

Abyssinia marches with a large part of the frontiers of the Sudan. I would ask you, when in that area to examine the situation with care, and to enter into negotiations with the Abyssinian authorities in order to settle outstanding questions.

I conclude by thanking you, my dear Gordon Pasha, for your kindness in continuing your valuable services to Egypt, and I am completely persuaded that with the conjunction of your great experience and your devotion to duty, we shall bring to a sound conclusion the work upon which we are engaged.

Believe, my dear Gordon Pasha, in my high appreciation and sincere friendship.

Your affectionate

ISMAIL

In spite of the cordial directness of this letter, the Khedive had not intended to dismiss Ayub without notice or cause shown. As Gordon expected, he had baulked at making a Christian the Viceroy of a vast number of Mussulmans. What had changed his mind was a last-minute representation from Vivian, perhaps inspired not only by Foreign Office instructions in the ordinary way, but also by desire of the Duke of Cambridge. It was a fateful step, and an action for which

Gordon ought to have been grateful. But he disliked Vivian—
'that stuck-up donkey'—and gave him no credit, still less
gratitude; probably because he knew that he was trapped
again. He did not want to be Lord of the Sudan, and made a
private last-minute effort to have Ismail's son, Tewfik, appointed in his place. So the first course was laid of a wall of
suspicion and misunderstanding which grew, and continued
to grow after Vivian had been succeeded; until neither Gordon
nor the British Government could see over it to appreciate the
other's situation.

Attenuated to a shadow, Gordon left Cairo for Massowa on
the Red Sea. At forty-three he was the almost absolute ruler
of a million square miles. His basic salary was £12,000 a year,
with allowances, and unlimited opportunity to make a fortune. He was the equivalent of a field-marshal in two armies,
the Chinese and Turkish, while in a third, the British, he was
still a half-colonel worth less than £1000 a year. 'A prophet
is not without honour, save in his own country and among his
own kindred.'

From the first he had no illusions about the practical difficulties of his position. Though he still trusted the Khedive as a
friend, he realised that Ismail was using him as the bankers
were using Ismail and the Powers were using the bankers.
Even so, it was comforting to receive at Massowa a present of
his Marshal's uniform, his 'golden armour', a coat that cost
£150. It impressed the Abyssinian raiders so much that he
was able to buy them off his north-eastern frontiers for £1000
a month, an essential preliminary to the reorganisation of the
Sudan administration.

Though he had himself claimed that who commanded the
Sudan controlled the slave-trade, he realised that, surrounded
as he would be from the beginning by hostility and treachery,
it might be beyond even his capacity to make even the best of
laws effective. It had been suggested in the English Press that
because there was a Moslem minority in Bulgaria therefore a
Christian would not be suitable for the proposed governorship. How much more did that principle apply to the Sudan!
Except in so far as direct action, whether judicial or military,
was concerned, Gordon would have to operate in a vacuum.
Though he could pass any law and prescribe any punishment;

though he could rule by decree; between him and his people —even his staff—were three formidable barriers over which human understanding could hardly leap. For he spoke almost no Arabic, looked down upon the religion of Islam because it appeared to him to lack the principle of the 'indwelling' of God, and was already too set in his character to be able to make personal concession to new circumstances.

If it had not been for the increased conviction that he was an instrument of God, even he would surely have tried to find an honourable way out; for experience in China must have taught him that the basis of good government is mutual understanding between the ruler and the people, a two-way resonance without which there can be only paper loyalty and an imposed order, which, instead of welling up out of the community, is little better than prison dress, to be stripped off the moment that authority weakens.

The sense of his mission, however, overruled all doubts, among them one which might have saved so many lives besides his own. This, the Great Doubt, he could not afford to entertain for a moment, for if he did so it would kill his daemon and his whole philosophy would collapse. To doubt that he had a mission, that he was a predestined instrument of divine purpose, would have been like a cyclist doubting his balance—Governor and rider alike would find themselves in the ditch. A similar delusion of genius was already gaining ground in the mind of Mohammed Achmet, who in due course would announce that he was the Mahdi of Allah, claiming parallel authority with that of Gordon, and from the same source. If either of the two men had dared to doubt, there might well have ensued peace and not war, prosperity and not starvation, liberty and not slavery. It is a tragedy reserved for the brave that in performing their admirable actions they are seldom bold enough to question whether they are right. Gordon never did, nor did the Mahdi, nor did Tien Wang; though each proclaimed, at least early in his career, that all men are brothers as the sons of God. An exclusive dogma of salvation, whether religious, political, economic or military, necessarily becomes neurotic, and, if incorrigible, those that are obsessed by it go morally mad, bringing war for peace, pain for joy, hatred for affection, and defeat for victory.

This is the *herrenvolk* principle, upon the denial of which the great religions of the world were founded. Their followers, however, frequently adopt it, nor perceive the fundamental perversion of which they are guilty. The Devil, who does most of his work in the name of God, was preparing to make Gordon his instrument, as he had done with Tien Wang and would do with the Mahdi.

At first, however, the pressure of immediate business was too great to allow the thin, strong threads of motive to be seen among the thick ropes of government. Administrative affairs submerged Gordon in the kind of day-to-day endurance which had carried him safely through the mental perils of Equatoria. Yet, as he began his task in the Sudan with 'The Negro, the Arab, the Bedouin's course, their meeting with me is decreed'; so, on a river journey, he could write of the undimmed vision: 'I entirely take that prophecy of Isaiah for my own and work for it as I can . . . "and it shall be for a sign, and for a witness unto the Lord of Hosts in the land of Egypt, for they shall cry unto the Lord because of their oppressors, and He shall send them a saviour, and a great one, and he shall deliver them"'.

Gordon set about their deliverance with a phenomenal expenditure of energy and confidence complete if not sublime. 'I have no easy task before me, but (*D.V.*) I have solved the difficulty. My scheme is not yet matured or approved. You have little idea of the great difficulty and the many questions involved in it, viz. in domestic slavery. First, I have to disband some 6000 *Bashi-Bazouks*, who are the frontier guards, and who must be replaced, for they let the caravans pass. You might as well order the sea to stop the caravans as these men. Now, think of disbanding suddenly 6000 men. You must do it neatly: you must see to replace them with trustworthy men. Let me ask, who that had not the Almighty with him could do that? I have the Almighty with me and I will do it. Secondly, consider the effect of harsh measures among an essentially Mussulman population carried out brusquely by a Nazarene—measures which touch the pocket of everyone. Who that had not the Almighty with him would dare to do that? I will do it. . . . As Solomon asked, I ask wisdom to govern a great people; and not only will He give me it but all else besides. And why? Because I value not the "all besides".'

This was just as well, for when he arrived at his palace he found every window broken and the divan of state ripped and slashed. The gesture was an effective one, for there was hardly another pane of glass in the whole country, still less suitable fabric to repair what was virtually a throne. Hundreds of apprehensive servants, including a eunuch for the safe-guarding of his harem—he must have been a sadly puzzled man soon afterwards—in ghostlike robes padded about the building, 'the size of Marlborough House'. Nor was there any demonstrative welcome from the people in the streets. If they had neither the strong feelings nor the courage of Ayub's sister, who had been responsible, in a fit of understandable jealousy, for the damage to the palace, they had no reason to welcome this white-skinned unbeliever. They suspected from the beginning that there would soon be uncomfortable altera-tions in the old way of life. For the income of most of the citizens was connected with ivory, whether white or black, and now that the former was a Government monopoly while harvesting the latter was illegal, there would soon be less money circulating even between honest men.

'With the help of God, I will hold the balance level,' Gordon told his people, 'the reign of the whip is ended.' Even he did not then realise how difficult the first part of the pledge would be to fulfil, nor did he have immediate opportunity to do so. There was no time in which to get to know the economic ferment which surrounded him, still less to understand the springs of fate which caused the vast majority of his subjects to surpass Augusta by praying five times a day. A consequence was that, contrary to the principles of war and the hard lessons of his own experience, Gordon began his greatest operation without adequate reconnaissance, for lack of which, like the nail of the proverbial horseshoe, the kingdom he won was later lost. Meanwhile anarchy prevailed over a large part of it and superimposed upon this was a dynastic quarrel in the western province, Darfur. It first flared up because Ismail had decided that the Sultan was too independent, and ac-cordingly resolved to depose him, making use of the Black Khedive, Zebehr, for the purpose. Zebehr was glad of the opportunity to become the effective Lord of Darfur with nominal allegiance to Ismail, for he well knew that the regular garrisons were no match for his own men, even before the few battle-worthy Egyptian units had been withdrawn to fight Russia in Bulgaria. Not only would the campaign give him more prestige and wealth, it would serve to blood his son Suleiman, to test the discipline of the troops and, not least, would force the Khedive to confer some signal honour upon him, perhaps even the Governor-Generalship of the Sudan, which Zebehr had long coveted.

The campaign easily succeeded and Zebehr, to make sure that the opposition was finally crushed, had every member of the Sultan's family killed; all except one, Haroun, who managed to escape. It was this man who, Gordon was now told, was in revolt, and against whom he moved before he had been a fortnight in his capital.

It may be doubted whether at the time Gordon had any intention of catching Haroun, who withdrew before the small force which was all that Gordon was able to muster; for bigger game was afoot. Zebehr was now under open arrest in Cairo, where he had gone to collect the honours which he had counted before they hatched. His fate was another demonstration, if one were needed, of the murky depth of Ismail's craft of state. But Gordon could not be concerned at this juncture with the ethics of the question. What mattered was that the lion was caged, and the cub, as he called Suleiman, was out in the open. To catch him before the balance of power changed for the worse was the first essential.

To reach Dara, the government post nearest to Suleiman's encampment, and four hundred miles from Khartoum, Gordon rode 'like the telegraph', wearing out his escort, camels dying under him, making eighty-five miles in a day and a half, arriving alone, save for his interpreter, to startle the garrison. They had been shut up for six months without news and were understandably amazed to see a dusty, red-faced man, wearing the glittering uniform of a Turkish Marshal, and escorted only by a cloud of flies, ride into their mud-walled fortress to announce that he was the new Governor-General.

Not that he always wore his 'golden armour', but put it on when a formal meeting was imminent. His riding clothes usually consisted of a fez, which is small help under the sun, a high-buttoned dun-coloured drill tunic, with collar and tie, breeches, puttees and boots. He dispensed with the usual tight body-binder and consequently suffered considerable pain, 'as though my heart and lungs were displaced'. Even so, he covered nearly five thousand miles, camel-back, in his first year of office.

Gordon concluded that the garrison troops were little better than those which he had found in Equatoria. 'The scum of Syria, Egypt and Asia Minor demoralised by unchecked pillage and frequent reverses', they were afraid to venture outside their post, unless in force. They then added to the hostility of the natives by foraging, cattle-raiding and ravaging. In consequence every man's hand was against them. They were equally despised by the warrior tribes and by Zebehr's disciplined troops. Gordon decided that to risk any considerable body of such men in battle would be to invite defeat. Accordingly he had recourse to the one weapon which had never yet failed him, his own inspired personality.

Ignoring Haroun, whose revolt he sympathised with, since it was directed against the corrupt garrisons and the slavers, creatures of Zebehr, Gordon set out to surprise Suleiman while he was still in conference with his sheiks. In one sense the vastness of his bailiwick was an advantage, for no one could tell where next he would be likely to appear. The effect was as though he were in several places at once. A new wind was blowing in the waste Sudan, a searching wind which, while it chilled the evil-doer, scattered the embers of religious nationalism wider than any tribal boundaries, and there were many. North of Khartoum were Nubians and Berberine Arabs. North-east were warlike tribes, the Bidharin and Hadendoa. South were the ineffective peoples he already knew, Shilluk, Dinka, Nuer, Bari, Madi and Moogie, primitive and of small account though some could be trained to war. But in the west, even to where the desert approaches Lake Tchad, were organised warrior-horsemen, fearless, proud and predatory; capable of enduring harsh discipline, having great courage and heroic loyalty. These felt the new wind as did the others, but it meant something different to them, a challenge. Why should the Sons of the Prophet have to watch, while an infidel purged the land of corruption brought out of Turkey, Egypt and the West? Only because there was as yet no focussing power, no leader in the name of Allah. Before ever Gordon gained his first success, the white-robed Baggara and Rizighat, round their desert fires or astride their well-bred horses, bare-back, or with only a toe-hold in a leather loop, were waiting for the leader who would kindle them to power.

Gordon, in full dress, went alone, on horseback, to the headquarters of the enemy he had been fighting from Equatoria, the military power behind the slavers. Three thousand hardened troops were drawn up, and he passed on foot and unarmed between their hostile ranks. To each of them he was a personal enemy, since if he succeeded in breaking Suleiman they would be disbanded, and could expect small mercy from the peoples they had formerly oppressed, even though many of them were slaves.

He entered the big tent at the door of which Suleiman was waiting to receive him, as hospitality required him to do. For technically his irregulars were still the allies of the Khedive, though Zebehr, his father, was a prisoner who might soon disappear for ever; and though, as slavers, they were the declared enemies of the Egyptian Government. Suleiman was boyish enough to appeal to Gordon's susceptible sentiments, 'nice-looking lad, an attractive boy of twenty or twenty-two, clearly a spoilt child, who would be all the better for a shaking. Poor little chap! How bitter for him to be suddenly nothing after having been accustomed to do exactly what he liked, even to killing people. "And David said, 'Deal gently for my sake with the young man'." I will try to do so if I can.'

Within the tent, sheiks in their white cotton *jibbas* sat cross-legged upon carpets. Gordon would not be seated, though he obeyed convention to the extent of drinking a glass of water, which he must have known was a risky procedure, since treachery was in the air. He then invited Suleiman, with his chosen aides, to Dara on the following day. Having said this in broken Arabic, he left the assembly 'dumbfounded that I had come among them'.

The following morning, Monday, the slavers appeared punctually, but, contrary to custom, retained their arms on

entering his presence: '. . . sitting there in a circle I gave them
in choice Arabic my ideas: That they meditated revolt; that
I knew it, and that they should now have my ultimatum, viz.:
that I would disarm them and break them up'. This from a
man who had five hundred unreliable troops against several
thousand with reinforcements handy and the certain knowledge that if Gordon were killed, or better, taken as a hostage
for Zebehr, the last semblance of order and discipline would
disappear, to their profit.

Yet Suleiman and his sheiks gave in and offered their
allegiance to Gordon, 'the cub' even kissing Gordon's feet to
beg for a post under the Government. The magnitude of this
personal triumph for a man handicapped by lack of knowledge of the language—he said he had to make much use of
gestures and tones of voice—is increased by the fact that even
before Gordon arrived at Khartoum, Suleiman had resolved,
in retaliation for his father's arrest, to plunge the whole province into anarchy and spread disaffection into the other
northern provinces. This had not been a mere random
decision, arrived at out of a passion of frustration. Orders had
been precise to the sheiks who were leaders of military districts
in the 'kingdom' of the Black Khedive. All that was required
on Gordon's arrival at Khartoum was the passing of a code-
phrase from mouth to mouth: 'Obey the orders given under
the fig-tree'. That Gordon had not wasted his initiative and
effort in hunting Haroun, but had gone straight to Suleiman,
must have seemed to the slavers to be further proof of an
almost magical power. In the trials to come he would have
need of it, and more.

For the problem before him was only military in the sense
that there must be an efficient power by which order could be
created and maintained, the new laws enforced and insurrec-
tion deterred. The Gordonian knot was tied in the chains of
the slave-trade, which were so complex that even at law the
situation was far from clear. Thus, although slave-hunting
was punishable by death as being equivalent to theft with
murder, slave-owning was not a crime. In theory it was at
first hoped to bring the trade to a standstill by preventing
slave-raiding, but it was soon apparent that as the children of
slaves were slaves, and as slaves could be freely purchased, the

mere ending of *razzias* would accomplish very little. The problem was further complicated by the attitude of the people themselves. Whether slaves or not, they regarded the institution as part of the traditional social order. Gordon encountered a man with seven slaves. 'My wives', he said, nor would any of them contradict him. Even the interception of slave-caravans had little more effect than still further to increase the horrible sufferings entailed by the long trek from the interior. Gordon frequently encountered a hundred or more, often women and children, dying of thirst because their masters had tried to march them clear of wells likely to be picketed, on Gordon's humane orders. Even when the slaves were rescued alive, what was to be done with them?

So great were the losses on the devious routes now in use that Gordon caused the wayside skulls to be piled up to bring home to the traveller what the traffic involved. It was later calculated that for the province of Darfur alone in five years 156,000 people perished; by no means all of them slaves, but all indirectly the victims of the trade. The figures were: Egyptians 16,000; Natives 50,000; Slaves 90,000. Since it is at least doubtful whether the whole of the Sudan could then muster a million people, the proportion is high. So was Gordon's indignation, and it was principally directed not at the slavers, who could hardly be expected to have scruples, but at the saccharine humanitarianism which was fashionable in England, the bedfellow of social oppression and imperial exploitation. He parodied the dinner-hostess discussing slavery: It is very shocking: have some more salmon'.

With typical inconsistency, he was at the same time complaining about interference from home, and not only from his usual butt, the Anti-Slavery Society. Even the Foreign Office, to which he owed his job and, as an Englishman, was still duty-bound, he accused: 'What have the F.O. to do with me, or I with them? I do not want their aid. I should be unfaithful to H.H. were I to accept it.'

His frustration showed in protests even within the context of religion. Comparing Arabs with Abyssinians to the latter's disadvantage, he had taken another step towards Islam and might well have agreed that, 'In the name of God, the merciful, the compassionate', a prayer would hardly be likely to go astray whether the worshipper was in the habit of naming the deity as Allah or Jehovah. He evidently confided this trend to Mrs. Freese, who promptly reprimanded him and eventually received an apology: 'Yes, you were right. They could not know Christ.' At the same time he was aware that while they could not be among the elect, 'there are those who are perfect gentlemen, and who, though they may not be called Christians, are so in spirit and in truth'.

*   *   *

Perhaps the strangest factor in this grim situation was that had Islam lived up to the precepts of its founder, it would long ago have outgrown slavery; just as Christians, had they honoured the spirit above the letter, would have done. For it is written in the Koran that there is no act more acceptable to God than the manumission of slaves. As to their status, it was protected by such injunctions as 'See that ye feed them as ye feed yourselves and clothe them as ye clothe yourselves'. In law there was not even a word equivalent to slavery, but rather a term appropriate to the status of a chattel, much as European wives were then regarded as the chattels of their husbands. This is borne out by the prescribed form of address 'my young woman', or 'my young man'.

Historically, therefore, the concept of slavery with which Gordon had to contend was different to that underlying the Western institution, which had grown the horrors of the Plantations out of Roman and Hebrew practice, a brutal and alien concept from the standpoint of the Mussulman. The ancient Hebrews were hard masters, and when Rome adopted Christianity it was only natural, in the absence of any specific contrary instructions in the New Testament, to revert to ancient practice over the slaves which still formed an essential economic element in the Empire. To dramatise the contrast between Islam and the West, under the former's law a slave who married a free woman himself went free; but in the shadow of Jehovah the woman was killed in an unspecified manner and her husband was burned alive. To quote General Butler: 'Domestic slavery is part and parcel of Mohammedanism. Mohammed was himself a servant before he was a prophet; and many of the greatest leaders and most devoted soldiers that the creed of Islam has produced have been slaves. There is a vast gulf between the domestic and the predial slave. The rights of the first named were carefully guarded under Mohammedan law; and once within the pale of Islam the lot of the slave was a very different one from the fate of his brother negro under a West Indian planter. . . . The higher the so-called civilisation becomes, the deeper grows the villainy of the traffic.'

Whatever the historical sequence, the most important fact in the whole course of slavery as it affected the Sudan was undoubtedly the failure of Christians to realise the anti-Christian nature of the institution. Having failed to see the principle, it was inevitable that the stupid cupidity of man would brutalise the practice. Of this the Sudanese were by no means ignorant. In their fathers' days the Europeans were running the 'racket' which they now wanted to suppress; apparently because there was no longer sufficient profit in it. Nor were the white men rich enough to pay compensation to the owners. How, therefore, could Gordon Pasha dare to demand the freedom of slaves? To do so was unjust.

His reforms in progress, Gordon pondered this problem as he watched the Nile and tried to keep track of the bribery which was going on among his staff. . . . His personal secretary, whom he completely trusted, was broken for receiving £3000. His Maltese major-domo, he said, gave him nothing to eat and got drunk on his brandy. He soon came to the conclusion that, at the risk of offending the Anti-Slavery Society, there would be no sense in failing to recognise the fact that whatever might be done about the export of slaves, their existence, even their status, could not be changed over-night. Accordingly he issued a decree designed to constitute the first stage of a gradual reform, while at the same time his patrols and 'purged' garrisons did their best to paralyse the traffic flowing from the interior of the continent. He was, of course, in action himself, and displayed the same courage which had characterised him in China, but by far the greater part of his time was spent travelling, or coping with the vast administrative problem. To his brother William he wrote:

'It is my firm conviction that I am only an instrument put in use for a time that enables me to bear up; and in my

N

present state, during my long, hot, weary rides, I think my thoughts better and clearer than I should with a companion. Any European would be at a disadvantage at present. They are not always wise, are apt to be too energetic, and would thus get us into scrapes. I have upset so many vested interests that the only people I can count on are the Ulemas, to whom I have given back all their ancient privileges, which had been taken away from them by Ismail Yacoob. If I take officers I make the army antagonistic, and only hold my place on sufferance. When I have laid a bit of a foundation, and mastered the alphabet of the province, then I may want men and shall take them. I hope I have solved the slave question by recommending to H.M. Consul-General, Mr. Vivian, the following scheme:

' 1st. By enforcing the law which compels runaway slaves to return to their masters except when cruelly treated. 2nd. By requiring masters to register their slaves prior to January 1, 1878. 3rd. By not enforcing law No. 1 if not so registered. 4th. By stopping all registration of slaves after January 1, 1878. By this I prevent, after January 1, 1878, any new slaves being considered as property, which they are rightly considered to be until either their masters are compensated or a term of years has elapsed—we here being in the same state now as the West Indian colonies were at the passing of the Abolition of Slavery Act. I also meditate an attack upon the European holders of slaves in these parts. If they declare they are foreign subjects I mean to liberate their slaves; if they say they are Egyptian subjects I shall tax them heavily. Europeans come here, hold slaves, cultivate the ground, and pay no taxes. I won't have this. You will think I might do more. I cannot.

'. . . I have an enormous province to look after; but it is a great blessing to me to know that God has undertaken the administration of it, and it is His work, and not mine. If I fail, it is His will; if I succeed it is His work. Certainly He has given me the joy of not regarding the honours of this world, and to value my union with Him above all things. May I be humbled to the dust and fail, so that He may glorify Himself. The greatness of my position only depresses me, and I cannot help wishing that the time had come when He will lay me

aside and use some other worm to do His work. You have
reached your happy eventide. I would that the heat of my
life-day was over; but He will aid me, and not suffer me
again to put down anchors in this world.'

After three times refusing the Khedive's request, Gordon
left Khartoum to become Chairman of an enquiry into the
national debt, a position which required a man with many
anchors in this world.

*   *   *

en route from Dongola to Cairo
February 28, 1878

I do not like at all going to Cairo, but there is no
help for it. I have now been one year (on February 17)
Governor-General, and I have lived a very rough sort of
life, so much so that I have lost all my civilised tastes, and
have an aversion to my meals which I can scarcely express.
I do not exaggerate when I say ten minutes per diem is
sufficient for all my meals, and there is no greater happiness to me than when they are finished; and this though I
am well.

*   *   *

Gordon arrived tired, travel-stained and irritable, to be met
by a state carriage and conveyed to a palace, where he was
installed in a suite once honoured by the Prince of Wales. He
was not even allowed to bathe and change before being conducted into the presence of the Khedive, who had been waiting dinner over an hour because the train was late. Gordon
sat at his right hand and listened to the tale of woe which His
Highness poured out with the same lavishness which characterised the service. Gordon evidently got up from the table
determined to rescue his friend from the machinations of
the Powers, who were implying with distressing clarity that
Ismail should abdicate, leaving the effective control of his
country in the hands of his creditors.

Touched by the faith which the Khedive had in him, and
apparently unconscious of the disapproval which his championship of the lost cause would arouse in England, Gordon
accepted the assignment; and the following day interviewed
the Consuls-General of the Powers with the largest interest

in the debt, England, France, Germany and Austria, each of which had appointed a Commissioner. Gordon's plan was to forestall their proposals by making negotiations a matter for discussion only between Egypt, represented by himself, the financial advisers of the Khedive, and the bankers. He would not allow the Commissioners to attend.

Major Baring, later Sir Evelyn and finally Lord Cromer, was the British Commissioner. He could hardly have been expected to welcome Gordon's assumption of authority over what was, after all, right out of his context. Vivian, who reciprocated Gordon's dislike, was of the same mind; so from the beginning Gordon lost the only allies who might have carried his ideas against the opposition of the other interested parties. As if their defection was not in itself sufficient, de Lesseps, the French Commissioner, also refused to cooperate.

Gordon's plan was simplicity itself, but quite unacceptable in an age before the gilt edge had worn off international funds. He proposed to suspend payment of the interest then due, to devote the money to arrears of pay for army and civil servants, and to arrange for the 'lost' dividend to be made up in future payments, which would carry a lower rate of interest. It would probably have made little difference to the outcome if Gordon had propounded a diplomatic solution to the problem, for the financial crisis as a whole was secondary to political, economic and strategic considerations outside Egypt. If the Powers thought Ismail unfit to govern, it was less because of his weakness than because of his strength. 'That splendid Leopard', as Gordon called him, was of a dangerously independent nature in an atmosphere charged with rumours of war; particularly since the great Canal was in his power.

If Gordon, fresh from his vast yet relatively parochial labours, appreciated such wider issues, he chose to ignore them out of personal loyalty to his employer, for whom he was prepared to offend both Vivian, whom he recalled as a 'pretty, black-eyed boy' who had been with him at Woolwich, and Baring with the 'pompous, patronising manner'. Both were, after all, the representatives of Queen Victoria, whose subject Gordon remained in spite of all his international adventures. Had Gordon's recommendations been accepted,

England might have been saved much blood and treasure. Probably Ismail would have kept his throne. Then there would have been no revolt by Arabi Pasha, no bombardment of Alexandria, no British occupation. In fine, Gordon's life might have been more valuable in Cairo than was his death in Khartoum.

It may be that the Commissioners appreciated that Gordon was working along the right lines in principle, but they could not accept his arbitrary methods. The climax came when he offered to take full responsibility for the results, and wired Goschen, spokesman of the creditors, to that effect. The financier, who at twenty-seven had been made a Director of the Bank of England, wired back, 'I cannot look at you: the matter is in the hands of Her Majesty's Government'. Undaunted, Gordon then offered to telegraph to the Foreign Secretary to the same effect, making it appear that Egypt and the Khedive were being tucked under his wing. Surely experience ought to have warned him that financiers and politicians, no matter what their nationality, would not take kindly to such summary methods, well though they may have worked in China and the Sudan! A week later he was complaining 'everyone laughs at me'; and he could make no more headway. Nor did he make any effort to get round what amounted to an unofficial boycott. He might, for instance, have met the right people socially, and so said in private what he could no longer say in council. But he would not go out at all, and took to his bed at eight o'clock every evening 'wishing and wishing that my end had come'. For once he was completely out of his depth. Here was a situation to which the principles of war did not apply and where other-worldliness was a serious handicap. Even the forthright speech of the soldier appeared only naïve.

Meanwhile de Lesseps, who had immense prestige owing to the achievement of the Suez Canal, opened in 1869, was determined to get rid of the Englishman. According to his own *Recollections* he told the Khedive: 'Gordon is a man of great ability, very intelligent, very honest, and very brave; but he keeps all the Sudan accounts in his pocket, written on small pieces of paper. All that he pays out he puts in his right pocket, and all that he receives in his left. He then makes up two bags, sends them to Cairo, and money is sent back to him. He is not the man to regulate the affairs of Egypt.'

With characteristic cynicism Ismail promptly dropped the man whom he had so recently set at his right hand. Even so, he had to hide for two days in his harem, about the only place which could afford sure sanctuary from Gordon, who wrote to his brother William: 'The sun which rose with such splendour set in the deepest obscurity. I calculate my financial episode cost me £800. His Highness was bored with me after my failure, and could not bear the sight of me, which his surroundings soon knew. I have no doubt it is better as it is.'

Hardly a fortnight after his arrival, the novice financier was on his way back to his post. This time there was no special train, not one official to see him off. He had to buy a ticket, a sharp humiliation because he had recently insisted upon halving his salary. Nor could he relieve his feelings until he entered his own dominions, where he went on tour among many bowed heads and bended knees. But no amount of earthly worship could give him back the self-respect he had lost in Cairo. 'Search myself as I will, I find that in all my career I can lay no claim to cleverness, distinction or wisdom. My success has been due to a series of (called by the world) flukes. My sense of independence is gone. I own nothing. I am nothing. I am a pauper and seem to have ceased to exist. A sack of rice jolting along on a camel would do as much good as I *think* I do. But how different it is in appearance to the world!'

His tour completed, Gordon settled down for the first time in his life to be an administrator rather than a man of action. He did so in spite of the fact that the campaign against the slavers was again in full swing, with the relapsed Suleiman as the chief enemy. Gordon's field commander was the faithful Romulus Gessi, whom he had first met in the Crimea. In spite of shortages of ammunition, including rockets and supplies of all kinds; in spite of Haroun becoming a second enemy, and the inferior troops which were all that Gordon could give him, the Italian did brave and brilliant work. Finally, after privations from which he later died, he succeeded in capturing Suleiman and his eleven principal lieutenants by a ruse. The slavers outnumbered Gessi's troops by ten to one, but thanks to a skilful night attack followed by an heroic bluff, they were induced to lay down their arms before the true balance of power became apparent.

Suleiman and his sheiks were well aware that, if they could rejoin their forces, the battle might yet go the other way, and so they planned an escape. Gessi caught them before they could get clear of his lines and had them all shot. When Gordon heard of it, he is reported as saying, 'Thus does God make gaps in the ranks of His enemies'. Since the day when the Governor-General was minded to 'deal gently with the young man' Suleiman had made himself as notorious as his father Zebehr, a black Prince to the black King. He was reputed cruel even among his cruel people, shooting prisoners who might be liberated and slaves which might become another's property. One of his battle-flags was dedicated in the blood of a sacrificed child, and it is said that the last shot fired under Gordon's régime killed the man who officiated at that black-magical ceremony. Witchcraft is indigenous to the Sudan, with Islamic institutions superimposed. It is not improbable that, as in China, part of the secret of Gordon's success lay in recognition by superstitious people of a magical element in him. To the cynic this might be explained solely as delusion: people thought he must have supernatural power to be so miraculously preserved, and so believing, they then had no choice but to be ruled by him. The social psychologist, however, still less the priest, would not be satisfied with such a negative interpretation of this aspect of Gordon's extraordinary influence over primitives, and some civilised individuals also. Did Gordon believe in magic—no matter how much it was wrapped in pious Christian phrases? He always prayed for sheiks whom he was to meet on the following day, and found, when in their presence, 'that something had already passed between us'.

The same factor in his character may explain why his creed, which should have been a peaceful refuge, became from time to time an almost unbearable torment; why he sowed peace and reaped war. If a man has *mana*, the magical power which runs through all cultures in all ages, he can hardly fail to use it, if not for good, then for evil. He is by it set apart from others, whether they recognise it or no. He is fated above and beyond the ordinary pattern of life. Was this the root of Gordon's fatalism, that if he did not resign himself to his God, then his own power would rise up, and, worshipping it, he would become a tyrant? The temptation was certainly there, but he always fought it, refusing to rule in his own name or to accept reward. Yet there is a note of triumph in a comment he made on leaving his kingdom: 'Not a man could lift his hand without my leave in the whole extent of the Sudan'.

Sadism, slavery and satanism go together; for anyone who revels in mastery tends to become the slave of his enjoyment. At first sight Gordon had nothing to do with such a neurotic attitude, yet why did he spend his life fighting against it? It is difficult not to believe that he enjoyed his self-imposed privations, for otherwise he would hardly have pursued them so devotedly. In trying to liberate others he came close to enslaving himself. Is a person less sadistic because his cruelty is to himself?

The nature of Gordon's God is becoming fairly clear, that indwelling light which led him kindly towards love as a horse to water, but could not make him drink. The nature of his daemon is beginning to show, the Shadow over against the Shepherd, the black against the white. Yet one thing they both had in common, power. Gordon was tempted to worship power, and not least when he turned away from the world; for the prophet is stronger than the king, and the magician richer than Midas.

*   *   *

In Khartoum as at Gravesend, even Gordon could not spin out his day's work so as to leave him with no leisure at all. In England he could at least go out to visit his various pensioners, the sick, the dying, his boys and Mrs. Freese. But in the Sudan the people were so importunate that he refused to leave his palace and be met by their vociferous demands. Even when he sailed down the river, they ran along the bank wailing, 'We are miserable'. He wanted to retort, 'So am I'. So he stayed at home, and from four o'clock in the afternoon the sun hung heavily over him. He did not take a siesta but worked on through the heat of the day, and when the tasks were done had recourse to one of his two hobbies, the dismemberment of the palace clocks and the welfare of his small zoo. He had grown out of his indifference to animals, and his comments on them are refreshingly light amid so much gravity over this world and the next:

Khartoum, August 8th (1878)

The hippopotamuses are very well—like fat pigs, not a crease in their skins—and they have such huge mouths, which they always open to you, showing little bits of teeth. They lie in the water, with their heads under it for hours. They do not smell a bit, and are lovable animals.

Not all his pets were such a success. A pair of ostriches which were loose in the garden attacked a servant and one of them kicked off the man's nose. Gordon had to compensate him, and says that he sentenced the ostrich to be sold, thereafter to live as a slave and be plucked every year to provide a pension for its victim.

While this shut-in existence would have irked in any case after the freedom of his interminable rides, it was rendered the more uncomfortable by excessive heat and a plague of mosquitoes, bred from standing water left behind after an unusually high Nile. There was a great deal of sickness, and Gordon concluded that Europeans would never be able to live permanently in the Sudan. If his health stood the strain, his temper did not. It was now that he began to acquire a reputation for being feared where before there had been only respect, and it is significant that he does not seem in the least perturbed about it. He wrote to Augusta: 'The people in the Sudan tremble before your brother. . . . Some are ceremonious, and when told to sit down will not. They are sometimes dragged to a seat and seated, and that quite upsets them; or else yelled at till they forget their mission from fear. Altogether, scenes are constant, and cause great amusement to the bystanders.'

Probably a rising sense of frustration accounted as much as the climate for this development, because he was gradually coming to the conclusion that although order could be restored and maintained by force, there was little or no prospect of succeeding in what he believed to be his primary task, the amelioration of the lot of the common people. The territories were so vast that to carry out a programme of reform would require men and money which could never, he thought, be forthcoming. Even to appoint a European to look into the method of tax collection was beyond the capacity of the exchequer, which could afford only £150, while anyone, says Gordon, would want £500 and all sorts of extras. Even the administration of justice was, it seemed, beyond his power to cleanse. Riches could not be convicted in any court in the land, and so he himself had recourse to sentence by *lettre de cachet*, without judicial procedure of any kind.

Alongside the growing sense of failure, in spite of his military and administrative reforms, went an increasing fatalism based upon the latest development of his personal philosophy, which now finally broke away from orthodox Christianity: 'You ask me what my ideas are of a future life. I think that this life is only one of a series of lives which our incarnated part has lived. I have little doubt of our having pre-existed; and also that in the time of our pre-existence we were actively employed. So, therefore, I believe in our active employment in a future life, and like the thought. We shall, I think, be far more perfect in a future life, and indeed go *towards* perfection but never attain it.'

This view is the more remarkable in that there does not appear to have been any available source, such as the literature of Hinduism or Buddhism, from which he could have derived the essential idea of a series of personalities. It suggests rather the kind of direct insight which might be expected to grow out of such mystical experience as motivated his life at Gravesend, and perhaps before. Whether he formed these opinions for himself, or whether they were borrowed, they undoubtedly confirmed his faith and courage in adversity. To his practical turn of mind there was much more to be said for a future in understandable terms of personal experience rather than in the improbable cloudland of a symbolic heaven. And if in the future, then surely in the past also: common sense. He believed that 'human beings are the transient embodiment of souls which have existed through an infinite past and will continue to exist through an infinite future'.

On Bismarck's initiative Ismail was forced to abdicate in July 1879. The brutal instrument was a telegram from the Sultan of Turkey addressed to the ex-Khedive. Gordon immediately determined to resign, as much in protest against the cavalier treatment of his friend as because his interpretation of that prophecy from Isaiah seemed now, even to him, to have been premature. Evidently the time was not yet when 'the desert shall blossom as the rose'.

By the time Gordon reached Cairo, Ismail had already steamed out of Alexandria harbour with a last salute ringing in his ears. Gordon had not even been able to say good-bye and his resentment turned naturally against Tewfik, at once the focus for the *coup d'état* and its beneficiary. Invited to stay at the palace, Gordon considered a curt refusal and going to an hotel instead; yet, having accepted, within a few days the new Khedive had not only induced him to delay his departure but to undertake a difficult mission to the King of Abyssinia. Tewfik must have inherited his father's charm.

*　　*　　*

Johannis, King of Kings, was a monster and perhaps mad. For smoking he cut off his subjects' lips, for taking snuff their noses; while for serious offences he filled their ears with boiling tallow. The claimed effect was to make them blind while the eyes appeared undamaged. Presumably they were deaf as well. He used to carry them about in his retinue when he travelled through his flea-ridden kingdom, *pour encourager les autres*. For really minor matters, such as taking a dislike to someone, the usual practice was chaining, with or without banishment to one of his peculiar hill-top prisons, to which the only access was by basket on a rope over a pulley. He had no fear of anyone or anything except women, who were not permitted to approach within three hundred yards of the palace; and he regarded himself as the equal, if not the superior, of the monarchs of Europe: this in spite of the fact that he was barely literate, lived in a palace made of two round huts without doors or windows, and under conditions so squalid that everyone had tapeworms. It was a usual excuse to say that one had 'taken Kossoo', a local vermifuge without which the parasites would have got the upper hand. He was proud

of his baths, which consisted of a hut built over a warm spring,
the water piped through bamboo.

As to the habits of Johannis, Gordon says he was psalm
singing every morning and drunk every night, between which
he was amused to receive deputations and particularly pre
sents. He badly wanted, he said, a port on the Red Sea, and
Gordon thought the little black man believed that the im
mediate result—and therefore the justification for the projec
—would be a steady flow of presents from his 'brothers' th
Kings in Europe.

The portents for the visit could hardly have been les
favourable even if Gordon had been a man of tact. As it was
he began by making himself unpopular through refusing t
sit where he was told. He took the chair and set it beside th
King, a gesture making him an equal. Johannis asked whethe
Gordon was aware that he could be killed for it, and Gordo
said he cared not at all, for there was nothing that Johanni
could do to make him afraid. 'I am always ready to die,' h
is reported to have said, 'and so far from fearing your puttin
me to death, you would confer a favour on me by so doing
for you would be doing for me that which I am precluded b
my religious scruples from doing for myself—you would re
lieve me of all the troubles and misfortunes which the futur
may have in store for me.' 'Then my powers mean nothing t
you?' Johannis asked. 'Nothing', said Gordon, and change
the subject to the business which had brought him so far i
such discomfort. It then transpired that the risk of losin
his head had been greater even than he had supposed, fc
Johannis had not the least idea who he was. The Khedive
letter of credence had not been opened, an oversight fc
which the secretary to the King received a large number c
blows upon the soles of his feet, perhaps with Gordon's ap
proval, for the King so disliked strangers that he was qui
capable of killing them for being unknown to him.

Apprised of Gordon's status as an ambassador, Johann
demanded impossible concessions in territory, and a larg
loan. Gordon, realising by now that owing to the ugly litt
man's brutality no one ever dared to tell him the trutl
remedied that deficiency. The audience soon ended, an
Gordon started on his way back to Egypt as soon as he coul

get his escort together. He had not gone far before he was ambushed, searched, robbed and put under close arrest by order of Johannis. He must have thought then that his death-wish would not long be denied fulfilment, because it had become clear that the King had no notion of the strength of the European nations and believed that he could withstand them all—except Russia, he had added as an afterthought. Therefore if he believed himself to have been insulted by this, the first man who had dared to treat him as an equal, he had no need to fear the consequences of killing him. He might even desire to kill in order to provoke a diplomatic incident, for Gordon had been at pains to tell him that there was not the slightest chance of any of his grandiose claims being met, particularly the one for some millions of money from bankrupt Egypt.

But Johannis did not do more than humiliate Gordon by keeping him a close prisoner. When he slept at night, he had three Abyssinian guards, one each side of the bed and one at the foot. They confirmed his opinion of the great superiority of Arabs over such as these who called themselves Christians. After a few days, and without having a further interview with the King, he was released and lost no time in getting out of the country. This journey was made the more arduous by the intense cold of mid-winter at such an altitude, especially after so much heat in the Sudan. Perhaps it was the King's intention to have him die from exposure, for the road to Egypt was closed and he had to march to Massowa, where, by someone's providential order, he found the British gunboat *Seagull*, in which he returned to Suez.

By the time he reached Cairo his mission had lasted four months, an illustration of the difficulties of travel, since Gordon never dawdled. He had by then driven himself into a state of nervous exhaustion which caused an Alexandrian doctor to offer him a serious warning before he sailed for home. 'I have recommended him to retire for several months for complete rest and quiet and that he may be able to enjoy fresh and wholesome food, as I consider much of what he is suffering from is the effect of continued bodily fatigue, anxiety and indigestible food.

'I have insisted on his abstaining from all exacting work, especially such as implies business or political excitement.'

This physician seems to have been ahead of his time. His diagnosis would not have included the word psychosomatic, but he clearly understood his patient's debility, irritability, sense of desperate fatigue and 'false angina' in terms of a complex reaction between physical and mental elements, all driven too far, too fast, for too long. As to the results of Gordon's efforts, they are fairly summed up in his own words: 'I am neither a Napoleon nor a Colbert; I do not profess to have been either a great ruler or a great financier; but I can say this, I have cut off the slave-dealers in their strongholds and I made all the people love me'.

It is fair to add that he also demonstrated two great principles, the first that imperialism can be a blessing to subject peoples, the second that only when they appreciate the blessing can they hope to keep it for themselves. Until then alien administration is as desirable as are adult masters in a boys' school.

In the knowledge that he had done his duty to humanity, Gordon was able largely to ignore the complaint that he had failed Ismail and embarrassed Her Majesty's representatives. Gossip added drama to the humiliating way in which Ismail's affairs had been wound up. So merciless was the action of his creditors that the ladies of the harem had nothing to eat until they opened the doors and sought asylum in the alien world. One of the first to go was a pygmy acrobat named Ticky-Ticky, who had been given to Ismail by Gordon because there was nothing he could do which would be better for her. She had been a great success as a clown.

The servants of Ismail also fled, unpaid. Those who had charge of the animals in his private zoo were so precipitate that some of the beasts, including a zebra presented by Chaillé-Long, starved to death. The officers of the army might soon have been in the same case, for many of them had been without pay for two years and their credit was exhausted. They demonstrated vociferously outside the Abdin Palace, where Tewfik from a window promised them not only their arrears but also alternative employment. With reason he feared a military *coup d'état*. The house of Rothschild gave him a special loan of £400,000 to allow him to keep his pledge about the pay.

As for inanimate objects, they were auctioned as circumstances allowed, and with every squalid accompaniment that a compulsory sale can have. Yet His Highness of yesterday had fallen through extravagance, not so much in his personal interest, for he enjoyed a private income of nearly half a million pounds, but for the development of his country. And he had paid out sixteen millions for the Canal. Though the experts concluded that he had attempted to carry out too many projects too soon, it was admitted that the pace was not so fast as it had been in England in the early years of the railway boom. Most informed people were willing to give Ismail their condolences as the victim rather than the villain of the financial jungle which he had entered when he began to get into debt to the West. Yet once he had fallen, and the wolf-pack began to howl, it would have been too much to expect anyone close to the throne to have escaped. Gordon was no exception. General Sir William Butler wrote: 'It is only true to say that every man's hand was against him, the hardest blows coming from his own countrymen. His cipher telegrams to the Khedive he was soon to read in the London papers, with his proposals clipped and changed to suit the objects of the men who were now in power in Cairo. Quick as steam and electricity could carry the warped messages, they were sent to demonstrate to England that this great son of hers was not only inconsistent, disobedient and insubordinate but that he was also mad!'

A telegram which Gordon sent to one of the Pashas may have contributed to this assessment. It read: MENE MENE TEKEL UPHARSIN. At least in his own opinion, he still held that balance in which, as the Ancient Egyptians believed, a man's heart is weighed against 'the feather of truth'. That being so, what had he to fear in the scales of the world which he so much despised? He had himself weighed against the feather the world's values, and, with the Pasha to whom his telegram was addressed, had found them wanting.

Chapter 9

ROLLING BOULDER

GORDON was in no hurry to get home. He visited both Athens, where he lunched with the exiled Ismail, and Rome. Understandably he seems to have been in a mood of bitter depression, but even so he made at least one shipboard acquaintance, Monsieur Reinach, to whom, from Disraeli downwards, he poured out his detestation of Tory 'mounte banks', authors of the cruel policy in Egypt and the suicida fate of his own career. Reinach evidently tried to alleviate th 'doles' by showing him something of the beauties of the tw great cities, but Gordon would not, or could not, respond He despised not only the world of man but also the natura world, and the grand pathos of ancient monuments made him even more depressed. Seen from the Bay of Naples, the Co losseum or St. Peter's, the charm of Rockstone Place was mor effective than ever. He decided to hurry home by train, in tending to keep himself in strict seclusion until his resignatio became effective.

He reached Southampton early in January 1880 and th dreary cold did nothing to lighten his spirits. Nor, presumabl did Augusta. The stimulus came from a very different quarte Queen Victoria. He was summoned to attend a levee at S James's Palace at which she would invest him with the on Order he was ever to receive from his own country, th Companionship of the Bath. As such a command could n possibly be disobeyed, Gordon duly presented himself in fu dress uniform, no doubt with contending views of the cer mony which lay ahead. For though he endeavoured to co ceal the fact, he gloried in the trappings of power, and thoug he advertised his contempt for the kingdoms of this world could play an impressive part among courtiers. No dou on this 17th day of February he was anxious to do so, for intended it to be the last time that he would wear Briti uniform. As to the decoration, though he probably h qualms about the propriety of accepting it while holding t

views he did about the policy in Egypt, he evidently concluded that it had nothing to do with finance but was in recognition, Tory recognition, of his administrative work. There
his conscience was clear. He had done his duty and more than
his duty. So, unlike Lawrence of Arabia, with whom he
would have had much in common, he obediently stood in
line for insignia of which he would be properly proud.

He was announced to the Queen not as brevet Colonel but
as plain Captain Gordon! He must have resented the mistake
and perhaps showed it. At all events the Prince of Wales
asked him to luncheon, another request which could not be
refused. And when Gordon duly attended at Marlborough
House, he found not only the portly Prince but also the Duke
of Cambridge, Commander-in-Chief. This, it seemed, was to
be more than a merely social occasion. Wondering what the
matter was, Gordon probably spent a miserable hour or so
over the meal. But then most of his meals were miserable. His
forebodings were justified. The Prince had followed his career
with interest and was convinced that he was a most valuable
leader of men. England had need of such. If the Duke would
give him indefinite leave, even a year or more, would he not
reconsider his decision to resign, a proposal which was perhaps understandable after what had happened in Egypt, but
was hardly in the interests of the country? As always when
confronted with a choice between some personal desire and
duty, Gordon agreed. The Prince promptly asked him to
dinner. Gordon had the effrontery to refuse, saying that he
always went to bed at nine o'clock. The Prince merely suggested luncheon instead. Gordon was again trapped in the
social net.

But not for long. He fled, first to Southampton, where he
went so far as to hide from visitors under the dining-room
table, which with its heavy cloth hanging low would be as
good a place as any in a small house, and then to Switzerland.
His health was still bad. Switzerland was bracing yet tran-
quil. It represented no ties and concealed no obligations. But
it reminded him of Belgium, and the King of the Belgians, a
cousin of Queen Victoria, to whom he had been presented by
Lord Wolseley. Leopold appreciated Gordon as England did
not, for even the Prince of Wales could not alter the bias

o

which had grown against him in high places. Perhaps the King would employ him? If so there would surely, with Wolseley and the Duke behind him, be no difficulty about getting free from the clutch of Whitehall? Fighting slavers was the great contemporary crusade for which Gordon was a uniquely qualified leader. No one dare put obstacles in his way if he were to go, say, to the Congo to continue the battle for humanity's sake.

*　　*　　*

Hôtel de Belle-Vue, Bruxelles
Tuesday, 2nd March 1880

. . . A huge card from His Majesty awaited me, inviting me to dinner at 6.30 P.M. It was then 6.20 P.M. I wrote my excuses, telling the truth. King has just sent to say that he will receive me at eleven A.M. I am obliged to say that I cannot come if my baggage does not arrive.

I picked up a small book here, the 'Souvenirs of the Congress of Vienna', in 1814 and 1815. It is a sad account of the festivities of that time. . . . They are all in their 6 feet by 2 feet 6 inches.

. . . Horrors, it is now 10.20 A.M. and no baggage! King sent to say he will see me at 11 A.M.; remember, too, I have to shave, dress etc. etc. No baggage!!! It is getting painful. His Majesty will be furious. . . .

12.20 P.M.—Got enclosed note from palace, and went to see the King—a very tall man with black beard. He was very civil and I stayed with him for one and a half hours. He is quite at sea with his expedition (Congo), and I have to try and get him out of it. I have to go there to-morrow at 11.30 A.M. My baggage has come.

During the interview Gordon evidently made a promise that if and when H.M. called upon him he would, if free from obligation to the British Government, undertake a mission to the Congo in much the same circumstances which had led to his post in Equatoria, the suppression of the slave-trade. This at least promised a way out of the impasse which threatened, for without such an offer he had little to look forward to; since it was clear that his record in Egypt, however justifiable on moral grounds, had led to his being labelled as unreliable and tactless.

Nor was he yet completely free of his responsibilities, for

when he asked a guest into his room at the Lausanne hotel where he was staying, on the table were death-warrants from the Sudan awaiting signature. Presumably he signed them, then, having broken the last link with responsibility, fell into the 'doles' and wrote that the boredom of leisure was insupportable. At the same time he reported that the numbness in his arms, which he had associated with 'angina', had cleared up. Either the angels were leading again, or else devils were driving. If so, they drove him into accepting a most inappropriate appointment. He said it meant that the independent comet (himself) had become a chained satellite, but he did not explain why he should so sacrifice his independence, so that it is reasonable to suggest the motive was *faute de mieux*. His employer was equally at a loss to explain how it happened, yet at the shortest notice after returning to England, Gordon found himself *en route* to India as the private secretary to the new Viceroy, Lord Ripon, whose Jesuit chaplain Gordon found more congenial on the long voyage than the rest of the *entourage*. Even before the ship docked at Bombay, both Gordon and Ripon realised there had been a mistake.

They were both proved right in short order, and though accounts differ as to the cause of the break, just as they do about circumstances of the appointment in the first place, it is probable that the reason was a shared idealism in disregard of the practical clash between two very different temperaments. Ripon's work was necessarily imperialistic, while Gordon had become a confirmed believer in the baleful influence of alien administration except in the service of all the people, in which sense Gordon was himself a great imperialist. In this he was nearly half a century before his time, and could hardly have expected any sympathy; though he did expect his motive of service *to the people* to be understood.

The catalyst of the reaction by which the satellite broke away was the Afghanistan problem, to which the orthodox solution was that England should annex the country, or at least garrison Kandahar, against possible Russian infiltration southward into India. It was a clear issue of shady imperialism versus enlightened internationalism, without the least need for sentiment on either side; but equally without need for hypocrisy or injustice. In Gordon's view the British case was both hypocritical and unjust, but as a mere negative that is now of so little importance that it can be ignored in favour of his positive thesis, applicable to the whole panorama of mercantile development under the stimulus of a mission to the 'lesser breeds without the law'. He wrote: 'Some say that the people of Kandahar desire our rule. I cannot think that any people like being governed by aliens in race or religion. They prefer their own bad, native governments to a stiff, civilised government, in spite of the increased worldly prosperity the latter may give.'

No wonder Gordon was not welcome, nor happy in his post! Ripon may have been disappointed, but he had no reason to be surprised, for he had been warned by Sir Charles Dilke that Gordon was 'too excitable to be possible as a private secretary'. An even more potent warning had been conveyed by Gordon's behaviour at a London dinner in farewell to the new Viceroy, who was going out to implement the new policy of the recently elected Liberal Government under the ageing Gladstone, after six years of Disraeli's cash-conscious Conservatism. No more formal occasion, even in that formal age, can well be imagined. Gordon insisted on taking the food for each course upon the one plate, remarking to his neighbour, 'We shall have to rough it in India, you know, so we might as well begin now'.

The idea of a Viceroy 'roughing it' must have been almost as startling to the elegant company as the idea of his private secretary being a barbarian. Yet the barbarian was distressingly Christian in an age when adultery was fashionable though divorce was anathema, and charity was laudable while fair wages were subversive. Gordon's view of India was in terms of basic humanity. He believed that only by raising the standard of living could peace in the long run be assured, while in the past the effect of British rule had been rather the opposite. General Butler says, 'It was only a year before this date, 1880, that a military officer of high rank and deep insight into Indian affairs had said that there could never be another rebellion in India, because the people were too weak from want of food to fight. That one fact would have been sufficient for Gordon. State-craft, official tradition, the policy of predecessors, all would have gone down before the simple

reality of the first village he came to being in want of bread,
while the vessels at the nearest port were shipping wheat to
England or sending rice to China. It was necessary for him
to be on the side of the weak.' Even so, in case it might be
thought that he had quarrelled with his employer, he wrote
for publication in the Press an effusive letter virtually giving
his blessing to the new Viceroy: 'Depend upon it, this vast
country will find that, in spite of all obstacles, the rule of Lord
Ripon will be blessed; for he will rule in the strength of the
Lord and not of men'.

As with most of his prophecies, he was not so far wrong.
Meanwhile he must get another job, but where? His first
thought was Zanzibar, again on anti-slave duty. Before he
could make any move in that direction a fateful telegram
arrived. The news of his break with Lord Ripon had not only
reached England, but thence China.

'I am directed to invite you to China. Please come and see
for yourself. This opportunity for doing really useful work on
a large scale ought not to be lost. Work, position, conditions,
can all be arranged with yourself here to your satisfaction.
Do take six months leave and come.'

The sender was Sir Robert Hart, with whom Gordon had
quarrelled, and later made it up, over the affair at Soochow.
Gordon, perhaps reasonably, now thought that the originator
of the message was really Li Hung Chang and not Hart, who
might well have been acting as a go-between, since Li had
written to Gordon while the latter was in Khartoum, and had
left it as likely that there would be a post for him in China if
he ever wished to return.

Gordon's reply was prompt and typical: 'Inform Hart
Gordon will leave for Shanghai first opportunity. As for conditions, Gordon indifferent.'

He was so indifferent that he left India without even small
change in his pocket, for he had used up all his money in re-
paying Lord Ripon the amount of the passage outward from
England. As for the conventional present due to Li, why, he
should have the viceregal coat which Gordon had never un-
packed. He left Bombay on the 12th of June and arrived, via
Hong Kong and Canton, at Pekin within a month. There he
found a hotbed of intrigue and two wars pending, a civil one

and one against Russia. He also discovered that he had not been summoned by Li Hung Chang but by Hart, who demanded that he should not even see Li before being briefed on the British view of the situation. Gordon ignored him and proceeded direct to the *yamen* of his old friend and ex-enemy, now one of the chiefs of the Celestial Empire, Senior Guardian of the Heir Apparent, Senior Grand Secretary, Viceroy of Chihli, holder of the Third Degree of the Yellow Jacket and wearer of the Double-eyed Peacock's feather.

Li Hung Chang was being worked upon by the German Minister, aided by his European colleagues, to the end that he should attempt to seize the Dragon Throne, using Gordon as his Commander-in-Chief. The plan was magnificently expedient, but because Gordon had no expediency in him, it failed. Instead of seeking to profit by the situation Gordon threw himself between the opposing forces, between Li and the party of the Literary Class, between China and Russia. Such a rôle could hardly have been played by any other human being with any chance of success; yet, so far from approving his move, Whitehall telegraphed in reply to his request for leave: 'Reasons insufficient. Your going to China is not approved.'

Gordon untrusted was as truculent as a woman unloved. The effect of the message was to confirm him in his decision to do what he thought best in China without becoming the catspaw of any party or individual. He replied to Whitehall: 'Arrange retirement, commutation, or resignation of service. . . . My counsel, if asked, would be for peace, not war. I return by America.'

He followed this with a public proclamation designed to make it abundantly clear that he had not the least intention of trying for a new dividend of military glory from his old investment in Chinese affairs. But the British Government was still uneasy, and took the unprecedented step of telling the Minister, Sir Thomas Wade, to prevent Gordon from carrying out his plan, as one authority says, by putting him 'under moral arrest'. Presumably the strange phrase was used because no charge could be brought against him. The effect, however, was much the same as if it had been. He was instructed not to leave the grounds of the British Legation in

Pekin or to have an interview with any person without the Minister's express consent. Gordon ignored the whole cat's cradle of red tape and, as usual, reduced the issues to one of personal loyalty. Much as he had tried to take responsibility for Ismail the Khedive, he said that he stayed in China for the safety of Li Hung Chang; and in Pekin he succeeded where in Cairo he had failed.

He followed up his previous telegram, to which there had been no reply, by another one resigning from Her Majesty's Service. In this way he thought to relieve the British Government of all responsibility for his actions, which were likely to be contrary to official policy. The situation was one of approaching crisis, to which Germany, France and England were by no means averse. If through their encouragement Li Hung Chang became the ruler of China, it would be to the advantage of importers and to the Powers by which they were protected. If China became embroiled with Russia, the effect would be to draw Russian attention away from the ruins of the Turkish Empire in Europe, during a period when the Western Powers were planning an arch of diplomacy over the whirlpool of new nationalisms; and also to distract attention from Afghanistan, an unlocked door to India.

Cairo had sickened Gordon of diplomats. Equatoria had sweated off him the glamour of 'civilisation', 'progress', 'the White Man's Burden'. He had been in the false position of being an official representative of a system which he had outgrown. Now at last he was free, or so he believed. He was not Colonel Gordon, or Gordon Pasha any more, but a private individual who happened to be so placed that in helping a friend, nations might have peace instead of war.

Yet this new freedom was qualified by more than the disapproval of diplomats. Perhaps he felt a twinge of conscience such as all men have who are forced unwillingly against patriot authority. By resigning he had to a large extent put himself outside the protection which he would otherwise have had through diplomatic channels. He was fair game, and knew it: '. . . Having given up my commission I have nothing to look for, and indeed I long for the quiet of the future . . . if the third party hear of my recommendation before the Court Party acts, then I may be doomed to a quick exit at Peking.

Li Hung Chang is a noble fellow, and worth giving one's life for; but he must not rebel and lose his good name. It is a sort of general election that is going on, but where heads are the gage.'

From this it appears that Gordon was the filler in a sandwich, not only between parties but also between individuals, one of whom was Li, still a dangerous man to cross whatever Gordon may have thought about the worth of his personal friendship. Yet it is likely that the very fact of his refusing to accept Li's views was a potent factor in the seemingly impossible agreement which he achieved, single-handed, against what appeared to be irreconcilable differences, hell-bent. Alone he went to Pekin. Alone he was received by Prince Chun, father of the boy-Emperor and leader of the war party. In council the only foreigner, Gordon showed forth the folly of war in both contexts, internal and external. So forceful was his speech that the interpreter was frequently embarrassed, and finally refused to translate a word, upsetting in his agitation a ceremonial cup of tea. Gordon seized the wretched official's dictionary and with a firm finger pointed to the ideograph for the offending word. It was 'idiocy'. In shocked but impressed silence the highest authority in the Empire accepted this barbarian's appreciation of the situation and sat meekly while he wrote out, under five headings, the basis of a Sino-Russian settlement.

He followed this up with a paper on the future of the country, written, as he says, 'as a Chinaman for the Chinese'. Commenting on it to his friend and biographer, Boulger, he makes these prophetic remarks:

'I painted this picture to the Chinese of 1900. "Who are those people hanging about with jinrickshas?" "The sons of European merchants." "What are those ruins?" "The Hongs of the European merchants," etc. etc.

'I wrote the other day to Li Hung Chang to protest against the railway from Ichang to Peking along the Grand Canal. In making it they would enter into no end of expenses, the coin would leave the country and they would not understand it, and would be fleeced by the financial cormorants of Great Britain. They can understand canals. Let them repair the Grand Canal.'

In two memoranda, equally forthright, he gave his views upon the foreign policy, the armament plan, the economic future of the country, and then went quietly off to Shanghai; presumably intending to take passage home via America as he had intended when leaving India. He must at that moment have felt that he deserved well from every quarter, not least from his own country, which otherwise could have benefited only if Li had successfully seized power; and this Gordon was convinced he could not have done. A telegram had arrived during his stay in Pekin, and had not been forwarded: 'Leave cancelled. Resignation not accepted.'

The blow, which would have felled most officers, glanced off Gordon's new sense of independence. He had believed that he was free. He had behaved as though he were free. There was now nothing to lose but his pension, and he had already made up his mind to sacrifice that. Had his efforts in China led to embarrassing consequences, especially warlike ones, he might well have had to face disciplinary action; but as he had clearly succeeded, and in just the way which would be most impressive to the sentimental public at home, there was small risk of any action being taken against him.

Already on his way home, he replied to the telegram: 'You might have trusted me. My passage from China was taken days before the arrival of your telegram which states "leave cancelled". Do you insist on rescinding same?'

The answer was six months leave. Gordon had won again. Nor, when he came home, did he alter his views to suit his masters, though he did refrain from publishing them, having already found it more effective to write privately to friends and let them, if they thought fit, publish the letters. One such, also to Boulger, reads in part: '. . . I also say that it is not fair to force anything on your neighbour, and, therefore, morally, it is wrong even if it was eggs.

'Further, I say that through our thrusting these eggs on China, this opium, we caused the wars with China which shook the prestige of the Peking Government, and the outcome of this war of 1842 was the Taeping Rebellion, with its deaths of 13,000,000. The military prestige of the Mantchous was shaken by these defeats, the heavy contributions for war led to thousands of soldiers being disbanded, to a general impoverishment of the people, and this gave the rebel chief, Hung-tsew-tsiuen, his chance.

'A wants B to let him import eggs, B refuses, A coerces him; therefore I say it is wrong, and that it is useless discussing whether eggs are good or not.

'Can anyone doubt but that, if the Chinese Government had the power they would stop importation tomorrow? If so, why keep a pressure like this on China whom we need as a friend, and with whom this importation is and ever will be the sole point about which we could be at variance? . . .

'China is the only nation in the world which is forced to take a thing she does not want. England is the only nation which forces another nation to do this, in order to benefit India by this act. Put like this it is outrageous.'

*   *   *

Holding such anti-imperialist views, it was hopeless for Gordon to expect congenial employment, in spite of the number of individuals who were beginning to realise that if he was a little queer, he was also a man of penetrating vision in which there was no room either for compromise or sentiment. Almost alone of his generation he saw the eggs which looked innocent enough, and often were laid innocently, but which were no more nourishing in the long run than was opium.

Accordingly, Gordon looked to fields afar, the farther the better. The Sultan of Zanzibar had recently concluded a state visit to Queen Victoria, and so, without offending Whitehall any more, it was an attractive idea to enter the Sultan's service and disappear again into Africa. What made the possibility even more attractive was that, thanks to the kindness of Sir William Makinnon, Gordon had been given the extraordinary privilege of going wherever he wished on Peninsular and Oriental ships; free travel almost anywhere in the world. There was another reason for getting out of the country. A book about him was about to appear under the editorship of Dr. Birkbeck Hill, who had gained permission to publish some of his letters on condition that the author and editor never met and that the author was not praised. The idea of the book fanning the flames of notoriety was too much for Gordon as he waited for a chance to get away to some paid adventure so in the end, when the Sultan failed to take advantage of the offer, he took the economical step of going to Ireland, ostensibly to shoot snipe through Kerry and Connemara.

Yet Gordon's constitution was such that he could not take a holiday. He had to have some serious end in view. This time it was the condition of the tenantry, and, as usual, he went at it like a bull at a gate. Within a matter of weeks he was deep in the troubles of 'the poor, distressful country', and within a couple of months had fallen under the ancient spell of Caitilin ni Houlihan. There was an echo of Irish pugnaciousness—he is alleged to have had the blood in his ancestry—in his conclusions; which were published through the action of friends to whom he wrote. These are typical excerpts: 'I must say that from all counts and my own observation, that the state of our fellow-countrymen in the parts I have named is worse than that of any people in the world, let alone Europe. I believe that these people are made as we are, that they are patient beyond belief, loyal, but at the same time broken-spirited and desperate, living on the verge of starvation in places where we would not keep our cattle.

'The Bulgarians, Anatolians, Chinese and Indians are better off than many of them are.'

Nor was he content to drive against the chronic public opinion of the English, which has ever considered poverty to be quaint in Ireland though terrible anywhere else. He made a practical suggestion, as efficient as it was impossible. He proposed that, on the precedent of buying out the slaves of the Plantations, the Irish should be bought out of the hands of their English landlords. He calculated that for all Ireland eighty millions of money, representing twenty years' purchase, would compensate the owners, leaving the soil as Crown Lands, to be allotted at fair rents for decent dwellings on adequate acres. O the brave voice crying in the wilderness! Gordon might as well have proposed to the Khedive that he buy out Zebehr.

If he was not officially reprimanded, it was conveyed to him that such activities were not welcome. The incident made it even less likely that he would be given an appointment worthy of his record. Owing to a chance meeting at the War Office between Gordon and a Colonel in his own Corps, Sir Howard

Elphinstone, both Gordon and the Adjutant-General were saved from the embarrassing deadlock of his further unemployment.

Elphinstone had been told it was his turn to be Commandant R.E. in the Army's least popular station, Mauritius. Two officers had already gone on half-pay rather than take up the appointment, and Elphinstone considered retiring rather than go out there, to be socially buried alive. As an indication of the unpopularity of the place, the usual consideration for substituting for an officer posted there was between £700 and £800. Gordon refused the money, saying he might as well be there as anywhere else. He was in the 'doles', for he had received no acknowledgement of a telegram he had sent to the Cape Government. It read, 'Chinese Gordon offers his services for two years at £700 per annum to assist in terminating war and administering Basutoland'. It was a bargain offer, and even to Gordon's way of thinking, something of a last resort. He was, for all his humility, the last man to go round touching his hat to politicians in the hope of employment; and it must have galled him that, with all the trouble now coming to the international boil, he was not at all appreciated, officially, in his own country.

Nor was this a temporary judgement. As time went on he seems to have confirmed it until he believed himself to be something of an outcast from England; and in that belief planned never to return except out of necessity. Even when he undertook his last mission, it is probable, no matter what happened to Khartoum, that he would never have come home.

So, in the mood of a wallflower at the dance of State, Gordon took ship for his new command, where at least he could look forward to solitary meditation. For what duties there were in that passé paradise took up little even of conscientious time; while the garrison officers got by with a duty, according to Gordon, of two hours a week. Even in Mauritius, however, he complained of social activities thrust upon him, 'I strike against garden parties, archery and lawn tennis meetings! I cannot go through these fearful ordeals of hours' duration.' Nor did he club with other senior officers, but rather seems to have avoided them, presumably because of their flippant attitude towards boredom and the few local antidotes for it. Instead, he sought the company of subalterns, whom he used to invite over to his quarters after dinner for serious talks. As part of his duty he visited the Seychelles, reporting that fortifications were undesirable in comparison with the protection which could be afforded by four gunboats based on East Africa. He also speculated upon the islands as representing the site of the Garden of Eden and drew a sketch map showing how rivers might have flowed westward to the Red Sea, and north-west up the Persian Gulf.

* * *

Chaillé-Long, on his return from the M'Tesa mission, had claimed the discovery of real-life lotus-eaters in the neighbourhood of the Great Lakes; a people who, like those in the poem, did nothing all day long, nor ever had a streak of duty or desire. Gordon accused the Mauritius garrison of the same sin. He called it their 'deadly sleep', and countered it in himself by writing articles for publication. So the months passed, until he found himself gazetted Major-General, which meant that he would have to leave his post, since it could be held only by a Colonel.

Whether they had been waiting for this promotion or not, the Cape Government now telegraphed urgently to H.M. Government asking for his services. Gordon promptly accepted and took passage on the *Scotia*, a sailing ship. As when he left China, he avoided a send-off in what might reasonably be regarded as a thoroughly discourteous way. He went on a twelve-mile walk—presumably his baggage was already embarked—and then had himself rowed to the ship from an unsuspected place on the coast. The *Scotia* was not a good sea-boat, and he was very sick on his way southward.

Arrived at the Cape he, as usual, cut his salary, which in spite of the previous offer had been set at £1200 p.a. Then, having made the gesture, he found that London had framed a new regulation by which he would not be able to draw basic pay parallel with his special service pay. For the first time he felt he had pinched himself too hard; but this did not in the least diminish the zeal with which he applied his unique talent to the work in hand.

The situation was a stalemate after two years of campaigning against the Basutos and the expenditure of five million pounds. There seems to be little doubt but that, though the bait had been administrative, the real reason for the Cape's invitation was for Gordon to lead their forces to victory. Not only did he refuse, he took the view that the Basutos had every reason to resist, and that the operations hitherto conducted against them had been based upon injustice.

On leaving India he had written: 'My views are diametrically opposed to those of the official classes, and in the face of the vested interests I could not hope to do anything really to the purpose'. Now, in Cape Colony, he takes much the same stand: 'The natives were goaded into rebellion by the badness and inefficiency of the magistracy'.

Excerpt from 'Memorandum' dated 26th May 1882.

'There are four points which stand out in relief:

1. That the Basuto people, who date back generations, made treaties with the British Government, which treaties are equally binding, whether between two powerful states or between a powerful state and a weak one.
2. That, in defiance of the treaties, the Basutos lost land.
3. That, in defiance of the treaties, the Basutos, without being consulted or having their rights safeguarded, were handed over to another power, the Colonial Government.
4. That that other power proceeded to enact their disarmament, a process which could only be carried out with a servile race, like the Hindoos of the plains of India, and which any one of understanding must see would be resisted to the utmost by any people worth the name; the more so in the case of the Basutos, who realised the constant contraction of their frontiers in defiance of the treaties made with the British Government, and who could not possibly avoid the conclusion, that this disarmament was only a prelude to their extinction.'

This forthright championship of native rights could hardly have commended itself to the Cape Government of that day —or this; and Gordon followed it up by a thorough personal reconnaissance. At length it was officially suggested that he should go to try to persuade an unamenable chief to cooperate with the authorities. Gordon accepted the charge and went alone to the 'rebel' kraal, only to be put in danger of losing his head because while he was talking peace, a war-party had formed up in a neighbour's land with the conniv-ance of the authorities. Masupha, the Chief, was finally con-vinced of his guest's innocence, less by Gordon's frank de-nunciation of the white man's plot against the black man than because of his intense indignation. It may well have been an impressive spectacle, for Gordon certainly believed that he had been sent to Masupha as a mere blind, while a surprise attack was planned. Perhaps because of his firm stand on the side of Masupha, not only was the attack not launched, the whole question of the Basutos was re-examined: unfortunately to no good purpose.

Even the personal friendship of Cecil Rhodes could make no difference to the official view, though Rhodes remained Gordon's staunch supporter. The two men must have made a curious contrast at meals, for Rhodes was something of a glutton. This attitude was not confined to food, and Gordon is said to have dramatised the contrast between their views by telling Rhodes how in China he had been offered—and of course refused—'a whole room-full of silver'. He demanded, 'What would you have done?'

'Why,' said Rhodes, astonished to be asked such a silly question, 'taken it of course! What is the earthly use of having ideas if you haven't got the money to carry them out?' Gor-don's reply, if any, is not on record. The thrust must have penetrated to the heart of his philosophy of investment beyond the world, which was incomprehensible as witchcraft to the solid citizens of the Cape; whose Ministers demo-cratically concluded that he was a dangerous, even sub-versive person, who had not only failed to subdue the natives, he had befriended them. How else were the men in power to read some parts of his report? The narrow range of their vision, blinkered by that old misinterpretation of Genesis about the status of the black man, was insufficient to re-cognise Gordon for what he was, a pioneer, not for a nation, but of humanity, a builder of Empire on the principle that among nations as with individuals, 'he that is greatest among you, let him be your minister'.

'Government by coercion', he wrote, 'is essentially rotten. The Duke of Wellington said that any fool could govern by that means. And it is still more rotten when Government governs by the rule of coercion without the power of coercion except at great expense. . . . Nothing can possibly be worse than the present state of affairs in native administration, and the interests of the Colony demand a vertebrate government of some sort, whoever it may be composed of, instead of the invertebrate formation that is now called a government, and which drifts into and creates its own difficulties.'

With such rough speech, it was hardly likely that Gordon's detailed proposals for establishing and keeping the peace would be taken seriously. The immediate preoccupation of Authority was to get rid of the man they had so recently welcomed. Gordon, as usual, cooperated with them to the extent of offering to resign. The offer was welcomed by the Cape Prime Minister: '. . . after your intimation that you would not fight the Basutos, and considering the tenor of your communication with Masupha, I regret to record my conviction that your continuance in the position you occupy would not be in the public interest'.

To which Gordon replied rhetorically: 'Is it likely that I would fight against a man with whom I am life and soul?'

So the spring of 1882 found him unpopular and facing un employment. He was moneyless again, and even remarked wryily to a fellow-passenger on the ship taking him home, 'Do you think it right for a British Major-General to set out on a journey like this without sixpence in his pocket?'

He must have known that the chance of being offered any responsible post was now remote, though Lord Dufferin had urged that he be sent back to Egypt to try to avoid the coming storm, which broke in the revolt of Arabi Pasha. Officially Gordon was now regarded as too unpredictable for any independent command, because he would always do what he thought right with small regard for what the laid-down policy happened to be. To the men behind the big desks con formity and blind obedience were more valuable qualities than genius for leadership and administration; but their view was not shared by Leopold, King of the Belgians, who re newed his appeal to Gordon: '. . . I now again request you as you are at liberty, to enter my service. For the moment I have no mission to offer you, but I wish much to have you at my disposal, and to take you from this moment as my counsellor. You can name your own terms; you know the consideration I have for your great qualities, and you cannot doubt the extreme pleasure I should always have in bearing witness to it. I shall be delighted to receive verbally or in writing a favourable answer. The cause which I hope to make succeed in Africa is that for which you have already done so much.

'Believe, my dear General, in my sincere friendship.— LEOPOLD.'

Gordon's reason for refusing this handsome offer, at a time when he was so much in need of something of the sort, was visionary, but eminently practical when viewed from a later date. He said that he would gladly go if he could operate under an international flag, but not otherwise. Under international rule of law the lighting of the 'dark continent' could be carried out to the mutual benefit of all concerned, not least the natives; but under competing nationalisms the result could only be darker even than before. What other man of his era could foresee the result of the patriotic rivalry of Europeans and its effects upon the bewildered Africans?

Whether Leopold agreed or not, the creation of a United Nations authority was so clearly premature that there was no alternative but to allow Gordon his eccentricity; which, in the absence of any other job, led him to the first and last real holiday of his life, in fulfilment of an old dream of his, to meditate in Palestine.

Thanks to a free P. & O. passage, he arrived in Jaffa on the 16th of June 1883 and went at once to Jerusalem, where he settled down, Bible in hand, to re-create in his mind's eye the potent history which he had studied so assiduously. He lived on bread and fruit, and was even able to give up cigarettes except on special occasions. Nor were all his speculations concerned with biblical matters. He found it impossible not to continue to think about Egyptian affairs, and wrote long letters and articles to support his contention that it was strategically stupid as well as morally wrong for England to support Tewfik against the will of the people. Such a régime

P

would mean, sooner or later, government by coercion, and that would involve the occupation of Egypt, which in turn would produce, sooner or later, an inevitable patriotic reaction. Better, Gordon argued, to get out while yet commitments were not so great as to make it impossible. As for the Canal, the only sensible course would be to recognise that it might well be lost to the Powers through Egypt's hostility; and so he proposed an alternative waterway over which Egypt had no control. Gordon went into this possibility with professional attention to details, and succeeded in showing that such an alternative waterway could be constructed from the Gulf of Akaba to the Dead Sea, thence to debouch into the Mediterranean.

'Such a canal would close all attacks from Russia upon Palestine, except upon the line between Haifa and Zerin, and strangely enough would force her to attack at Megiddo (Armageddon).

'These are my views. Anything is better than the wretched want of sympathy between us and the Egyptians, which is now daily increasing into a deadly hate. We must have a Nemesis unless we show more sympathy. What single good thing have we done the people?'

In the previous year they had risen against their oppressors under Arabi Pasha, only to be defeated by Lord Wolseley at Tel el Kebir after the bombardment of Alexandria by the British fleet. England now ruled Egypt, yet Turkish-Egyptian oppression remained virtually unchanged. No wonder the Sudan was aflame from Equatoria to the Egyptian frontier! There could be no lasting peace on the banks of the Nile save a just peace, a righting of wrongs. There should be England's task, not in propping the rotten throne of Tewfik, the hub of the wheel of Cairene corruption. No doubt the voice which had proclaimed Islamic 'holy war' was a challenge to Christendom, but its owner was only a poor Dongolawi, one of Gordon's own people, whose grievances and sufferings cried to heaven. Let the wrongs be righted, Gordon said in effect, and the Mahdi will melt away.

For all his clear-eyed strategy, much of his speculation was at best erudite, being concerned with such matters as the exact location of the construction of the Ark and its probable

course. His style, too, has something of the profuse improb-
ability of those who write interpretations of prophecy, whether
from pyramids or sacred books, tending to forget in their
multiplication of signs and portents that the Promised Land,
for instance, is more likely to be a state of mind than a pattern
of acres. The following excerpt from a letter to his brother is
typical:

'Aden: is it not Eden? Bab el Mandeb through which the
cleft passes, means "the gate of the world".

'The Red Sea coast presents uniform strata on both sides,
and ancient sea-terraces are to be observed. It is in the Gulfs
of Akaba and Suez we must search for Gihon and Pison,
for down those gulfs or clefts those missing rivers must have
flowed.

'Pison means to overflow, or increase; the changing,
doubling, or extension of mouth. Nilah is the Sanscrit for
blue. The Hebrews called the Nile the Nachel of Egypt, which
signifies a stream or torrent, dependent upon mountain rains,
or upon melting snow. The eastern confluent of the Nile is
the Bahr el Azrek, or Blue Nile, rising in Abyssinia, flowing
through the Lake Tzana, encompassing Godjam, a province
of Abyssinia, and joining the White Nile at Khartoum. It is
this river which by carrying down the alluvial soil of the up-
lands, fertilises Egypt; and it is this river which causes the
inundation from the mountain rains of Abyssinia. In Godjam,
from remote time, gold has been found. Bdellium is supposed
by Josephus to have been a yam, as manna is compared to it,
and from Godjam yams were exported.

'Godjam I identify with Havilah. Genesis x 29 says Havilah
was the son of Joktan, and brother to Sheba and Ophir; they
dwelt "from Mesha as thou goest unto Sephar, a mount of the
east". Sale's Koran says Mesha is Mina; and Dhafair, or
Zafar, north-east of Aden is supposed to be Sephar. The Bay
of Zeylah, south of Perim, was in ancient times called Sinus
Avalatis, and Gesenius considers this to have been a Joktan
settlement. Arrian, who lived in the time of Alexander the
Great, also so considered it. . . .'

In contrast, the style of his ordinary letters is clear and
brisk: 'The priests found a Crusader buried in his armour,
and out he came. . . . It is nice sauntering about, conjuring up

scenes of days gone by—real scenes, actions on the stage of life; all gone! It quiets ambition.'

Knowing that he was uniquely qualified to quell the chaos rapidly deepening from the Delta to the Equator, he must have been sorely tempted. It would have been a simple matter to write to Wolseley, his friend from Crimean days, asking for an appointment. He was probably held back from this obvious step less by reticence than by the recognition that his political views would be unacceptable. He was too much inclined to side with the rebels, an old failing of his when justice demanded it, as in South Africa.

When staying with Laurence Oliphant in his house at the foot of Mount Carmel, he made it clear to his host that the only policy likely to succeed in the Sudan required an end to Egyptian hegemony. He seems even to have foreseen a native administration, though presumably it would have been at first under English direction to ensure an ordered development and the completion of the anti-slavery reforms. He believed that with such a prospect put before them the native ruling class would prudently avoid the Mahdi, preferring office to camp, and peace with prospects to war with none.

Oliphant wrote of him at this time: 'What was so extraordinarily attractive to me in him was his underlying meekness and contempt for himself, except as an instrument for divine ends'. The meekness, however, was not so much underlying as superimposed upon a grandiloquent pride, much as Cyrano de Bergerac's appearance of humble simplicity was piped with arrogance.

Yet it is doubtful whether at this time Gordon had any specific ambition left, though with the autumn came a new summons from 'the tram of the world'. Whatever had passed between Gordon and the King of the Belgians, he had left the latter with the impression that under certain circumstances he would, when asked, go to the Congo. The situation was an echo of that which had arisen between him and the Khedive years before. So when Sir William Makinnon, to whom Gordon owed his free P. & O. passages, invoked the alleged promise and brushed aside the objection about an international authority, Gordon felt bound to comply. His task would be to succeed Stanley, who was coming home in the following spring, and to this effect the Foreign Office was duly informed before they received Gordon's telegraphed request for permission. He was by no means eager: 'As for going to the Congo at all, I am indifferent; and unless the king had had my promise, I do not know whether I would go at all'.

He may even have hoped that permission would be refused. If so, the hope died with the receipt of the following message:

'The Secretary of State has decided to sangdon [*sic*] your employment in the Congo.'

With that, the aura of other-worldliness faded, and the practical man in a hurry took over arrangements with all his old drive. He had to go back to England, but said he would not stay a day longer than he could help. Accordingly he did little more than change ships, and arrived in Brussels on the first day of 1884.

There he learned that the clerk in the Jaffa telegraph office had made the all-important message read the opposite of what had been intended. The Secretary had not *decided* but *declined* to *sanction* his employment.

If the King was surprised, he did not blame Gordon for failing to anticipate such a decision because he must have suspected that, in Baker's words, 'The Authorities neither themselves employ him, nor allow others to do so'. Though Whitehall had upset his plans and perhaps made him feel foolish, Leopold generously recognised that Gordon was the chief victim, and even went so far as to offer to pay to him the whole value of his commuted pension, £7288, if he would resign his commission and then, being a free civilian, go to the Congo as already arranged. Gratefully Gordon accepted the offer—he could hardly look anywhere in the world for suitable employment except to H.M. of Belgium. Accordingly he sailed for London, and wrote out his official letter at Southampton, dated 7th January, in answer to the written communication which had confirmed the original wording of the fateful wire.

SIR,

    I have the honour to acknowledge the receipt of your letter of the 5th inst. informing me that the true decision of the Secretary of State for War was that he declined to sanction my going to the Congo, and further, that if I retired from the army of Her Majesty, I am entitled to no pension.

I assume that the decision of the Secretary of State for War was based upon his reluctance to grant me leave while on the active list of general officers, and if that obstacle was removed, Her Majesty's Government would have no objection to my entering the service of His Majesty the King of the Belgians.

I have, therefore, the honour to request you to forward to His Royal Highness the Field-Marshal Commanding-in-Chief, for the gracious approval of Her Majesty the Queen, this, my humble petition to be allowed to retire from Her Majesty's service.

I quite understand by the warrant quoted by you, that should Her Majesty graciously accept my resignation, I have no claim whatever for pension from Her Majesty's Government.

His Majesty King Leopold II has most kindly assured me that His Majesty will compensate any pecuniary loss I may incur in leaving Her Majesty's service.

I have, etc.,

C. G. GORDON

Bitterly hurt and terribly alone, Gordon made his will, dividing his estate between Augusta and twenty-five nephews and nieces. There were twenty-eight of them in all, but of three he did not approve.

Chapter 10

LION'S DEN

SINCE by convention an officer's resignation was treated as though it were effective immediately it had been handed in, Gordon evidently considered himself already a free man; for the very next day he gave to Mr. Stead, editor of the *Pall Mall Gazette*, his detailed appreciation of the situation in Egypt and the Sudan. He would hardly have done so had he considered himself to be still a serving officer, particularly since his opinion was contrary to that of official policy: 'Whatever you may decide about evacuation, you cannot evacuate, because your army cannot be moved. You must either surrender absolutely to the Mahdi, or defend Khartoum at all hazards. The latter is the only course which ought to be entertained. There is no serious difficulty about it. The Mahdi's forces will fall to pieces of themselves; but if in a moment of panic orders are issued for the abandonment of the whole of the Eastern Sudan, a blow will be struck against the security of Egypt and the East, which may have fatal consequences.'

Gordon went on to suggest that the Mahdi was a puppet, not a prophet, whose strings were pulled by Zebehr, still hankering after his kingdom, still at large, and with great influence at Cairo now that Ismail was gone. And then, consistent with his championship of the under-dog: 'The Sudanese are a very nice people. They deserve the sincere compassion of all civilised men. I got on very well with them, and I am sincerely sorry at the prospect of seeing them handed over to be ground down once more by their Turkish and Circassian oppressors. Yet, unless an attempt is made to hold on to the present garrisons, it is inevitable that the Turks, for the sake of self-preservation, must attempt to crush them.' As the alternative, Gordon believed that Zebehr would become the ruler of the Sudan, than which nothing could have been more unpalatable to the man who had fought his slavers to a standstill, and shot his son. Gordon wrote to Baker to urge him to go to Egypt as the 'only man who knows his own mind and has decision'. He added, as to the Congo: 'I do not want to go; but neither do I want to go to the Sudan: it is too late'.

The article, as it was meant to do, created a ferment, for England was already becoming sentimental about the prospect of the loss of those vast dominions which Gordon had won out of oppression and chaos. Moreover the sentiment was backed by a surge of patriotic fervour, rebounding from a serious reverse at the hands of the Mahdi's fanatics, who had been promised the support of twenty thousand angels. It seemed an insult to the flag that at the very moment when England had won Egypt, some unkempt heathen out of the desert should so far presume as to slay General Hicks, a retired British officer in command of an Egyptian army. That Hicks died like an engraving out of the *Illustrated London News*, astride his charger and with drawn sword, made for flashing eyes and puffed-out chests; but not for critical insight into the situation which had produced out of a cowed and unarmed rabble a fighting force strong enough to obliterate ten thousand well-armed men, of whom only one survived to start the news for Cairo. To the democratic mass, which had elected Mr. Gladstone to put a brake on Disraeli's dashing foreign policy, glory beckoned out of Egypt and common sense took a back seat. Hicks' troops had been betrayed by their guides. Not force of arms but fatigue and thirst had defeated them. No ordinary civilised person, it seemed, could bring himself to believe that savages with swords were able to stand against disciplined troops—even Egyptians, with modern firearms.

Mr. Gladstone himself thought differently. On the very day that Hicks fell—before the fact was known, there took place a Mansion House banquet at which the ageing Prime Minister had declared, amid a disapproving silence, that England would evacuate Cairo. He appreciated, if the public did not, that principle of Gordon's about government by coercion, and he had no intention of committing to Egypt sufficient forces for such a purpose, recognising that sooner or later they would become too weak to sustain their rôle, even against natives quaintly dressed and picturesquely armed.

Thus before Hicks died, and while Gordon was still preoccupied with the exact site of Golgotha, the Government, or at least the Prime Minister, were opposed to the policy which the public forced upon them in a juvenile spirit of 'Rule, Britannia'. Nor was this view conditioned only by party considerations: far from it. A British officer, who had been in command at Khartoum, Colonel de Coetlogon, telegraphed from Cairo: 'Khartoum and Sennar cannot be held. In two months there will be no food. All supplies are cut off.'

Le Poer Power, Consul and *The Times* correspondent at Khartoum, wired: 'It is perfectly useless to attempt to hold this place, where the population is a slumbering volcano. The land line of retreat is closed. The river line may be closed tomorrow.' A Pasha wrote to Baker: 'What fanaticism! All this will appear to you who know the Sudan, strange enough, even incredible. Yet these are the very people who, but eighteen months ago, bowed in the presence of a *tabush*; when a whole village could have been frightened out of its wits by a rusty old flint-lock—the only danger in which was that it might kill the man who fired it. But so it is. All those who sacrificed themselves really believed that Mohammed Ahmed was the Mahdi. They were told that those who were killed would go at once to Paradise; and they were led by Dervishes, who were always in the front ranks ready to throw away their lives by the thousand.'

That was in November. Now, in January the river was still navigable and the telegraph wires uncut. Cairo breathed again, sent a stream of cipher messages to London, and began recruiting to replace those who with General Hicks had not returned. The new intake inspired little confidence, for the men had to be press-ganged to the depôts, sometimes fettered, and already mourned by their families as though they were as good as dead. There was at least one mutiny in spite of these penal conditions.

While Gordon was going on with his arrangements for Congo service, the Fates began to weave over the official decision not to re-employ him. It happened that a Colonel Edwards wrote to his friend General Clarke, that in his opinion 'there is one man competent to deal with the question—Charlie Gordon'.

Clarke, who also felt strongly about Britannia, sent the letter on to another friend, who happened to be the Chancellor of the Exchequer. With it was a covering note, which includes the potent commendation: 'If the Mahdi is a prophet, Gordon, in the Sudan, is a greater'.

The Chancellor wrote to the Foreign Secretary, who wrote to the Prime Minister: 'Do you see any objection to using Gordon in some way? He has an immense name in Egypt—he is popular at home. He is a strong but sensible opponent of slavery. He has a small bee in his bonnet. If you do not object, I could consult Baring by telegraph.'

On the day that telegram arrived in Cairo—for Gladstone raised no objection—Zebehr had taken another step towards his kingdom, and to that master of expediency the task might not have seemed one of great difficulty. He had, after all, every reason to support the Mahdi, but no need to be ruled by him. It is a measure of the muddle in Egypt that Zebehr, of all people, should have been proposed for a command which caused Power to wire from Khartoum: 'it will nullify Gordon's and Baker's work'. Even *The Times* was 'astonished'. The Government vetoed the proposal. Meanwhile Baring, who did not want Gordon any more now than he had on the Debt Enquiry, failed to find anyone to undertake a mission to Khartoum which was not only dangerous but almost impossible to fulfil. The whole Egyptian Cabinet had already resigned in protest against the British decision to withdraw, and no one had any confidence in the ability of Egyptian troops to effect the evacuation, or to withstand the Mahdi. Though there were twenty-one thousand soldiers in the Sudan they were islands in a hostile sea, easy for the Mahdi to overwhelm, incapable of offensive action and powerless to fight their way home. The Christians in Khartoum alone numbered eleven thousand, and in magazines up and down the country lay warlike stores which in the Mahdi's hands would give him the power to threaten Egypt. He promised his followers all the lands of the Nile, but without modern equipment his hordes inspired no fear for Cairo. With the contents of those magazines it would be another story.

In this hopeless situation even Baring turned to Gordon. He telegraphed to London: 'My telegram (No. 44) of today and your telegram (No. 28A) of yesterday, General Gordon would be the best man if he will pledge himself to carry out the policy of withdrawal from the Sudan as soon as possible, consistently with saving life. He must also fully understand that he must take his instructions from the British Representative in Egypt and report to him. He was in Brussels early this month and is now believed to be in England. If so, please see him. I would rather have him than anyone else, provided there is a perfectly clear understanding with him as to what his position is to be and what line of policy he is to carry out. (Otherwise not.) Failing him, consider Stewart. Whoever goes should be distinctly warned that he will undertake a service of great difficulty and danger.'

And still no one had thought fit to tell Gordon that he might be needed, nor had his advice been officially asked in any context. The only intimation he had that some employment, alternative to the Congo, might be in mind, was the failure to return any answer to his official letter of resignation.

Inured to discourtesy and double-dealing, Gordon went ahead with his arrangements, but before returning to Brussels he went to see Baker, urging him to accept the burden of the Sudan, and at the same time to assist his brother Valentine Baker, who, as Chief of the Gendarmerie in Cairo, was certainly in need of help. Baker evidently refused because he believed the task to be impossible. The physical difficulties in the way of evacuation were too great. Gordon agreed with him: 'Where are you going to get the camels to take them away? Will the Mahdi supply them? If they are to escape with their lives, the garrison will not be allowed to leave with a coat on their backs. They will be plundered to the skin, and even their lives will not be spared.'

The desert journey was made necessary by the Second, Third and Fourth Cataracts. To cut, overland, that huge loop of the Nile between Abu Hamed and Wadi Halfa, some two hundred miles, was the only alternative; and the only means were camels, as necessary for the desert as ships for the sea.

Yet, when Baker in turn suggested that Gordon should attempt the impossible, he was evidently fired by the ambition he thought had died in Palestine. Barnes, the parson who accompanied him on his visit to Baker, remarked his eager-

ness, but Gordon told him: 'That was myself—the self I want
to get rid of'. In which spirit he sailed again for Belgium.

This time he did not intend to return to England, ever. It
may have been for that reason he took with him a friend and
a brother officer, Captain Brocklebank, who had been the
only other person present at the interview with the editor of
the *Pall Mall Gazette*. Brocklebank may have been carrying a
secret, for that night and the following morning, the 16th/17th
January, Gordon's attitude changed so markedly that from
deep depression he became 'in the highest spirits' and wrote
to his brother asking for various items of uniform, including
patent-leather boots, which were hardly required for the
Congo. He added to the hurried note: 'I saw King Leopold
today; he is furious'. And well he might be! For Gordon
must have told him that, through Brocklebank, it had at last
been suggested that before taking up his work for Leopold he
should first visit the Sudan to report what, if anything, could
be done. He was not being asked to do the impossible; but he
had an opportunity to succour his people and perhaps for
martyrdom. At this, however, even his own brother could
only guess, for the Cabinet had not yet decided what was
to be asked of him.

The same day he left for London again, and was promptly
taken by Brocklebank to Knightsbridge Barracks, which he
was not allowed to leave, being, according to his friend
Boulger, who had met him at Waterloo, 'in honourable
custody'. 'At 12.30 P.M. Wolseley came for me. I went with
him and saw Granville, Hartington, Dilke, and Northbrook.
They said, "Had I seen Wolseley and did I understand their
ideas?" I said, "Yes", and repeated what Wolseley had said
to me as to their ideas, which was: "they would evacuate the
Sudan". They were pleased and said, "That was their idea,
and would I go?" I said, "Yes". They said, "When?" I said,
"Tonight", and it was over. I started at 8 P.M. The Duke of
Cambridge and Lord Wolseley came to see me off. I saw
Henry and Bob; no one else except Stokes—all very kind. I
have taken Stewart with me, a nice fellow. We are now in the
train near Mont Cenis. I am not moved a bit and hope to do
the people good. Lord Granville said Ministers were very
much obliged to me. I said I was much honoured by going. I

telegraphed the King of the Belgians at once and told him, "Wait a few months". Kindest love to all.—Your affectionate brother, C. G. GORDON.'

The scene at Charing Cross Station that evening had been such a tribute to Gordon that at the same time it was something of a caricature, both of his character and of his mission. The Duke of Cambridge held open the carriage door for him. The Foreign Secretary, Lord Granville, gave him his ticket. Lord Wolseley handed over a watch and chain. As the train began to move off it is said that a bag with £200 in gold was handed through the window, presumably delayed until Gordon could not longer refuse it. And none of these gestures were empty. On the contrary, they were typical of the nation's pious hope that Gordon would again be Saint George, to subdue a dragon which would succumb only to the magical hero. *The Times* observed: 'It is impossible to exaggerate the feelings of relief and satisfaction universally inspired by the knowledge that General Gordon has undertaken the pacification of the Sudan'.

But while her subjects sighed with relief, the Queen's instinct warned her that the time for satisfaction, if it were ever to come, was certainly not yet. 'His attempt', Victoria wrote in her journal, 'is a very dangerous one.' Of the many responsible persons involved only Baker and Baring seem to have agreed with her. After all, he was not being sent to Khartoum, and all he had to do was to report. His orders were in the following form:

'Her Majesty's Government are desirous that you should proceed at once to Suakin to report to them on the military situation in the Sudan, and on the measures which it may be advisable to take for the security of the Egyptian garrisons still holding positions in that country, and for the safety of the European population in Khartoum.

'You are also desired to consider and report upon the best mode of evacuation of the interior of the Sudan, and upon the manner in which the safety and good administration by the Egyptian Government of the ports on the sea coast can best be secured.

'In connection with the subject, you should pay especial consideration to the question of the steps that may usefully be taken to counteract the stimulus which it is feared may possibly be given to the slave-trade by the present insurrectionary movement and by the withdrawal of the Egyptian authority from the interior.

'You will be under the instructions of Her Majesty's Agent and Consul-General at Cairo, through whom your reports to Her Majesty's Government should be sent, under flying seal.

'You will consider yourself authorised and instructed to perform such other duties as the Egyptian Government may desire to entrust to you and as may be communicated to you by Sir Evelyn Baring. You will be accompanied by Colonel Stewart, who will assist you in the duties thus confided to you.

'On your arrival in Egypt, you will at once communicate with Sir Evelyn Baring, who will arrange to meet you, and will settle with you whether you should proceed direct to Suakin or should go yourself or despatch Colonel Stewart to Khartoum via the Nile.'

There was no need to communicate with Baring, for on arrival at Port Said, Gordon was met by Sir Evelyn Wood, Sirdar of the new Egyptian Army, who told him that, instead of going at top speed to Suakin, he was to proceed to Cairo for consultations. Clearly it had been Baring's idea in accepting his appointment that he would go to Khartoum, but, perhaps owing to telegraphic confusion, the Cabinet, while putting Gordon under his orders, did so on the assumption that he would go to Suakin, a very different proposition to Khartoum, and relatively safe.

Already the vacillation which was to characterise the whole struggle was beginning to delay the initial operation; while with every day that passed the Mahdi became stronger, his followers more numerous. It is probable that he could already count upon a hundred thousand adherents, though not, for the most part, either organised or battle-worthy. Yet they were enough to seal off the Sudan from Egypt whenever the divine inspiration intimated to Mohammed Achmet that the time for such a bold stroke, which would certainly invite reprisals, had come. And they were fanatics to a degree which no one in authority, not even Gordon, seems to have appreciated: '. . . la flamme du fanaticisme dans les yeux, la rage et l'amour au cœur, brûlant de courir au combat sous la conduite de l'ang-

Azräel lui-même, méprisant et appelant une mort que devaient suivre des délices éternelles, ils attendraient, tremblants d'impatience'. (Délébecque.)

Baring was aware that Gordon's inspiration might at any moment modify his policy, no matter what instructions he had been furnished with. In a private letter to Lord Granville, Baring wrote: 'It is all well that Gordon should be under my orders, but a man who habitually consults the prophet Isaiah when he is in difficulty is not likely to obey the orders of any man'. Baring had probably heard that Gordon's arrival in the capital was unimpressive: 'When the special train came in, one solitary passenger alighted, a small man in a black greatcoat, with neither servant nor portmanteau'.

Baring, the Consul-General, distrusted informality. He was more the ruler of Egypt than was the Khedive, for since England had occupied Cairo it was hair-splitting to pretend that Egypt was anything but a conquered country. What more natural, therefore, than that Egypt should seek to shift the burden of responsibility for the Sudan to British shoulders? They were, in the first instance, Baring's shoulders, who in turn had to pass the weight to Gordon. Years ago Gordon had remarked that when oil and water mixed, so would he and Baring. Here was the meeting, and superficially all was well, yet deep down they must have despised one another, than which it is difficult to imagine a worse augury for Gordon's mission. Gordon thought of Baring as a man without a soul, albeit a master of expediency. Baring thought Gordon at best theatrical and at worst crazy, though undoubtedly sincere.

*   *   *

And so the stage for tragedy was beset by paradox and misunderstanding until the principal actors become almost unrecognisable because of the complexity of the action, which began with a clash over Zebehr. Gordon first told Baring that the great slaver should not be permitted a command and should be exiled to Cyprus, to get him out of the way of temptation to join the Mahdi. Two days later he proposed that Zebehr should accompany him on his mission and be installed in Khartoum as the ruler of the Sudan. Not only was he to have Gordon's own kingdom, but the old slur of slaving was to be covered up with the scarlet and blue of the Order of Saint Michael and Saint George; and he should receive half a million pounds to keep the state which Gordon had previously stripped from him. The suggestion was parallel with his selection of Abu Saud when first he came to Egypt; but whereas Ismail had let Abu Saud out of prison to go with Gordon to Equatoria, Baring by no means approved of a similar gesture to Zebehr, who, though not in prison, was being followed by secret police.

Gordon insisted. The proposal was put to Gladstone, who evidently liked it in principle, but would not sanction it, on the ground that the electorate would never approve the appointment. Zebehr had been too much built up as a monster, 'the greatest slave-hunter who ever existed'. It would be wrong to seek his help, no matter how great the need or how weighty the practical arguments. In Gordon's view, and presumably Gladstone's, the 'Black Khedive' offered the only real chance of peace. His influence was still enormous and he controlled the only disciplined fighting force in the Sudan. Whichever side he fought for would win—if he were allowed to fight; so at all costs he must be weaned from the Mahdi lest Egypt herself should fall, and all the British capital be lost, together with control of the Canal. No doubt Baring appreciated this better than most people, and realised that Gordon would never have made such a suggestion if there were an alternative. If it were shameful for England to honour an ex-enemy, how much more so for Gordon to hand over his own office to someone he had hunted?

At least he persuaded Baring to accompany him on a personal call to Zebehr, the suggestion for which had, surprisingly, been accepted. The Black Khedive received them with the dignity characteristic of that ageing man. His long, lined face was squared off by a grizzled beard, and his eyes had something of the power-glint which occasionally lit Gordon's, though here was no gentleness. Zebehr's eyes were hard with bitter memories. Nevertheless he spoke politely, until Gordon impulsively brought into the open the greatest of all bars to their cooperation, the death of Suleiman, his son. Gordon sought to evade Zebehr's accusation of murder by saying that he killed only traitors. He did not attempt to shift the responsibility on to Gessi, whose order had been the direct cause of Suleiman's death. The Black Khedive scorned argument. He salaamed to Gordon. One account says that he prostrated himself. 'If that be true,' he said, with all appearance of humility, 'I am your servant.' Then, drawing himself up and raising his voice. 'But it is not true. The blood feud is between us.' And so the interview ended as common sense would have foreseen; nor was Gordon's stature increased in Baring's eyes, to which the scene must have been acutely embarrassing. He had no use for 'mystic feelings' such as the one which had guided Gordon to seek the help of the criminal he had hunted as the enemy not only of Man but of God.

On the broad issue of Gordon's mission, it now appeared to both men that the main point of his appreciation in the *Pall Mall Gazette* was correct; Khartoum must be held 'at all hazards'. Only from there could the required influence be exerted over sheiks, provincial sultans and the general population, in such a way that the Cabinet policy had any opportunity for success. Already the chance was slender, but only in the sense that the garrisons might not be movable without first coming to terms with the Mahdi, a situation for which Gordon was already prepared. He remained convinced that if the system of tribal government which had existed before the Turkish conquest were reintroduced, then the reappointed rulers, in all grades, would have everything to gain by remaining at least non-belligerent. Without them the Mahdi would not be strong enough to force the capitulation of Khartoum, or even of Berber, so that 'at all hazards' did not anticipate even a risk of final defeat but only that the terms of the evacuation might not be easy to arrange or comfortable for those involved.

With such ideas Baring and Gordon must have immediately realised that the key to the problem was Gordon's personal authority over the men who would be promoted to administrative posts vacated by foreigners. To such men his present status was wholly inadequate. They would not treat with, nor be influenced by, a mere messenger; but only by a man holding high office, from which alone they could derive their initial authority. This had certainly been foreseen by Gordon, who had suggested, in a memorandum on ways

Q

and means, that he should reassume the now ironic title of Governor-General. The point was evidently appreciated in London, for no objection seems to have been raised. Similarly, there was no opposition to a change of destination and route, an indication that all such details were consistent with the general idea and the written orders which embodied it.

Yet it is the apparent inconsistency of the chief actors in the drama of Khartoum which has inspired the greater part of the relevant literature; and in the process their basic attitudes, which remained constant, have often been overlooked or too much taken for granted. One does not adjudge the captain of a sailing ship inconsistent because he tacks to the wind.

Gladstone had publicly stated at the Mansion House that it was intended to evacuate Egypt. He remained convinced that the policy of non-intervention was both right and expedient: all else was subordinated to it. The War Office, long distrustful of Gordon, remained so. It was not out of naughtiness that the staff moved slowly, but from caution only natural in view of the General's record. In their view anything would be preferable to military commitments in his unwanted wilderness; whence only slowly, at risk and with difficulty, troops could be recalled in time of crisis.

Gordon himself was supremely consistent. Though he perished in trying to serve two masters, and in so doing embarrassed his superiors, he retained his integrity of purpose and did not alter his basic military appreciation, which the *Pall Mall Gazette* had published at length. He may well be forgiven for thinking that the views there set out were familiar to the men who appointed him, but this may not have been the case. No one in high office seems to have recalled, when it was so necessary, Gordon's succinct summary that either Khartoum must be held or else the occupying forces must come to terms with the Mahdi. From the very beginning, everyone was, or should have been, aware both of this, Gordon's aim, and of his character, which would drive him on to its fulfilment or to death. No, it was not inconstancy so much as *idées fixes* which made the muddle which made the sacrifice, which made the Hero.

He, of all people, failed to realise how an ideal can transform a man or a movement. He still believed in the Sudanese as an amenable, peaceable people, who trusted him because he was only nominally a servant of the oppressor. His policy had always been against alien administration in the Sudan. Surely God had now summoned him to that task, when, even at the price of re-established slavery, there was for the first time an opportunity to carry it out?

To England he owed a soldier's duty but no more. To Egypt he owed honest administrative effort; but Egypt was the tyrant, the cause of that despair which had called the Mahdi into being. Small wonder that Gordon considered himself almost a free agent, under God. The Mahdi would go the way of Tien Wang. Then the Congo would receive the too famous General into comforting anonymity.

While he was walking the diplomatic plank, it is probable that he remained unaware of two factors which would have shaken his confidence, the first political, the second military. The first was a powerful if secret body of opinion which regarded the British withdrawal from Egypt as disastrous. Better far to continue the occupation than to lose the vast sums of capital which had been invested in the country. Butler says, 'Nine-tenths of the official world of Cairo were against a peaceful evacuation of the Sudan, and so were a large majority of the permanent government of England'. Later, it was alleged that not only civil servants but Ministers were involved in something hardly less than a plot to get England embroiled. An extreme view was that Lords Hartington, Granville and Northbrook, backed by Rothschild interests, intrigued with Sir Charles Dilke to influence Baring against a peaceful issue. They must have been grateful for the Mahdi! The second factor was the personality of the Mahdi.

* * *

That, during Gordon's first tour of duty, a particularly good-looking young man, son of a Dongola carpenter, and nephew to one of Gordon's guides, should have chosen to live like a hermit on an island in the Nile, was not remarkable in a country addicted to dervishes; who are, or ought to be, members of one of the thirty-six monastic orders of Islam, vowed to poverty, humility and chastity.

Even when the neophyte became a sage, there was no great

stir. Sages were also common enough, and who had the heart
to listen to them amid the manifold miseries of life? Talk fills
no belly, nor are the wisest words acceptable to the tax
gatherer. It seemed that Mohammed Achmet would remain
as other Mahdis before him, an obscure if erudite hermit, with
power to inspire enthusiasm and devotion. Then he changed
his way of life, and his method of applying religion to life. He
travelled widely, speaking less of the grace of Allah than of the
damnation which awaited tyrants. This was talk which the
people understood and welcomed, as always happens when a
man of vigour and intensity offers them heaven to come, after
hell on earth. They believed in Mohammed Achmet's heaven
as though he were a representative of it, with his compelling
features, his voice that moved hard-bitten peasants to tears
and the magical grace of his presence. Rumour spread that
here was a focus for the simmering forces of rebellion, and
recognising the truth of the charges against them, Egyptian
and *bashi-bazouks* heard with misgiving about the prophet
who told their subjects that Allah would bring them low.

As confidence grew around him, so it grew within him, and
one day Mohammed Achmet was asked the great question
he had probably been waiting for: 'Are you the promised
Guide, the liberator foretold by the Prophet?' He replied, 'I
am the Mahdi', meaning no ordinary prophet—there have
been many Mahdis—but Mohammed ben Hasan al'-Askari
supposed to have been in hiding for ten centuries.

This Messianic claim could not be ignored by the authorities, because it implied active rebellion, even though they
were also of Islam. For the Mahdi was the law, according to
the prophetic tradition, and he, the supreme authority, would
bring about, not some other but his own kind of universal
peace . . . after universal war. Though there had as yet been
no sign that Mohammed Achmet was organising his following, nor even inciting the people to take up arms, it was
decided to nip his pretensions in the bud by summoning him
to Khartoum, where they could be conveniently ridiculed
and, if necessary, he could be put quietly away. The order
was contemptuously disobeyed, and Raouf Pasha, sitting in
Gordon's seat, promptly sent soldiers to fetch him. The date
was August 1881.

In stealth and at night two companies of troops closed upon Mohammed Achmet's humble retreat on the island, *Abba*, only to be beaten off by a few devotees, for the most part armed with nothing better than sticks. Nor did they renew the attempt, but steamed back to Khartoum, while on the strength of this 'miraculous' deliverance the Mahdi declared *jehad*, the holy war. He could hardly have done anything else. He had to resist or face imprisonment.

This abortive raid detonated the explosive situation which had been slowly becoming more and more unstable since Gordon went away. A shock-wave traversed the country and blew Raouf Pasha out of the palace at Khartoum. The garrisons everywhere trembled. Cairo, realising that without British help they were doomed, yet loath to strengthen foreign power in Egypt, hesitated while the myth of the Mahdi throve on petty victory and the rumour of the marvels by which he was surrounded. The mole on his cheek was the sign of the Mahdi, a divergence of front teeth the promise of victory. The Prophet walked and talked with him. A flock of angels shaded him from the sun. Such were the tales which made the illiterate wonder, and administrators smile tolerantly, not yet realising that under this hyperbolic froth was a strong brew, enough to intoxicate thousands. Within a year they caused the mobilisation of every available man in government service, the raising of irregular levies, the fortification of towns, and the offer of a reward for every dead rebel: £2 for other ranks, £18 for a chief.

These measures failed to stem the rising tide, and with each feat of arms the magical reputation of the Mahdi grew, until his most fantastic visions were instantly believed, and even the most level-headed among the tribes began to concede that he must be at least semi-divine and therefore ever victorious. Events continued to support such a point of view, for by the end of 1883 the impossible had happened and the Mahdi virtually ruled where before the Khedival writ had limped. Only the fear of reprisals kept the minority loyal after a fashion. They would not go over to the Mahdi until they had to, for the arm of Egypt was still long, and that of England longer. Even the surrender of the province of Darfur, with the capture and conversion to Islam of its Austrian governor,

Slatin Bey—after fighting twenty-three battles—did not convince those who had yet escaped the direct attentions of the rebels that all was over. They awaited some specific action by Egypt and England, and saw the first stirring of it with the arrival of Gordon, who accepted his Governor-Generalship soon after his subordinate had sworn fealty to the Mahdi in the following terms:

'In the name of God the most compassionate and merciful, and in the name of the unity of God, we pay God, His Prophet, and you, our allegiance; we swear that we shall not associate anything else with God, that we shall not steal, nor commit adultery, nor lead anyone into deception, nor disobey you in your goodness; we swear to renounce this world and look only to the world to come, and that we shall not shrink from holy war.'

Chapter 11

LOST CAUSE

WHILE Gordon was on his way out from England, Sir Samuel Baker's brother Valentine had been put in command of an expedition to relieve garrisons near the Red Sea. His force consisted of two thousand Egyptian infantry, five hundred and twenty cavalry and a hundred European policemen, with ten British officers. The force had been recruited in the old way, with some of the men dragged from their homes in chains. Training had not been effective. There had been a mutiny, and after a Khedival review, all the Turkish officers had resigned. Yet the project was pursued, and as Gordon sailed down the Nile on the first stage of his journey to Khartoum, the force was utterly defeated with a loss of two thousand three hundred and seventy-five killed.

The news of this fresh disaster struck English sentiment as though with a maul, and Gladstone, always sensitive to the changing mood of the electorate, promptly offered Gordon what was in effect an opportunity to cancel his mission. When the message reached him, he had absorbed first impressions of the Sudanese and believed that their attitude confirmed his notion of the realities of the situation. He thought they were more concerned to get foreigners out than to fight a sectarian feud. It was his job to get the foreigners out, therefore the people would support him first and go over to the Mahdi afterwards, if at all. For Gordon would have stolen his best card, the promise of liberation from the alien yoke, and the country would offer no military objectives, for the garrisons would be gone. Thus the rebel armies might indeed melt away, and Gordon's vision would again be justified, though it differed considerably from the view of his superiors. They saw first the threat to Egypt and the vast investments therein. He saw the principle of self-determination budding on what had seemed a dead branch. So he replied through Baring, 'I must say it would reflect discredit on our name to recall me after having seen these people. Also I firmly believe, in spite of all, that God will bless our efforts.'

Unjustifiable optimism can so easily masquerade as faith, and faith itself be turned to justify action contrary to fundamental moralities. Though the regional name of God was Allah, not Jehovah, Gordon and the Mahdi shared the abstract principles of a common allegiance; yet in the name of mercy and compassion they made a vast blood-sacrifice. It is problematical whether the humility, towards God, of Gordon or of the Mahdi was the greater; or whether toward men the pride of the one exceeded that of the other.

Khartoum had been more or less under siege since the previous July, and the news of Baker's defeat had taken out of the populace what little heart they had left. Pride sent a telegram, 'Do not be panic-stricken. Ye are men, not women. I am coming.—Gordon.' Twelve hundred miles south of Cairo a fall was prepared for him, when already he was beginning to feel that inspired loneliness which had driven him so far and so fast on his previous tour of duty. The scene of the fall was Berber, and though the incident may not in itself have prevented the evacuation, it certainly handicapped Gordon's mission and contributed to the final tragedy.

Berber was the tactical key to the Nile as a line of communication. The considerable town was situated above the Fifth Cataract, a natural focus for the forces which might by loyalty make the evacuation practicable, or by defection prevent it.

Summoned to the divan of the Governor-General, who had made his word law where no law had run before, the sheiks of the surrounding country flocked into the town. It mattered little whether they inclined to the Mahdi or not. They hoped to learn something more fundamental to their lives than the profession of an allegiance. Were the foreigners going to stay and rule, or were they going to withdraw? Remembering Gordon's reputation and record, and having vague ideas about the ultimate war-power of England, that almost mythical country whose great ships had blasted the forts of Alexandria, they intended to play safe. The Mahdi came second. And this Gordon knew, or sensed. He planned a bold stroke to turn it to his advantage.

Presumably on Baring's advice, the Khedive had furnished

alternative decrees; one spoke only of the re-establishment of
the ancient form of government as it had been before the
Turkish conquest; the other announced the evacuation of the
whole country by Egyptian interests. Gordon had the second
read aloud to the assembly, and was gratified, but hardly surprised, to observe the enthusiasm with which it was received.
He had, he believed, given the people what they wanted and
what they deserved. He had been honest with them, keeping
nothing back. He had shown them the dawn, and now out of
gratitude they would support his policy; particularly as he
formally declared the Anti-Slavery Convention to be null and
void. There would soon be no one to enforce that law, so why
be such a hypocrite as to pretend that it was still valid?

Thus, in Wingate's words, Gordon began 'to loose the
bonds of every system he had laboured to construct, to
authorise the slave-trade which he had fought so many battles
to suppress, and, it might be, to collect the scattered sheep
and lead them home to their own pastures'. Before he left
England he had stated that it would be 'fatal' if the news of
the withdrawal of Egyptian authority were to leak out. Now
he boldly announced it. To account for the seeming contradiction it has been suggested that he did not realise the full
meaning of the decree, for he still neither read nor clearly
understood Arabic. It is more likely that when he saw these,
his people, he experienced a surge of protective feeling towards them, reminding him that it was his private destiny
to rescue them rather than their oppressors.

But for once he had overestimated his personal influence, as
well as underestimating that of the enemy. These men came
to Berber not out of love for him but because they wanted to
hear whether he would stand between them and the Mahdi.
His answer was clear. With protestations of devotion they
dispersed across the desert, for the most part convinced that
the sooner they were under the Mahdi's protection the better;
for soon there would be no other power in the land, and the
Mahdi was in the habit of confiscating all the worldly goods
of those who were slow to acknowledge him.

So when Gordon left Berber for Khartoum it was as though
the 'emergency exit' was secretly barred behind him. Even
his baggage, and the treasure in gold and silver which he had

brought to finance his office, never got beyond Berber. As usual he was far ahead of the heavy gear, and had with him little more than the service dress which he always wore. Yet he approached his old capital in high spirits. God, it seemed, was again working through His humble servant. If the desert was not to blossom as the rose, some at least of the crooked paths would be made straight.

In contrast to his arrival on first appointment, the streets were packed with hysterical crowds who hailed him as their Father and threw themselves in the dirt that they might make the gesture of kissing his feet. Mothers pushed their children into his way so that by an accidental touch he might bless them.

And the windows of the palace were all intact. The acting Governor-General had already left, prudently, before Gordon could find fault with him. Raouf Pasha had been dismissed after his failure to arrest the Mahdi at the beginning of his mission. Gordon was alone in enemy territory through which ran no communications but the thin thread of the Nile and a single telegraph wire, longest in the world. He had no troops other than the demoralised garrisons he was pledged to evacuate, and no allies save those sheiks over whom his spell was more potent than that of the Mahdi; yet he radiated confident authority and began his work with an assurance which worked wonders. He proclaimed: 'I came without soldiers but with God on my side, to redress the evils of the Sudan. I will not fight with any weapon but justice.' In proof of which he had bonfires lit, and into them were thrown the records of tax arrears, with the whips of the collectors. He strode to the gaol ahead of a crowd, and emptied the place of guilty and innocent alike. The chains were struck off the supposedly dangerous prisoners, and among the two hundred and fifty 'criminals' were discovered several who, though they had been acquitted in court, yet languished because they had been forgotten, or because they could raise no money to buy their liberty.

The people went wild with joy, for the cup brimmed over as the news went round that Gordon no longer opposed slavery: he was in favour of it. After Liverpool and Bristol, but lately turned to other trade, Khartoum—before Gordon

—had been the greatest slave-city in the world. Under Raouf Pasha business had thrived again, and there must have been many who dreaded Gordon's reappearance on that account. Now he announced:

'To all the inhabitants:

'Your tranquillity is the object of our hope. And as I know that you are sorrowful on account of the slavery which existed among you, and the stringent orders on the part of the Government for the abolition of it and the punishment of those who deal in slaves, and the assurances given by the Government for its abolition, seizing upon and punishing those concerned in the trade; according to Imperial decrees and the *firmans* forwarded to you. But henceforth nobody will interfere with you in the matter, but everyone for himself may take a man into his service henceforth. No one will interfere with him, and he can do as he pleases in the matter, without interference on the part of anybody; and we have accordingly given this order. My compassion for you.'

The lack of precision in the text was due, it is said, to the same difficulty with Arabic as contributed to the mistake at Berber, the English quoted above being, in all probability, a translation from the Arabic, which Gordon was not in the habit of checking. He required only that the sense of his orders be rendered in a way easy to understand . . . the opposite of modern governmental practice which often obscures the intention of an order in the quest for an accuracy of diction which cannot be misunderstood in detail.

In Mohammed Ali's time there had been no settlement at the confluence of the two Niles, the White and the Blue. Now thirty-five thousand people lived within their 'V' of water, of which the shape of the northern arm, the Blue Nile, was supposed to resemble an elephant's trunk, from which came the name Khartoum. With excellent water defence on two sides, the town was protected on the third by an elaborate series of earthworks six miles long, with a wide ditch filled from the rivers, making for its time an almost ideal defensive position. The palace faced due north to the defended island, and across the Blue Nile, to the east of the town, was the fort and town of Omdurman, also garrisoned.

The troops were officered by Turks or Egyptians, and

consisted, in addition to those nationalities, of Sudanese and negroes from further south. The total strength was under eight thousand, supported by some artillery, an arsenal and a dock-yard. Since a serious siege had long been anticipated ample reserves of all kinds of stores had been accumulated, and could be added to so long as the steamers moved freely and friendly tribes would sell their grain. The staple diet was a millet called *dhoora*. Nor could the steamers be stopped by rifle fire even if the enemy occupied both banks. Short of artillery capable of penetrating below the water-line they ought to be able to steam freely at all seasons, at least as far as Abu Hamed and the Fifth Cataract, rather more than three hundred miles to the north. From there navigation was fre-quently impossible, particularly at Low Nile, so that the usual route was from Abu Hamed across the desert, to join the river again at Wadi Halfa, making between five and six hun-dred miles from Khartoum. To reach Cairo, steamers must travel as far again, and when running upstream could make little more than walking pace. It was fortunate that Gordon revelled in a sense of isolation which would have unnerved most commanders in similar circumstances.

That first night, the 19th of February 1884, he must have felt a sense of homecoming, for he no longer considered him-self at home in Europe. He would have looked down from the palace roof, following the line of the principal street with its smoky lanterns lighted in his honour, sensing rather than seeing the meaner houses, their mud-brick walls with flat roofs huddling together as though in resonance to the fear of the people, the fear which already he had begun to lift.

Next morning Power sent a telegram to *The Times*: 'Every-thing is now safe here for troops and Europeans. He is giving the people more than they expected from the Mahdi.' Seldom was a more significant tribute paid to Gordon's influence over men and cities.

*   *   *

Gordon's orders, as the first paragraph clearly stated, re-quired a 'report on the military situation in the Sudan', and such a report would be a lengthy and complex document. That he does not seem even to have attempted it, could not have been due either to idleness or to insubordination, as

Gladstone evidently supposed, but to the rapidity with which the situation changed; until the single fact that Khartoum was invested was, at least in Gordon's opinion, all that England needed to know in order to see where her national duty lay. By then the Mahdi was the almost undisputed master of the whole of the rest of the Sudan's vast territory, which, to say the least, limited the scope of the required report, making it such a farce that Gordon never thought to begin it.

Gladstone can hardly be blamed for not seeing the absence of the report in a different light, or even for failing to send an order to Gordon to return. Baring was equally restricted to his own particular field of view. It was as though these three well-meaning architects of chaos worked on their common problem back to back. The Prime Minister could think only of Bismarck's threat to the peace of Europe, of the Russian approach to India, simmering revolt in Ireland, annexation in West Africa, and France approaching hostility because England might have to occupy the Sudan. Under such circumstances any fresh military commitments would be worse than foolish, they would be dangerous to the mother country. In comparison with such an issue the Sudan was small beer.

Baring could see the situation only through the sombre glass of Egyptian economics. For him the primary object was to safeguard and accelerate recovery from bankruptcy and the aftermath of the rebellion. Politically and geographically Khartoum seemed almost as far away as London—which was true enough.

Gordon, while apparently wholly concentrated upon the manifold problems of his office, was simultaneously and increasingly 'in tune with the infinite'. When the Mahdi, ignoring England's hostile actions further north, sent him respectful greetings, it must have come as confirmation to his belief that the hand of God was guiding, particularly as the 'salaam' had opened the way for direct, man-to-man negotiations, about the outcome of which Gordon was always confident.

So assured was he of peace to come, that he took immediate steps to evacuate not only foreign civilians but also the Commanding Officer, Colonel de Coetlogon, and his second-in-command. The Colonel was an experienced officer who had thought it proper to telegraph, as long ago as the 9th of January, urging immediate withdrawal. That it was Gordon's intuitive confidence rather than this officer's deduced foreboding which carried the more weight in Cairo, may further help to explain why from the outset there was a cumulative misunderstanding.

De Coetlogon was probably an angry man when he left Khartoum, for he may well have taken as a personal insult Gordon's injunction not to panic. If he did, he must have laughed grimly at the open letter which Gordon sent with the evacuees, informing all whom it might concern that he was as safe in Khartoum as he would be in Kensington Gardens.

As a practical demonstration of confidence he had the gates opened on the landward side, so that for the first time in many months the people could come and go freely. Under de Coetlogon the town had long been sealed against surprise attack.

Because Gordon was later accused of a belligerent policy, against orders, it is significant that the first crisis with which he had to deal was due to the citizens' protest that he was pacifist. They sent a deputation to wait upon him with what must also have been de Coetlogon's view . . . that no troops be allowed to leave. Gordon had already moved all the Egyptian soldiery to the fort in Omdurman across the river, where they were waiting for transport. He had to rescind that decision to keep the confidence of the townspeople, who within Khartoum relied upon three thousand Sudanese and negro levies, with some volunteers. They did not share his view that the revolt was 'trumpery' or expect that in a personal interview he would be able to overawe the Mahdi, flushed with victory. Yet he was not entirely to blame for this fatal bias, since presumably the intelligence upon which he relied had been furnished by official sources in Cairo. They alone knew, or should have known, what was happening in other parts of the country.

In the event, though the troops remained, nearly all the foreign element among the civilians was removed successfully to safety by the steamers, of which Gordon disposed eleven, from the hundred-and-sixty-foot *Bordein* downwards, in horse-power from thirty to ten. It is sometimes forgotten that had

Khartoum depended only upon land forces, the critics of Gordon's strategic and even tactical optimism must have been justified to a much greater extent. This iron flotilla altered the situation profoundly, and could have given Gordon the reasonable conviction that at need he could force his way, with the garrison, through any probable enemy concentration. For with the departure of the civilian evacuees there were virtually none but natives and soldiers left. The former belonged where they were. The duty of the latter was to stay at their posts until terms were agreed with the enemy, or they had to fight their way out. The swift developments which soon pinned them to the ground could not at this stage have been easily anticipated even by a commander completely free from preconceptions. And any commander, accepting Gordon's estimate that each steamer was worth a thousand men, would have been entitled to some sober confidence.

*   *   *

There were now in Khartoum's angular, echoing white palace, with its two institutional wings, flanked by tall palms, blindly overlooking the river, three Englishmen: Gordon, Stewart and Power. Besides the French Consul, Herbin, the only other white man left was his Austrian colleague, Hansal, of whom Gordon disapproved. It seems he lived with seven native housekeepers, and did not relish establishing them in Cairo, so stayed on when the other foreigners left. He belonged to the people rather than in the palace, and could do nothing to mitigate the foreboding loneliness of the three Englishmen; which rapidly deepened in spite of Power's confident telegrams, at four shillings a word. Soon the reassuring walls of Omdurman would no longer suggest to them Gordon's faith in victory through defence, but that thence had marched out seven thousand infantry, three hundred cavalry, thirty guns and some three thousand irregulars; none of whom returned. They were the doomed army of General Hicks.

Shadows multiplied rapidly. Enthusiasm died away when Gordon's fine words were not followed by forceful deeds, for it had been shrewd to allow that in spite of his protestations he had power enough behind him. Where was it? The sheiks, whom Gordon expected to come in as they had done at

Berber, held back. They were also waiting for Gordon to move, knowing that if he did not the Mahdi would.

Realising how opinion was turning against him and that the trend must be checked at once if at all, Gordon issued 'to the People of the Sudan' a proclamation which it would be an understatement to describe as wishful thinking. For the facts of the situation remained as on his first arrival. He had no reinforcements and none in near prospect; while the action of the British in the north-east was only hardening opinion against him in his rôle of peace-maker. The text read:

'Since my arrival here about seven days ago, I have constantly advised you to the effect that good treatment and justice would be accorded to the natives, and that they should desist from rebellion, which only leads to war and bloodshed. Finding, however, that this advice had no effect on some of the people, I have been compelled to have recourse to severe measures, contrary to my own inclinations, so much so that the troops of the British Government are now on their way and in a few days will be in Khartoum. Whoever persists in wicked conduct will then receive the treatment he deserves.'

Recently the Mahdi had occasion to issue a somewhat similar reprimand because his troops were getting out of hand:

'God has now sent me as your Saviour; join me therefore in my holy war. . . . Beware lest God punish you. If you persist in doing this you will be destroyed, God will burn you up with fire and the earth will open her mouth and swallow you up. I have warned you so that you may have no excuse. Return all the loot you have taken, for the Prophet has told me that any man who still keeps loot in his possession will be destroyed, and our Prophet keeps his word. Again I say, repent, for He who has destroyed the Turks will find it no difficult matter to bring you into subjection.'

Meanwhile Gordon had replied to the Mahdi's 'salaam' with a civil letter, offering him the sultanate of Kordofan, and symbolising that dignity by the gift of a rich ceremonial robe. It was a magnanimous gesture from the Governor-General to the carpenter's son who was fighting his co-religionists in the name of Islam—from the orthodox body of which he had been excommunicated. Mohammed Achmet came close to accepting the bait, but as he hesitated, waiting upon events, as usual they went against Gordon.

The offer arrived soon after the Mahdi had reason to believe that he had passed the zenith of his power; and he was clear-headed enough to realise that once the tide of victory turned, his promises of perpetual conquest would visit him with disgrace. On the last day of leap-year February his fanatics had for the first time come up against British troops, and found them of a very different temper compared to the Egyptian levies. Six thousand rebels attacked four thousand English, under Sir Gerald Graham, V.C., at El Teb in the north-east. The rebels lost fifteen hundred killed, and the rest withdrew before the still intact British, who were not only able to continue their advance, but on March the 13th signally defeated twelve thousand Mahdists who lost there, at Tamai, a further two thousand killed.

These two battles demonstrated, past even religious doubts, that the Arab forces, brave but undisciplined, and without modern arms, would not be able to withstand the determined intervention of England, which now seemed to be in its initial stages. After Tamai the route to Berber was clear, and once Graham held that town Khartoum could hold out indefinitely; but the Mahdi could not. So the Mahdi was the prey to indecision, unlighted by convenient visions, and heavily weighted by a swift fall in the morale of his troops, quite apart from Gordon's offer. It is difficult to tell the survivors of a defeat inflicted by Unbelievers fewer in number, that one's promises of invincibility were truly inspired by Allah.

The Mahdi, Gordon was told, wrote a letter accepting his present, a gesture which would almost certainly have led to a general armistice for which the Mahdi could have claimed credit; particularly as afterwards he would remain the paramount authority, not only in Kordofan, but in all the Sudan. The letter was never sent, but destroyed while he awaited inspiration. None came, and in the ominous quiet, Gordon confidently telegraphed urging the immediate occupation of Berber, which he believed could be held by a token force of two hundred men.

R

While the Mahdi meditated, General Graham and his staff weighed the situation as it appeared to them. Between their victorious force and Berber the enemy was not in strength. The wells were full, the weather relatively cool. Tactically the operation was practicable, but strategically the reasons against it were judged decisive. The move would involve just the type of commitment which the Cabinet was so anxious to avoid. It might only provoke the Mahdi and so tie Gordon's hands. It was not within the orders under which the force operated, for their task had been to relieve garrisons, not to take the offensive. Graham's force began to withdraw towards Suakin. The Mahdi tore up his second letter, and wrote a third in the full surge of mystical confidence. For indeed it seemed to him miraculous that the British were retreating in their hour of triumph. Allah drove them back. The Mahdi's words were true, his destiny was sure.

So he demanded Gordon's conversion as the price of a safe-conduct to the garrison and the lives of his citizens. The letter runs to five pages of small print, out of which emerges an argument so close to that which Gordon himself used, that, allowing for the Oriental flavour, it might almost stand, in part, for his own creed:

'From the servant of his God, Mohammed el Mahdi ibn Es Sayid Abdulla, to the dear one of Britain and of the Khedive, Gordon Pasha.

'In the name of God . . . Your letter has been received and understood. . . .

'I am a humble servant, a lover of poverty and of the poor, one who hates the pride and haughtiness of those rulers whom I wish to lead into the way of truth. . . . They seek after things which vanish instead of those things which remain for ever. They are taken up with the vanities of this world, and are forgetful of the sayings of God and His Prophet. . . .

'I do not believe that he who hankers after the pleasures of this world can believe in his heart that he is pleasing to God, nor can he hope to have a share in the world to come. Jesus has said, "Ye disciples, ye build up your worldly abode on the waves of the sea, therefore do not take it as your permanent abode". . . . Build up for yourselves that which will lead you to the Almighty God, obey Him, and seek for prosperity in the world to come. Do not consider this world your abode which you must work to obtain.

'If you would abandon your present belief, which is not contained in the religion of the Moslems, give yourself up to God and His Prophet and choose everlasting life, we would then accept you as a true believer and a brother, and the friendship which pleases God and His Prophet will exist between us. . . .

'The only object should be to inherit eternal life; to gain this should be the desire of everyone. No good can arise from the pleasures of this life, which bring in their train only sorrow and grief in the day of resurrection, and are great obstacles to gaining eternal prosperity and salvation.

'I have preached both by word and deed to all the chiefs, that they may duly value the kingdom of God, and cast off all vanity.

'All the principal people who have fallen into our hands have been treated with kindness and generosity, and those who have become faithful to us are now enjoying wealth and honour.

'If after this explanation you will deliver yourself up and become a follower of the true religion, you will gain honour in this world and in the world to come, and by so doing you will save yourself and all those under you. Otherwise you shall perish with them, and your sins and their sins will be on your head. . . .

'May God lead us and all creatures into the right path.'

With the long letter was a short note and a parcel, the contents of which dramatised the issue unmistakably and cut across the foliations of the argument. The note ran:

'From the servant of his Lord, Mohammed el Mahdi ibn Abdullah to Gordon.

'In the name of God . . . On reading my answer to your letter you will understand me. Herewith a suit of clothes, consisting of jibbah, cloak, turban, belt and rosary. This is the clothing of those who have given up this world and its vanities and who look for the world to come, for everlasting happiness in Paradise. If you truly desire to come to God and to live a godly life, you must at once wear this dress and come out to accept your everlasting good fortune.'

To almost anyone but Gordon such language would have meant no more than the wind in the palms, or else would be regarded as the sugar coating on a bitter pill. To Gordon, though surely unknown to the Mahdi, it must have been an arrow through the heart, and no amount of protestation, explanation or counter-affirmation could dislodge it. For such was the longing of his soul, which in life he had despaired of realising. This was his answer to prayer—out of the enemy's mouth!

Though power was already beginning to corrupt the Mahdi, his promises were often valid. Gordon knew that when Slatin surrendered El Obeid, the life of the community as a whole was hardly affected. He had been honourably treated, and though individuals suspected of concealing valuables were mercilessly flogged, the communal suffering was so much less than that which would have been involved in further resistance as to bear no comparison. The Mahdi would do the same, no more, in Khartoum; for according to his doctrine it was for the good of their souls that hoarders were whipped . . . for being too much attached to this world's goods. The Mahdi's reputation was such that already the loyalty of the majority of the citizens was at least questionable. Gordon had himself described how useless are fortifications to keep out a fanatical idea, as though there could be military defence against a pestilence. It was in the Mahdi's interest to allow the garrison and other foreigners to be evacuated.

Another of the Mahdi's prisoners, Father Ohrwalder, lived to write: 'The Mahdi was now honoured almost as a god. . . . The fear of his name spread like wildfire through every province and district of the Sudan. He was now regarded as the true Mahdi, every Moslem believed in him and all doubt was put aside. . . . He could not understand how it was that Gordon came to offer him what he already possessed some time ago; and he remarked that the very ground on which Gordon was standing was practically in his hands.'

Knowing that the least hesitation would by the people be regarded as a sign of weakness, Gordon summoned a council of notables. The Mahdi's messengers entered the room. Their master's letters were read aloud. The dervish dress was formally presented.

Gordon dropped the dress on the floor and spurned it with his foot. Then he had his reply read out:

'From Gordon Pasha to Mohammed Ahmed,

'I have received the letters sent by your three messengers, and I understand all their contents; but I cannot have any more communication with you.'

The telegraph line was already down, and soon the rebels might find a way of denying passage to his steamers. He had written to Augusta:

'This may be the last letter I send you, for the tribes have risen between this and Berber and they will try to cut our route. We have lots of food for five or six months. They will not fight us directly but will starve us out. Our Lord's promise is not for the fulfilment of earthly wishes; and therefore if things come to ruin here He is still faithful and is carrying out His great work of divine wisdom. What I have to do is to submit my will to His own, however bitter may be the events which happen to me.'

It is ironic that on the day the wire was cut, Cairo received from London, but could not forward, the final decision against sending either Zebehr or any military support whatever. Gordon was still counting on one or the other, if not both, as his own last message to Baring, sent that morning, suggests: 'I should like to express to you and Her Majesty's Government my sincere thanks for the support you have both afforded me since I took up this mission and to acknowledge that you have given me every assistance I could have expected. It is not in our hands to command success. I say the same for the Khedive and the Egyptian Ministers.'

It was a month before Gordon knew that he was to receive no practical assistance. By then there was no alternative but to keep the defence going on the basis of his original promise that the English would soon come. It had been in the beginning more than optimistic, and now it was downright misleading, except in the sense, which he profoundly believed, that London would eventually be forced by public opinion to alter a policy which had become dishonourable. It is a tribute to them that, once aware of the situation, the people of England did not hesitate to justify his faith in them. They forced a change of policy, forged an army, and sent it thousands of miles, at great cost of blood and treasure, to honour their obligation to a man who had failed to complete his mission. Anticipating something of the sort the War Office had already sent out, on special intelligence duties, a certain Major Kitchener, who was already in Dongola. He was the pin-point of a vanguard which, thirteen years later, was followed, under his own command, by the avenging army which swept the fanatic hordes into oblivion, destroyed the Mahdi's tomb, and made it possible to begin again from Khartoum Gordon's original task, but lately brought to conclusion with self-government.

Chapter 12

EXCELSIOR

THE irrevocable choice clearly made, Gordon threw himself into the practical work of defence with an application and fertility of contrivance which in any context would have been phenomenal. Burdened as he was by an over-centralised administration, it makes the siege of Khartoum a unique demonstration of what the energy, skill and spirit of one man can do.

He coped with justice, finance, food, stores and health. He issued paper money in lieu of the gold which had been intercepted by the enemy—it is a measure of his confidence that the first issue was for only £2500, redeemable in six months. The cost of administration was £500 a day.

He designed and built steamers. He improvised mines both for land and water, some of them made out of ancient alembics, but most out of shells. They were not very dangerous, but affected the Arabs much as the *Hyson's* whistle had intimidated the Chinese. He improved de Coetlogon's earthworks and added wire entanglements, which, with the mines, made assaults so costly that the enemy soon gave them up. Yet defences, no matter how effective, could only postpone, not prevent, ultimate defeat in the absence of a relieving force, which everyone, including Gordon himself, now regarded as a mirage. He would soon be writing: 'It is a sort of position where, one may say, one has no hope but in our Lord. . . . The revolt would be nothing if we had any forces at all, but these we lack, and I am (it is odd to write it) obliged to trust in God alone, as if He was not enough. Yet my human nature is so weak that I do worry myself about these things; not always but at all times. . . . "Is My hand shortened?" and "You have no possible way of escape" are continually contending with one another.'

With April ending, Khartoum became a tower of silence in a vultures' world; yet, unknown to Gordon, a message was on its way from Gladstone to Baring, which contained, within a reprimand, the first ray of hope. The message reached him in June. It read in part that Gordon 'advise as to the force necessary to secure his removal, its amount, character, route for access to Khartoum and time of operation; that we do not propose to supply him with Turkish or other force for the purpose of undertaking military expeditions, such being beyond the scope of the commission which he holds and at variance with the pacific policy which was the purpose of his mission to the Sudan; that, if with this knowledge he continues at Khartoum, he should state to us the cause and intention with which he so continues'.

Pacific policy! Apocalyptic horsemen already rode the bare, baked plains, and on the river banks papyrus reeds concealed leaf-bladed spears. Two champions, their people and their Gods, were locked in mortal combat, which, failing Gordon's forcible removal, could, in common sense at least, end only with his death. As for why he stayed when physically he could have escaped under the moral umbrella of 'to report', the people would not let him go beyond the fortifications, or even on the river. He was their sole defender, magical as much as military. No wonder, responding to their importunity, he felt an obligation above and beyond duty. As for the hope of the future; the English would come to deliver them all from the wrath of the Mahdi and his militant angels. Had not Gordon the Ghazi (Defender of Islam) been ever as truthful as he was staunch? They had every reason to trust him, and to fear a long siege less than the consequences of capitulation. For their orthodox priests, the Ulemas, had denounced the Mahdi on scriptural grounds, and so lent their loud voices to Gordon's exhortations, calling upon their flock to support the Un-believer against a messiah of their own faith. Would not the Sanhedrin have supported Pilate against a 'Christian' mass-movement?

The argument used by the Ulemas runs in part:

'Esh shar a'ni says that the Mahdi will be born in the year 255, that is, 1046 years ago, but this Mahdi is clearly not a tenth of that age.

'The Mahdi will claim sovereignty because people will follow him. But this Mahdi is only followed because he kills those who refuse.

'The Mahdists should not adduce as proof of their genuineness the slaughter they have made in Kordofan, for that is nothing compared to the slaughter described in the sacred books.

'A general once had thirteen reasons for not bringing up his guns. The first was that he had no guns. Thus, the first argument against the Mahdi is that there is no Mahdi.'

Such were the grounds on which, at the beginning of his ministry, the new prophet had been excommunicated; and in view of his subsequent success, it is hardly surprising that the people were not impressed by the schoolmen's denial of his authority. They were afraid of the Mahdi, whose victories spoke louder than the Ulemas. They were still more afraid of the English—so long as Gordon could maintain conviction of retribution for any who failed in their duty to him.

As pressure on the town increased, even his nights were broken by the necessity for rounds of the landward defences. Yet he still managed to write a flood of letters, which were taken by steamer, protected by no more than a quarter of an inch of sheet iron against rifle, and even gunfire, from the banks. Among official and domestic correspondence were letters addressed to the Emperors in Europe, to the Pope; and a suggestion that a fund should be raised by English and American millionaires for the financing of a relief expedition. . . . Not for himself, but for the people—an honourable discharge of England's duty to complete what she had begun.

By this time Gordon had not only evacuated civilians to the number of two thousand six hundred, but also some of the least reliable of his troops, for Khartoum was now held less by the three thousand Egyptians than by a thousand Sudanese Negroes—and by Gordon himself. Nor was he content to be passive in defence. The 'Principles of War', the need for action to keep up morale, and his own inclination, led to constant sorties; one of which failed so disastrously that he had the two senior officers shot for treachery, an act for which he was later contrite, referring to it as judicial murder; presumably because no officer could have been expected to put heart into those men, who would not fight 'even for their own lives'. It seems they were so apathetic that they continued to march with arms at the slope while rebels picked them off and cut down stragglers without a shot fired in reply of any action taken; an apathy surely less cowardly than pathetic. Two hundred and fifty of them were evacuated after the incident: most of the remainder stayed on, to earn their laurels with the Sudanese.

Other sorties succeeded brilliantly, so that Khartoum had more or less regular doses of the best tonic, success, to go with the food which the steamers still brought in from beyond the encircling horde. The enemy's incomplete investment, which made such success possible, was due partly to the Mahdi's preoccupation with his conquered territories and the developing threat of British intervention, reported through his Cairo agents. He remained confident, however, that Khartoum was virtually his already. When it was ripe the town would fall into his hands without a fight. Gordon's appreciation had been correct.

So thirty-odd thousand civilians, some three thousand soldiers and three Englishmen, settled down to wait. Power had no duties, for as a gentleman of the Press he was severely handicapped, and as a Consul he had no charges. Stewart, a Cavalry officer, could hardly have been in his element, though as Gordon's Chief of Staff he was given various independent missions. For the most part he must have fretted, as had done others before him, at his General's dislike of delegating authority. Under such circumstances personal stresses must have run high, and a molehill incident such as the difference in opinion as to whether it was proper for Gordon to give an official interview to Power, was capable of making a mountain of trouble. It is a tribute to all three men that there is no suggestion of their failure to cooperate, even over such a delicate matter as the Mahdi's second demand for surrender.

This occurred in May, soon after Berber fell, and with it Gordon's agent there, an Italian named Cuzzi, who, to save his native wife and child from reprisals, became a Mohammedan and adopted the dervish dress. Brought through the investing force, he was made to swear a solemn oath to be back by sunset, and led into the town, where he was taken before the acting commandant of the garrison, a Sudanese, to whom he represented that he must deliver to Gordon personally the Mahdi's letter. The commandant told him to leave the letter and go, but Stewart, who had known Cuzzi in the past and liked him, had a long and friendly talk, during which Cuzzi told him all he could of the Mahdi's forces. Gordon would not have approved, for he had refused even to admit Cuzzi to his presence, nor would he reply to the Mahdi's letter through him, an apostate. A day later he sent this answer by another messenger: 'Guiseppe Cuzzi brought me yesterday letters, in which you call on me to surrender. As you well know, the Mohammedans who are with me do not wish to surrender, and do you expect that I, who am a Christian, should set the example? If you have letters to send to me again, do not send a European but one of your own people.'

Cuzzi had told Stewart that in his opinion the Mahdi's forces were overwhelming. Whether Stewart passed on the opinion or not, Gordon, though worn thin by work and worry, continued to conduct himself with confidence and un-dimmed authority. He must have known better than anyone within the town, better even than the Mahdi, that by all reason Khartoum was now doomed. But reason did not rule in Gordon's world. He believed in miracles, and went on believing even when the strain of keeping up assurance before others became too great. Then he would shut himself into a room alone, to meditate, to pray; or, with characteristic meticulousness, to calculate diminishing supplies of food and warlike stores. For though the arsenal could turn out some fifty thousand rounds of small arms ammunition a week, ex-penditure was often higher, probably reaching as much in a single day. Native troops, he wryly reflected, put too much faith in noise, too little in marksmanship.

* * *

In England, Gordon's relief had become a heart-stirring concept for millions of people, including the Queen, who wrote secretly to Lady Wolseley to ask her to make her husband, the Commander-in-Chief, resign if the Govern-ment would not give him freedom of action over what was beginning to be known as the Gordon Relief Expedition though officially it was the Sudan Expeditionary Force. On the 5th of August Mr. Gladstone himself moved that

£300,000 be appropriated for that purpose, and a month
later hundreds of boats designed for Nile transport began to
leave England, by which time £750,000 had become the
estimated cost. It was then known that Gordon could hold
out 'with ease'—his own phrase—until mid-December. Even
allowing for the advance to take three times as long as would
an unencumbered journey, there was clearly margin enough.
If Khartoum could not be relieved in the time, at least it
could be reinforced by a small vanguard. Pending the arrival
of the main body such a tonic would certainly prevent, if not
a serious assault, at least its success; for when manned by
resolute troops the defences were virtually impregnable to the
Arab armies.

But Fate was still busy loading the dice with which
Wolseley, Gordon and Kitchener had to play against the
Mahdi. A major but typical incident was that, in spite of the
fact that the accessible Nile was now patrolled by stern-
wheelers manned by British sailors, the Army forgot that its
own steamers would require coal. Though the lapse is glaring,
such things do tend to happen in complex operations, and
here was one which Wingate—and who better qualified to
speak?—says was probably unique in world history. Men and
horses, with arms, ammunition and stores for three months,
were to push fifteen hundred miles through hostile and largely
unknown country, following for the most part a river flowing
against them in a series of cataracts which necessitated, if they
could be passed at all, the man-handling of the boats. Mid-
way, a camel corps would have to be formed from men who
had never seen such animals before, and they would trek
through hundreds of miles of almost waterless desert where
the occasional wells were in enemy hands. If and when
Khartoum was reached, the Expedition must be prepared to
feed thousands of starving citizens in a country already
stripped bare by the locust-like hordes of the Mahdi. Above
all, there must be no failure. Defeat would imperil Egypt,
with all the British capital there invested; and it would in
England provoke a major political crisis while seriously affect-
ing prestige abroad. Even the balance of power in Europe
might be affected. There must not be another Hicks.

There were two possible routes, both terribly slow and

hard, sharing the same torrid heat which would take such toll of unacclimatised troops. At first that from Suakin to Berber had been preferred, but experiments conducted at Aldershot suggested that a water line, upon which the movement would depend, was quite impractical. It could be laid. It would deliver drinking water a hundred miles inland, high in the bare mountains. But the water would be at boiling-point and would cost more than wine. Alternative transport would be by rail, and tenders were submitted for a line between Suakin and Berber, only to be abandoned in their turn. The Nile was surveyed, and that route became the only one, though the difficulties were hardly less and it was even slower. Within that context the task of the Expedition, in all some seven thousand men with eight hundred vessels, may be expressed as follows:

(*a*) With troops trained for European warfare in a temperate climate, advance against the current in boats with which the soldiers were quite unfamiliar. Then, for the vanguard at least, camels must be collected from more or less hostile natives before being allotted to the men whose ride, of about three hundred miles, would cut through the great C-shaped loop of the Nile from Wadi Halfa to Abu Hamed. There would then remain a further five hundred miles by river, the last section of which was completely dominated by the enemy. Gordon's steamers might be able to get down as far as Metemmeh, two hundred miles from Khartoum, and they might be able to embark the vanguard on that last lap. The rest of the expedition must struggle up as best it could with its own steamers, which might have to be taken to pieces to get them overland past the Cataracts.

(*b*) Defeat, without delay, any opposition to the advance.

(*c*) Protect a line of communication from the Egyptian Frontier, held by Egyptian troops, all the way to Khartoum.

(*d*) Clear the enemy out of Berber and garrison that town against his return.

(*e*) Garrison Khartoum in sufficient strength to allow the evacuation of the old garrison to take place without the risk of losing the town.

(*f*) Carry, in addition to all other stores, sufficient food with the vanguard to alleviate the starvation, and with the main guard enough to carry Khartoum until normal supplies could be resumed out of a country rapidly reverting to wilderness.

(g) Maintain at all times a sufficient mobile force to defeat the enemy's main body.

And all this had to be done without taking undue risks! Wolseley liked Gordon, even loved him, sharing his religious conviction. In addition to that compelling personal motive he knew the urgency of honour in jeopardy, his own, his army's and his country's. Yet he forced himself to plan and to move with the efficiency, necessarily slow, which the grave responsibility demanded. He was, as Churchill said of Admiral Jellicoe, the only man on either side who could have lost the war in an afternoon. If Wolseley lost the war to the Mahdi, Europe might soon be at bay before a new Islamic invasion.

And yet, on the day that Parliament voted the first £300,000 for the Expedition, a near-miracle had occurred which almost put Gordon in a position to do without it. Once again it seemed that God, in His mysterious way, had been trying him in the fire—surely to pull him out only at the last moment.

In July a brilliant sortie in strength and by steamer, under the command of a Pasha, had resulted in a severe defeat to the enemy, the repercussions of which allowed the clearance of both banks of the Nile as far as Shendy and the loading of ships with grain from areas hitherto out of reach. The way to Berber was open, and Gordon, riding the wave of enthusiasm, believed that he would not only be able to take that town but even to garrison it, with two thousand men brought from Khartoum for the purpose.

The gallant Pasha, under the highest pressure of professional zeal, then so far forgot himself as to disregard Gordon's order that in following up the enemy he was on no account to seek battle beyond the support of the ships' guns. Not only did he forsake the river, he even undertook a night march which, with treacherous guides and a subtle enemy, was in itself an invitation to disaster; and dawn brought it. The column, lost, sick with thirst and ragged from fatigue, was ambushed as Hicks had been and utterly destroyed. That the Pasha died 'standing on his fur', a pattern of heroism, could not soften the mortal blow which his over-confidence had dealt his chief. . . . (The gesture is performed by removing the sheepskin from under the saddle, and, standing upon it, remaining sword in hand until cut down.)

Thereafter there could be no more sorties and no incoming food. Khartoum had become not only a prison, but a condemned cell. The Lord gave and the Lord had taken away. It is the measure of Gordon as a man that his faith stood the shock, as did his practical mind. From the bitterest depths he had been raised to a height from which he must have seen his whole career as a demonstration of his trust in God against all odds, a trust mysteriously crowned for all to marvel at. And from that height, in a moment of time, by the speech of a sentence, he fell back into the pit and was not broken. Instead he determined upon an action of calm moral courage. He decided to send away his only companions, and on the 10th of September made the first entry in the journal which was thereafter to be their substitute, his confidant:

'Colonel Stewart, Mr. Power and Herbin, left during the night for Dongola via Berber.' It sounds as easy as taking the boat from the Tower of London to Margate! In fact it was to run perhaps the longest gauntlet imaginable, for though the steamer *Abbas* was armed and armoured, the Arabs had by this time Krupp guns capable of sinking her, and, apart from such action, there would be many opportunities to overwhelm her when tied up to take on wood fuel, when negotiating sandbars and rapids, or when anchored at night. Her only soldiers appear to have been a bodyguard of nineteen Greeks, who, save Hansal, were the last of the Europeans.

Yet Gordon, foreseeing death by hunger, by treachery and by the sword, could write two days later in the journal:

'The people are all against us, and what a power they have; they need not fight but merely have to refuse to sell us their grain. The stomach governs the world, and it was the stomach (a despised organ) which caused our misery from the beginning. It is wonderful that the central tube of man governs the world, in small and great things.

'One of Seyd Mahomet Osman's family, come from Shendy, reports Osman Digma as writing to Berber reporting the arrival of the English at Suakin.'

So the withdrawal of Graham's force was now safely accomplished. Where was the Expedition? His guess was Cairo, according to the journal, but the reference is probably facetious. Even so he was only ten days out. Wolseley and his staff left Cairo on the 27th to join the advanced base at Assuan, five hundred miles south; Gordon had guessed them in Cairo on the 17th. Definite news came on the 21st:

Debba, 22nd August 1884

DEAR STEWART,
Can I do anything for you or General Gordon? I should be awfully glad if you will let me know. The relief expedition is evidently coming up this way, but whether it will go by Berber or attempt the direct road from here I do not know. The Mahdi is in a bad way; he has abandoned Darfur, and has no reinforcements to send to Khartoum and Sennaar, which are asked for.

Yours always,
H. H. KITCHENER

With this warm, unmilitary note were enciphered telegrams which could not be read because Stewart had taken the key with him in the *Abbas*. Gordon guessed them to be 'of same import', *i.e.* that the Expedition was seriously on the move and that the Mahdi was discomfited. There was other equally cheering intelligence noted in the journal: 'Six more escaped soldiers came in with their rifles today. They say the Arabs are furious at losing their Peacock Dervish (who was one of their officers) yesterday, and also at the constant desertions, and have written to the Mahdi to ask whether they are to kill these blacks or not. The Mahdi hired one thousand camels to bring dhoora to the Arab camp, but the people who engaged to do this, bolted with the money and the camels into the interior. . . .

'Messengers have arrived at Omdurman, saying that a mixed force of British and Indian troops are at Debbeh, on the Nile, north of Dongola, and that they had defeated a party of dervishes.

'The Greek, who came in a few days ago from the Arabs said the Mahdi had given Cuzzi an ointment to rub on his body, which would keep him in odour of sanctity!'

Again the dice seemed to be falling Gordon's way, justify

ing his military predictions and his faith. Even at this late
hour the armies of the Mahdi might be melting away and red-
coats from England soon show themselves—that, he thought,
would be sufficient for the wavering remnants of the horde.
But he could not forget that so often before he had felt deliverance in the air and been disappointed. He kept his new
optimism under discipline of the vision of death: 'Haunting
the palace are a lot of splendid hawks. I often wonder whether
they are destined to peck out my eyes.'

He thought of mining the palace and going up with it,
but declared there was moral obliquity in the idea. It was too
near suicide. While writing often more than a thousand words
a day in his journal, he waited for better news, particularly
that Stewart had got through to Kitchener; and he filled the
broad pages with notes which fairly define the last calm view
he could have taken of matters great and small.

'I do not believe that fanaticism exists as it used to do in
the world, judging from what I have seen in this so-called
fanatic land. It is far more a question of property, and is more
like communism under the flag of religion, which seems to
excite and to give colour to acts which men would otherwise
condemn.'

'. . . My belief is that our future happiness is in being finite
intelligences. We will go on to all eternity, grasping the infinite knowledge of God which we are so formed as to be able
to do, but will last for ever in so much as He is infinite. When
one gets on these subjects, and has to come down to this
dreadful Sudan question it is depressing; so also is the thought
that misery here is our lot, for if we will be with our Master,
we must be like Him, who from His birth to His death may be
said to have been utterly miserable, as far as things in this
world are concerned: yet I kick at the least obstacle to my
will.'

Intolerance, except in the inevitable irritations of daily life,
seems to have left him. He has a few hard words for Baring
and others, but there is no quailing and no search for a scapegoat. He accepts his position completely, without excuse or
illusion. Perhaps it was this new calm which turned his spirit's
eye to the Koran, finding there the integrating root of Allah
in the meaning of 'Islam', '*i.e.* self-sacrifice: consequently a

S

true Christian is of the Islam religion, as far as the name goes'. And again, 'The God of the Muslims is *our* God'. The same quality of detachment allowed him to take pleasure in simplicities which before would not have been approved by his austerity:

'We have a Turkey cock and five Turkey hens. They were all very tame, but having put the Turkey cock's head under his wing and swung him into sleep, on one occasion, he is now too shy to come near me; however, if one goes to his wives and scratches them he is furious, and comes up with his neck all colours. . . .

'I am one of those who believe in the fore and future existence of what we call animals.'

There follows a biblical justification for the belief, and then, in the same journal entry, he is drawn back into worry and mystical despair, ending with an obscure but prophetic statement that the 'bond' between him and the people is limited in time, 'which I fix in January'. It was still September then. Long before the turn of the year the turkey he rocked to sleep would be in the pot.

With the news of the Expedition's advance confirmed, Gordon made a final effort to maintain morale, posting in the town pictures of British soldiers. A salute of a hundred and one guns was fired—as though victory were already won. Yet the mood of his private mind remained sombre if illuminated. Sacrifice had been the keyword all his life, *self*-sacrifice. And now, having apparently discovered that Islam hung upon the same concept, came the news that, far from melting away, the main forces of the Mahdi were approaching, buoyant with the prospect of that great festival of sacrifice, *Kurban Bairam*.

That feast commemorates how Abraham would have slain his son, a sacrifice to Jehovah, but that at the last moment the God accepted a scapegoat in his place. The Mahdi, for such a context, was an Abraham with many 'sons'; and either they would die in battle to pass the gates of Paradise, or else Allah would preserve them as he had preserved Jacob. Gordon must have seen a parallel in Church dogma: 'May our Lord not visit us as a nation for our sins, but may His wrath fall on me, hid in Christ. This is my frequent prayer, and may He spare these people and bring them to peace.' It would not have occurred to him, nor to the Mahdi, that the doctrine of salvation by suffering might be due to a perversion of symbols, turn love back upon hatred, and drown in the blood of pain the greatest principle of all, to which both religions give equal and prior allegiance. 'In the name of God, the merciful, the compassionate.'

Tolerance and clear-sightedness equally marked his political and strategic opinions: 'What have we done in Lower Egypt to make them like us? Not a single thing. We have foisted Europeans on them to the extent of £450,000 a year; we have not reduced taxes, only improved the way of extorting those taxes. The Mahdi says, "I will take one-tenth of your produce, and I will rid you of the 'dogs' "—a most captivating programme! If well led, and once he takes Khartoum, the combined forces of France and England will not be able to subdue him, unless they go at his nest. From a *professional military point of view*, and *speaking materially*, I wish I was the Mahdi, and I would laugh at all Europe. Query (believing all the above as I do)—would I be justified in coming to terms with the Mahdi, on the understanding that he should let go all refugees . . . while I should give over to him, unhurt, all warlike material in Khartoum?

'Certainly, according to the letter I would be justified in so doing; and *then* what! If what I feel sure will happen, *i.e.* a rising in Egypt occurs, what will my nation say? . . . They will say it is my fault; but (D.V.) they shall not say so, for I will not give up the place except with my life. It cannot be too strongly impressed on the public that it is not the Mahdi's forces which are to be feared, but the raising of the populations by his emissaries. I do not believe he had four thousand men when he defeated Hicks. We have to think what would a garrison of ten thousand men do in Cairo if the population rose.'

What a change is here, in seven months, since he dismissed the revolt as 'trumpery'! He was equally penetrating on the subject of the expedition and his resolve not to go back to England, whatever happened.

'I altogether decline the imputation that the projected expedition has come to relieve me. It has come to save our national honour in extricating these garrisons etc. from a position our action in Egypt placed these garrisons. I was relief expedition No. 1. They are relief expedition No. 2. . . . I am not the rescued lamb and I will not be.'

Not the *rescued* lamb, he might have added, but the sacrifice. Potent symbols come in opposing phases, and those whose deep minds are ruled by them, swing of necessity from one extreme to the other. For which reason it is foolish to underrate their angel-led, or devil-driven, accomplishments, and dangerous to allow them to sit in the seat of power. In the Grail myth the Knight of the Quest is necessarily of this temperament, for he would not have set out on his compulsive adventures without first being shaken by the apparently irreconcilable opposites in heaven and earth. It is appropriate therefore that in his achievement of full stature the place reserved for him is called the Siege Perilous. None but he dare sit there, for they would be broken in pieces by the contradictions in their own natures. And he, being able to receive the high voltage appropriate to his hard-won authority, must tend to break up the world around him through the projection of the power.

Of such was Gordon, a dedicated man whose traits were exaggerated by the power which ran through him, through *all* his traits. He emerges in quite another rôle than that of the frontispiece from a Victorian boy's book of heroes, but he is not on that account to be reduced by the modern cynic to the stature of a homosexual alcoholic with delusions of grandeur. In life he sometimes appeared ridiculous because he marched to music none but he could hear. In death he was graven into a figure of preternatural dignity, a template for Imperial Virtue in the manner of his times. Patriotic admiration would have made him a war-lord, but he was a peacemaker. National sentiment would have made him an empire-builder, but his country was the world. Piety would have made him a pillar of the Church, but he was a heretic. Idealists show him as bearing the 'white man's burden', but it was the black man's burden which he believed the white man ought to bear.

Time has defeated Victorian Gordon, shrinking his victories and his defeats, outmoding his political conceptions, and rendering his intense theological speculations merely quaint. All that in the world he strove for was taken from him, as though out of his strength came weakness. But out of his weakness, out of his soul divided, came a singular strength to drive his integrity through daunting circumstances, to become genuinely heroic in the terms of any age.

He did not fight against people so much as *for* principles, and, save perhaps in his first campaign, he hated the business of war, even against those who for the time being he was sure in his own mind were the vehicles of evil. If he suffered from an over-developed conscience, it was a benign malformation, akin to that of Cyrano de Bergerac's nose. There is much in common between the two characters, even the paradox of vanity in poverty. Both were ruled by the strictest concepts of honour, both fought, their lives long, without thought of reward, and therefore in the eye of the world their lives were equally futile. The judgement would not surprise them, nor in the least modify their conviction, of which the world has ever stood in need, that value is above price. Fighting his last battle Cyrano says:

> . . . *C'est inutile ? Je le sais !*
> *On ne bat pas dans l'espoir du succès !*
> *Non—non, c'est bien plus beau lorsque c'est inutile !*

Chapter 13

TORSO

WITH October half-way through, the turkey cock was still alive, and so was that hope deferred on which Gordon had kept his command since first the wire to Cairo had been cut. The rationing system still allowed two and a half months subsistence, if on nothing more than biscuit and millet. The Nile was unusually high, making defence easier and in theory assisting the advance of the Expedition. Within the town there was relatively little sickness and few wounded. Among the enemy, however, there was fever, dysentery and smallpox. With such a large, loosely coordinated force, their problems of supply were such that willing spies continually reported desertions due to lack of reward and grumbling at the contrast between the Mahdi's practice and his preaching. They must have reminded Gordon of his early opinion that if only Khartoum could be held long enough, the enemy would melt away. It seemed that he might yet be justified.

He was also optimistic about the rate of progress of the Expedition. Seen along the edge of a ruler, Dongola looked like a springboard for a dive into the desert, a dive for which Kitchener had planned and which Wolseley had at first approved; only to be forced to reconsider as the risk increased and the size and weight of his formations with it. Gordon was still thinking along such lines. They might, he considered, be bold enough to strike away from the river all the way. . . . No, that would be folly, for the enemy commanded the wells. First Berber must be retaken, an operation which would involve delay. Berber was the key to the gate of Khartoum, and it would not lightly be wrested from the Mahdi. Then there would be the Fourth and Fifth Cataracts for the troops to pass, not so difficult now, but as the river fell it would become an increasingly arduous task. Artillery would be most awkward to handle. He had always taught that guns were only a nuisance against an uncivilised enemy, but could Berber be taken without artillery support?

So, from his unique knowledge, he mulled over the situation, and evidently concluded that while within the time available he could not expect to see the main body, yet his first necessity would be met by a mere sliver of a vanguard. Morale would still be the dominant factor, and even a handful of English would make all the difference to it. Once they were in Khartoum, visible to the people and to the enemy, the defence could probably hold out, in spite of semi-starvation, until relief was complete. On this appreciation Gordon based his policy and his proclamations, assuring the people over and over again that soon, soon, their troubles would be over.

Trained in the same school, Lord Wolseley's mind had reached the same conclusion, to send a token force ahead of the main body with the object of 'showing the flag'. Twenty red-coats were to go with the leading boat so that the British uniform could impress itself upon the enemy, exactly as Gordon desired. Slatin, who as an honourable prisoner was now a member of the Mahdi's staff circle, and was uniquely placed for such an opinion, says that had those red-coats been seen by the enemy even the day before the final assault, it might never have taken place.

Largely owing to the first, unfounded threat of British reprisals against those who did not behave themselves, the population of Khartoum no longer believed Gordon's promises. Even the town notables, including the Ulemas, were turning against him. Having hedged with Gordon for their goods, they were now prepared to abandon them and him if the Mahdi would spare their lives. Nor was this swing of allegiance due only to the reaction against hope too often raised, too often dropped. Spies did not give their information only to Gordon, nor were all of them genuine. It was said that the English were hesitating again, just as they had done after their march from Suakin. They might retire, even now, as they had done after General Graham had won the victories which opened the route to Berber from the east. Also the Mahdi had had a revelation. His main army was on the move southward, bringing, it was said, inexorable doom on all those 'of the left hand', as shown forth in the Koran. There were many in Khartoum who had no intention of being found in that position for the sake of an Unbeliever, and among them were the town's Governor, the chief Ulema, a brother to the Governor, a senior Judge, and a dozen other leaders of opinion.

Gordon had the whole company thrown summarily into prison, and did not intervene when one man, accused of attempting to fire the magazine, was shot on a court verdict with which he did not agree. He knew, none better, that if ruthlessness is ever justifiable it is within the context of mutiny. Men who will no longer be led must be driven, and the first thwack of the stick must be at the first moment of hesitation. No wonder they hesitated now! Until lately the choice had been to live with Gordon and keep one's wealth, or go over to the Mahdi and be poor. For the Mahdi systematically confiscated all kinds of wealth, slaves, cattle, goods and money. He needed them to finance his war, and he claimed the virtue of poverty as particularly necessary for those who had been slow to acknowledge him. Now, however, the choice had changed: it was to live with the Mahdi or to die with Gordon, a very different matter, and one not to be obscured any longer by the conferring of decorations, the issue of promissory notes, or elevation to superior rank in a doomed hierarchy.

The arrests troubled Gordon's conscience in spite of his recognition of their necessity in terms of military efficiency. He wondered if he had the right to prevent people going over the river. What duty did they owe to England? Not even that of these alien troops who still obeyed him. He wrote that if he really believed the people wanted it he would give up the town; but he was aware that to do so would be to betray those who had been most loyal to him, such as the heroic Egyptian garrison in the sealed fort at Omdurman.

Mutiny! Another man might have shut himself up in the palace. Gordon was seldom there, unless on the roof with his telescope. He went continually among the people in the knowledge that his life was within the reach of many hostile hands; and so powerful was his presence that even in this extremity he could keep burning in the city of despair something of his own fierce flame—in the light of which his faults even now seem very small.

A worse blow fell. A letter came from the Mahdi saying

that the *Abbas* had run aground and Stewart, with Power and
Herbin, had been killed by local Arabs. All the correspondence, including the cipher key, had fallen into the Mahdi's
hands, who now knew only too well to what straits his enemy
was reduced. The letter ended: 'As to your expecting reinforcements, reliance for succour on others than God—that
will bring you nothing but destruction. . . . There is no refuge
but in God, and in obedience to His command, and that of
His Prophet and of his Mahdi.' The torment of such words—
to Gordon of Gravesend!

The Muslim New Year 1302 had begun the day before, the
21st of October, and Gordon recognised that the Mahdi would
now attack in force. The time of waiting for famine had gone
by. In the New Year the town must fall—before the relief
expedition could appear.

In view of the crumbling morale, Gordon must have
welcomed this development. Let the troops feel the thrust of
the enemy and they might yet rally. In holding the town they
would then commit the Mahdi's forces, so that when Wolseley
came up in their rear there would be an end to the false
prophet, surely the only human being who had ever dared to
lecture about God to His humble servant, C. G. Gordon, who
now took comfort from the coincidence of the New Year with
Trafalgar day.

To the final demand for his surrender Gordon replied indirectly: 'I am here like iron . . . it is impossible for me to
have any more words with Mahommed Achmed, only lead'.

And he put a candelabrum conspicuously in the window of
the room he used at night, an example, a symbol and a folly.
He claimed it publicly as a proof that he was without fear, but
to his journal he confessed that he no longer believed 'in the
unmoved man'. He was now brave enough to admit to fear
yet not to show it. Courage does not consist in being unafraid.

*   *   *

So the star-crossed prophets entered the final phase of their
conflict, inevitable by the world's standards as it should have
been unnecessary by their own, and futile in the eye of history.
Both must have been troubled by the contradictions in their
own characters, Gordon's unconscious, the Mahdi's now an

intent hypocrisy based upon the ancient heresy that ends
justify means. They may even have seen far enough into the
fog of war to read in it their own ignominious ends. Gordon,
always burdened by a death-wish, appeared now as an aged
man, for whom the kingdoms of the world were already dust,
and all his effort vanity. Not long ago he had written that
at least being shut up in Khartoum was better than going out
to dinner in London. War, until these last months, had kept a
certain glamour in the old sense. Now even that had gone,
leaving this tortured man, whose task was to undo all he had
laboured for over the years, bereft of the last illusion: 'As I
was leaving the hospital today, a dead man was carried out by
four men in chains (convicts) on a stretcher, accompanied by
two soldiers with fixed bayonets—to be buried as a dog! This
is part of the glory of war!'

*   *   *

As the Nile fell with late autumn, so did the level of stores,
and the morale of the garrison. The grass huts of the investing
horde made a city, out of range. Within it the Mahdi warily
sought to read into the signs of the times something more encouraging than the prophetic utterances with which he concealed from the faithful that, in spite of so much victory, the
winter of their waning power was close upon them. For the
Mahdi was well served by his agents, and he had with him
Slatin from whose well-educated head he took the European
knowledge which his native followers could not even imagine.
They thought of England, if they thought of her at all, as
another tribe whose intervention could present no greater
problem than that of the Egyptians, which was no more than
an invitation to Paradise. Allah was not only the God of the
Arabs, but of the world. The Mahdi, for all his convenient
visions, knew better than that. If Slatin had not given him a
sufficiently coloured picture of the armies of the West, then a
young Frenchman, a volunteer to help against the hated
Albion, would have supplied the deficiency before he died of
typhus.

By the beginning of December, the Mahdi must privately
have been almost as gloomy about his prospects as was Gordon about his. He knew that the invaders would be too strong

for his discontented, disease-ridden, bored and mutinous rabble, over which the mere reiteration of texts and the fabrication of personal interviews with the Prophet no longer exercised the customary discipline. Gordon knew this, for deserters still came to him, unaware of the lack of provision within the town. Half a dozen steamers were still in commission. On the 8th of the month came news that Berber had fallen. Gordon still did not believe that there was in wait for him no other fate than that invoked by the Mahdi's last message: 'Know, O thou enemy of God, there is no escape for thee from death at our hands, and death by lack of food'.

And had he been privy to the Mahdi's secret councils, he would have been heartened, for the besiegers were already meditating retirement, a move rendered the more prudent by a minor victory gained by the Expedition over the forces disposed to delay them. At this time Slatin was handed the following message and ordered to translate it: 'I have about 10,000 men; can hold Khartoum at the outside till the end of January. Elias Pasha wrote to me; he was forced to do so. He is old and incapable; I forgive him. Try Hajji Mohammed Abu Girga, or sing another song. Gordon.'

There was no indication to whom the message had been addressed.

Slatin, with great courage in the face of his probable fate if the deception was discovered, swore that he could not read the message which he insisted was in 'French cypher language'. In so doing he almost certainly saved Gordon from an earlier assault. He asked permission to write to his Consul, for Slatin was an Austrian. The Mahdi asked him also to write to Gordon, and this he did, but covered it with a secret note in which he offered Gordon his service and his life. Gordon did not reply, scorning the apostate who had so much faith in him even at this juncture. Pathetically, Slatin had excused himself for having embraced Islam, saying that 'perhaps unfortunately' he had not had a strict religious upbringing, and reminding Gordon that he had fought many battles on his behalf. No answer came from the man of iron who, like iron, was there over the river behind those pock-marked walls.

Slatin's overtures were discovered, and he fell into chains

from his honoured place: neck, wrists, waist and three separate fetters on his legs. He was starved in solitary confinement, his bell-tent was surrounded by a high zariba of thorn so that he could not see what went on in the vast camp, swollen not only with the faithful and the warriors, but with thousands who had drifted there for the food, or out of curiosity to see the man of miracles who walked and talked with the Prophet. When the assault was imminent Slatin was loaded onto a donkey, propped at each side by a man on foot, and taken to a place near Omdurman, which, in spite of the straits to which the garrison of the fort were already reduced, did not surrender until the 15th of January, and then only with Gordon's permission. The Mahdi pardoned the garrison, who marched out, though disarmed.

Within Khartoum Gordon called his last meeting of the town's influential people. He told them that any who wished might freely leave and go over to the Mahdi, for they could no longer be fed. There was talk of surrender, but he would not hear of it. The men of influence went sadly back into the hot and dusty streets, disillusioned. They had come to the conclusion that Gordon no longer told the truth. They did not believe in the Expedition any more. The gates were opened, and civilians, men and women, streamed out, crossed the river, and were absorbed by the ant-like aggregation of the enemy. But Gordon's will still held the garrison like glue.

January 1885 was to be the last month of the siege, and both besiegers and besieged knew it, for there was so little food in store. Though painfully slow, the Relief Expedition could still be in time to avoid capitulation through starvation. If only the Arabs continued to hesitate, it might also avert an attack in force, which was now only too likely to be successful against the demoralised troops, who, because of the fall of the river, had now a longer landward defence to man.

On the 14th of December Gordon made the last entry in his journal, and next day sent the thick manuscript down river on the steamer *Bordein*, now like a colander not only from shell, but because the enemy's better rifles could punch holes in her 'armour'. The holes were plugged with a special bolt and nut made in quantity for the purpose. The steamer was to join at Metemmeh three others, already there, waiting to bring the point of the vanguard up the last, critical phase of the river journey.

Even now Gordon was concerned for the future government of the Sudan, under Zebehr, and he could note, 'The buglers on the roof, being short of stature, are put on boxes to enable them to fire over the parapet; one with the recoil of the rifle was knocked right over, and caused considerable excitement. We thought he was killed, by the noise he made in his fall.'

What other man would see anything funny at such an hour! He set his limit now, expecting the entry to be read, perhaps on the morrow, or the day after—still time enough, just time enough. The journal ends drily: '. . . if the Expeditionary Force, and I ask for no more than two hundred men, does not come in ten days, the town may fall; and I have done my best for the honour of our country. Good-bye. C. G. GORDON.

'You send me no information, though you have lots of money. C. G. G.'

The postscript was a wry joke. He had been complaining of the way in which *he* had to pay the secret messengers who from time to time reached him from Kitchener, with whom, however, he was on good terms as man to man. He even offered Kitchener the Governor-Generalship, in a communication dated the 26th of November, which was the day after he boarded an incoming steamer expecting to meet at least an officer of the Expedition, to find only letters, one of them from Kitchener, a month old. The idea of Kitchener becoming the next Governor-General was suggested by a Khedival communication which Gordon read as though it were chiefly concerned with that matter of his successor. The Khedive's British-inspired intention was in fact only to limit Gordon's sphere of influence. He was virtually demoted to be governor only of Khartoum and its immediate vicinity.

Pushing such singularly unreal problems away, Gordon, though personally disappointed at the progress of the Expedition, posted another proclamation: 'If God will, in the next few days the siege will be raised and your alarm will pass away. Know also that, if Mohammed Achmed should call upon me for three years to surrender Khartoum, I will not listen to him, but will protect your lives and families with all energy and steadfastness.'

This was not a piece of wishful-thinking. He had passed through that phase. The combined intelligence at his disposal made it a reasonable hope, if not quite a probable forecast ... always provided that Wolseley followed the tactic of a light, fast vanguard. And that was no longer his plan, except in the last stage of the advance. Worse, he seems to have read confidence into Gordon's messages when there was only cheerfulness. Gordon, he thought, would be unable to hold out 'for many more *months*'. And still it was not quite too late. Gordon calmly recognised that much through the confusion of impressions and contradiction of rumours.

Such was the new Gordon, emergent from the dark night of the soul, finding a peace beyond the tormented world by which he was surrounded, a peace which even allowed humour and the kind of gentleness from which the turkeys benefited, neither of which had been characteristic of his relatively unchastened years. Though he would have reduced his own food to the absolute minimum there is no suggestion of impaired vitality or judgement, such as might have contributed to that less admirable detachment, fatalistic and selfish, which comes to most people on the threat of a personal end. Indeed, he was in this also a changed man, not accepting the fate which seemed so close, not wasting words to explain his attitude. The implications point to a man in some valid sense reborn, as though only such an extreme test as this could have made clear to his inward eye the hairline between vision and illusion, the profession of faith and its reality.

*   *   *

The ten days ran out. The 'few' days of the proclamation could be stretched no further. The year itself ran out. There was no food left at all, and still no definite news of the Expedition. Then, one morning, the Mahdi's guns thundered a hundred-and-one-gun salute for victory. Justifiably suspicious, Gordon saw through his French telescope that far from the camp rejoicing, the only movement came from groups of wailing women. The salute was a ruse, and that such a gesture was called for, suggested that the Mahdi was by no means so assured as he had seemed. Gordon's unextinguishable heart was lifted up. There had not been victory but defeat! Now there would be no obstacle to the last lap of the relief. The Mahdi would have to raise the siege or fall into chaos well deserved. After such hardship, such disappointment, the change of fortune seemed miraculous; as though God, having tried His servant in the furnace of salvation, had at last really begun to justify him. The people would soon know that Gordon had not betrayed them, and his reward would then be greater far than the laurels of victory, for they would give to him also the rose of earthly worship and affection.

His reading of the immediate signs was correct. On the 16th of January, at the wells of Abu Klea, the expected clash had taken place between the van of the Expedition and an Arab horde barring their route. The British were worn out with desert marching. Ten thousand Arabs would deny them water. Contact was made in the evening, and at dawn the Camel Corps (1800), a Naval Brigade and a detachment of the Royal Sussex Regiment, moved forward down a slight slope to encounter the enemy, who had drummed himself into frenzy during the night, and now flowed forward to meet the plodding square of which the fire-power was still unrealised.

This development was welcomed by Sir Herbert Stewart, commanding. His men dismounted and the camels were huddled within the square. The skirmishers withdrew before the advancing wave of white tunics splashed with coloured patches. The Mahdists carried two, or even three broad-bladed spears in the right hand, a bossed oval shield on the left forearm. A great iron sword was slung with its cross-hilt under the left shoulder, and in the sash of the tunic was a short iron dagger. They came barefoot, in silence save for the thudding of their drums, and then, nearing the square, which, imperturbable, held its fire, broke into the war-cry of Islam, *Fishan Allah wa Rasulahu*, For God and His Prophet!

Led by their Emirs, mounted, and in spite of the rifle fire, they came on, broke through. Hand-to-hand fighting suggested a battle in the balance, but, in the camel-lines, white turbans tumbled to rapid-fire bullets in enfilade. A thousand dead were left within the British square, and no prisoners were taken. The British casualties were in all seventy-four:

victory was complete.

While the exultant victors pushed on the last ten miles to the river, the Mahdi prayed for inspiration and it was revealed to him that he should withdraw in the face of this overwhelming force. His council, however, were not unanimous. To retire now might be interpreted as weakness, which, after so many promises of divine invincibility, would be too much for the faithful, already disenchanted. On the other hand, to take Khartoum only to be besieged there in turn, would be to enter a trap. Yet he must attack now or never, before his forces, as Gordon had foreseen, would melt away and men mock him for being, after all, a false prophet.

Meanwhile Gordon had again told his people that help was close at hand. They must hold out only a day, two days, a few days . . . what matter after so many? Again the balance hesitated towards Gordon's favour, and again an unforeseen factor tilted it the other way. Unknown to the Mahdi or to Gordon, the victory at Abu Klea had been marred by the death of the officer in charge of the vanguard, and as the advance was resumed on the following day, his second-in-command also became a casualty. So when, on the 21st, the tired, triumphant soldiers of the Queen saw again the gleam of the Nile and made out Gordon's steamers waiting near Metemmeh, their cheering must have seemed over-confident to the inexperienced staff officer upon whom the command now devolved, Sir Charles Wilson.

Unaware that Khartoum hung from hour to hour upon the brink of death, he paused. Prudent reconnaissance, as required by the principles of war and the dogma of staff duties, was duly carried out. If it were not, he would in defeat have no mercy from the War Office. Meanwhile the machinery of the steamers was overhauled, and all Egyptian troops, as Gordon required, were taken off. Thus passed three days, and still Khartoum held out. At eight in the morning of the 24th the steamer *Bordein* led *Telawieh* southward on the last lap of a nightmare race against time, the ancient river, unaccommodating desert and an enemy who welcomed death.

Bordein carried Sir Charles Wilson, Captain Gascoigne with ten other ranks of the Royal Sussex, a naval officer and petty officer, and a hundred and ten Sudanese infantry. In spite of the need to lighten draft because of shallow waters, she was heavily laden with grain for Khartoum, as was the other, though smaller, ship. Watched by the enemy, though not interfered with, they thudded against the swift current, while the Mahdi was announcing another vision—of victory by God; and Gordon faced a final collapse of morale among his troops who, after so many promises, read the delay since Abu Klea as meaning that again in the hour of victory the English had retired. There was no longer anything that even Gordon could do to raise their suffering spirits, imprisoned in wasted bodies, poisoned by abominable meat and indigestible vegetable fibre; their minds clouded by sleeplessness and fear.

But it was still not quite too late. The river was still open. Even at walking pace the steamers could reach Khartoum in time to prevent the attack, or at least to strengthen the despairing arms of the defenders long enough to gain time for the main guard to come up. Gordon was beyond hoping. He withdrew from the turmoil and sat in a room by himself. Bordeini Bey, a prominent merchant, who as Wingate's chosen witness deserves credence, was the last responsible person to speak with him.

'I found him sitting on a divan; and as I came in he pulled off his tarboush and flung it from him saying, "What more can I say? I have nothing more to say, the people will no longer believe me. I have told them over and over again that help would be here, but it has never come, and now they must see that I tell them lies."

'He was afraid that people would see despair in his face and so made his last promise through an intermediary, that in twenty-four hours the English would arrive. He said that he expected an attack that night, and ordered every male, from eight years to old men, to be forced, if necessary, to the defences. Yet, he added, if the commandant insisted he was at liberty to "open the gates and let all join the rebels".

'He ended the interview by saying, "If this, my last promise fails I can do nothing more. Go and collect all the people you can on the lines and make a good stand. Now leave me to smoke these cigarettes." There were two full boxes of cigarettes on the table. . . .

'It was a gloomy day, that last in Khartoum; hundreds lay

T

dead and dying in the streets from starvation, and there were none to bury them. At length the night came, and, as I afterwards learnt, Gordon Pasha sat up writing till midnight and then lay down to sleep.'

The English should have been coming some miles closer with every hour he slept, to dismay the Arabs poised for their attack; but the *Bordein* struck a rock in the Sixth Cataract, and though work went on all night, she could not be got off until next day, after being unloaded. With breaking backs the men reloaded her, but while they had been working in the dark the Mahdi had struck, and won. The attack had been launched where the river in falling had emptied a ditch. The sleepy soldiers, bloated from starvation, made small resistance, so small that it was believed, until a Court Martial acquitted the accused officer, that treachery had been at work. As angry dawn flared out of the desert, death came horribly for General Gordon; and in the next six hours three thousand of his people followed him.

Though the Mahdi had given orders that he was to be spared, they were ignored by men with a personal grudge, a further sign of the prophet's faltering grip. Accounts of the killing vary, but Wingate's witness is surely reliable when he says: 'Taha Shahin was the first to encounter Gordon beside the door of the divan, apparently waiting for the Arabs, and standing with a calm and dignified manner, his left hand resting on the hilt of his sword. Shahin, dashing forward with the curse, '*Mahoum-el yom yomek*' (O cursed one, your time is come!), plunged his spear into his body. Gordon, it is said, made a gesture of scorn with his right hand, and turned his back, where he received another spear-wound, which caused him to fall forward and was most likely his mortal wound. The other three men, closely following Shahin, then rushed in and, cutting at the prostrate body with their swords, must have killed him in a few seconds. His death occurred just before sunrise.'

The head of the body was hacked off. The trunk lay all day in the palace garden, exposed to mutilation by the followers of Mercy and Compassion, who blooded their spears in it for luck. At evening it was thrown into one of the wells which already were being filled with corpses. Of the fate of the head there is no record after it had been taken across the river in haste, while dawn was yet in the sky, to be identified by Slatin, who wrote: 'The sun was now rising red over the horizon; what would this day bring forth? Excited and agitated, I awaited the result with intense impatience. Soon shouts of rejoicing and victory were heard in the distance; and my guards ran off to find out the news. In a few minutes they were back again, excitedly relating how Khartoum had been taken by storm, and was now in the hands of the Mahdists. Was it possible the news was false? I crawled out of my tent, and scanned the camp; a great crowd had collected before the quarters of the Mahdi and the Khalifa, which were not far off; then there was a movement in the direction of my tent; and I could plainly see they were coming towards me. In front marched three black soldiers; one, named Shatta, formerly belonging to Ahmed Bey Dafalla's slave bodyguard, carried in his hands a bloody cloth in which something was wrapped up, and behind him followed a crowd of people weeping. The slaves had now approached my tent, and stood before me with insulting gestures; Shatta undid the cloth and showed me the head of General Gordon.

'The blood rushed to my head, and my heart seemed to stop beating; but, with a tremendous effort of self-control, I gazed, silently, at this ghastly spectacle. His blue eyes were half opened; the mouth was perfectly natural; the hair of his head, and his short whiskers, were almost quite white.

' "Is not this the head of your uncle the unbeliever?" said Shatta, holding the head before me.

' "What of it?" I said quietly. "A brave soldier who fell at his post; happy is he to have fallen; his sufferings are over."

' "Ha, ha!" said Shatta, "so you still praise the unbeliever; but you will soon see the result"; and, leaving me, he went off to the Mahdi, bearing his terrible token of victory; behind him followed the crowd, still weeping.'

The Mahdi did not gloat. He observed that he had hoped to convert his enemy. He may even have felt sorrow, as did the crowd of unknown and unconsidered people. The Koran would have been within reach. In Sura XXIII he would have found an epitaph:

'Happy now the Believers, humble in prayer, who keep aloof from vain words and are doers of alms-deeds; who restrain their appetites, tend well their trusts and their covenants, and keep strictly to their prayers: these shall be the heritors who shall inherit the silvan garden, to abide therein for ever.'

*   *   *

In Khartoum the Mahdi's troops went crazy with blood-lust. For money they might have hidden, men were flogged till the flesh hung in strips from their glistening bones. Among women too old to be useful in the harems which the Emirs, following their master's example, were ruthlessly collecting, there was a debauch of obscene torture. Looting was systematic for three days while the dead littered the stinking streets. When the Mahdi enforced discipline again, he himself withdrew, to drink from plundered chalices date syrup mixed with ginger, and, like Tien Wang, 'the Heavenly King', to keep close the bosoms of his women. A few months later typhus reached him there. He died in time to leave just a few shreds of the myth of the sincere ascetic which he had once personified.

Meanwhile in grief and shame the English had withdrawn, followed by a derisive chuckle from the Arab guns. The two steamers had reached Khartoum forty-eight hours after it had fallen. They were too weak to attempt a landing, so in danger and with difficulty made their way back. They were nearly lost, aground again in treacherous low water racing north. The Relief Expedition had no lack of courage, endurance or resource. The mere movement, so far and under such arduous conditions, was in itself an achievement; but it was overlaid by the bitterness of being too late, and by a mordant ardour to refurbish Britannia's tarnished sword.

In the England he had forsworn, Gordon was taken to the nation's heart as few men have ever been. Rage was mixed with sorrow, and cried out for vengeance which the army was eager to exact, but could not undertake soon enough to prevent cruelty, corruption and starvation from spreading from Khartoum throughout the Sudan; which under its own people became a vicious tyranny on a greater scale than ever was under alien administration.

The Queen led the denunciation of her Government which brought it down. She telegraphed to Gladstone: 'You have murdered Gordon', and wrote in her own hand to Augusta. The Government bowed before a democratic storm which reversed England's policy in Egypt and made further blood-shed inevitable in the Sudan: Gordon must be avenged.

So began the harvest of the whirlwind, sown in the Round Bright Garden by the wind of Gordon's consuming fire, when, because he had to turn a garden into a desert, he first chal-lenged the expedient ethics of this world. Thereafter he laboured to make a desert bloom, the setting for a temple he would raise to God in the name of humanity. A blinded soul, forced to pull down his own building, he believed himself to be an abysmal failure while the world conferred upon him the halo he has had to wear ever since.

Was Gordon perhaps not so much tragic as absurd? In his *Arthurian Torso* C. S. Lewis wrote: 'To Strachey, laboriously picking out every admission, every scrap of correspondence wrenched from its context, which can make it appear that his eminent Victorians were really very absurd people, the spirit of defeated irony replies, "But of course". Who ever supposed otherwise? Of course all great men, all men, are absurd. And now let us begin the rite of honouring these eminent Vic-torians. Let us run to succour their falling as we did to Virgil in his fall! And against that Strachey's work sounds like the flop of a large man who has tried to dive and failed. We can only hasten with all possible courtesy to rescue him also. He has not been ironical enough.'

Was Cyrano not absurd when with a rapier he hardly had the strength to hold, he prodded at the hallucinations brought by approaching death, come to wrest from him life's greatest gifts, Victory and Love? Equally absurd, equally sublime, Gordon echoes Cyrano's valediction:

> *Oui, vous m'arrachez tout, le laurier et la rose!*
> *Arrachez! Il y a malgré vous quelque chose*
> *Que j'emporte, et ce soir, quand j'entrerai chez Dieu,*
> *Mon salut balaiera largement le seuil bleu,*
> *Quelque chose que sans un pli, sans une tache,*
> *J'emporte malgré vous, et c'est . . . Mon panache.*

Surely it is for his panache, his incorrigible integrity, that Gordon is memorable. It is greater than his absurdity, greater than his tragedy. Nor did the tragedy consist only in what happened at Khartoum, but in that fundamental issue upon which he had always been divided. It is said that the Mahdi quoted to him from the Koran, 'And He hath said, the faith of man will not be perfect until he loves his brother as he loves himself'. Gordon tried so hard to love his brother and could not, because he despised himself.

CHRONOLOGY

CHARLES GEORGE GORDON

1833 Jan.	born at Woolwich
1843	went to boarding school at Taunton
1848	entered Royal Military Academy
1852 June	passed out of R.M.A.
1854 Dec.	ordered to Crimea
1855 Jan.	arrived at Balaklava
Sept.	(Russians evacuated Sebastopol)
1856 May	appointed to Frontier Commission, Moldavia
1857	appointed to Frontier Commission, Armenia
1858 Nov.	home leave then back to Armenia
1859 May	Captain and 2nd Adjutant, Regimental Depôt, Chatham
1859	(Palmerston Prime Minister)
1860 Sept.	landed at Tientsin
1861	garrison at Tientsin
1862	commanded Royal Engineers, Shanghai
1863 Mar.	Brevet Major (Army rank. He remained Capt. R.E.), commanding Ever Victorious Army under Li Hung Chang
Dec.	fall of Soochow, murder of the Wangs
1864 Jan.	tried to resign, the Emperor's gifts refused
Feb.	agreed to continue the campaign
July	end of war, Emperor's gifts again refused except titles
1865 Jan.	on leave in England
Sept.	commanded Royal Engineers, Gravesend
1866	(Lord Derby Prime Minister)
1868	(Disraeli Prime Minister)
1868	(Gladstone Prime Minister)
1871	appointed to Danube Commission based on Galatz
1872 Nov.	met Nubar Pasha, Prime Minister of Egypt
1873	at home on leave, mother dying. Nubar offered Governorship of Equatoria

1874 Jan.   to Cairo via Paris

1874 Apr.   arrived at Gondokoro via Khartoum, began anti-slavery campaign

1874   (Disraeli Prime Minister)

1876 Dec.   resigned Governorship of Equatoria because of corruption in Cairo and Khartoum (Ayub Pasha). Home for Christmas

1877 Jan.   returned to the Sudan as Governor-General

June   summoned by the Khedive to Cairo for a financial conference

July   returned to the Sudan

1879   (Suleiman, son of Zebehr, shot by Gessi)

July   Khedive Ismail exiled, Tewfik appointed. Gordon resigned, but first went to Abyssinia

1880 Jan.   arrived home

Feb.   attended levee at St. James's Palace to receive C.B., tried to resign his Commission, was prevented by intervention of Prince of Wales, left for Lausanne on holiday for health

Apr.   returned home (Gladstone Prime Minister)

May   appointed Private Secretary to Viceroy of India, Lord Ripon, travelled out with him and resigned on reaching Bombay. Invited to take service in China again, accepted; averted war between China and Russia, reprimanded

1881 Apr.   offered to serve Cape Government over Basutoland: no reply. Took Sir H. Elphinstone's place in Mauritius

May   (Mahdi resisted arrest and proclaimed *Jehad*, Holy War)

July   arrived in Mauritius

1882 Jan.   became General Officer Commanding Mauritius and was promoted Major-General. Cape Government asked for his services, accepted

May   arrived Capetown

Sept.   negotiated with Chief Masupha, resigned by telegraph. (Arabi Pasha's rising put down)

Oct.   left the Cape for home

Nov.   arrived in England, unemployed. King of the Belgians offered anti-slavery appointment in

Congo, went to Palestine on holiday when plans fell through

1883 Jan. arrived in Jaffa

 May (Evelyn Baring appointed British Resident, Cairo. Annihilation of Hicks' Force of 10,000. The news reached England the day after Gladstone had announced that England would evacuate Egypt)

1884 Jan. summoned to Brussels, where he heard that the War Office would not sanction his employment by Belgium. Resigned, surrendering pension. Interviewed by editor *Pall Mall Gazette* on situation in the Sudan

1884 Jan. 15 arrived in London and left next day for Congo via Brussels

 Jan. 17 ordered back to London. Interviewed by Cabinet

 Jan. 18 left London with Col. Stewart for Sudan via Red Sea. Diverted to Cairo where he was again appointed Governor-General in succession to Raouf Pasha. His task was to evacuate garrisons and leave stable government behind

 Jan. 26 left Cairo for Khartoum. He was killed exactly a year later

 Feb. 18 arrived Khartoum, given great welcome, burned tax records

 Mar. 1 having evacuated 2500, telegraphed that he expected to be besieged

 Apr. 16 telegraph to Cairo cut, Khartoum invested

 May 26 Berber fell, key to communication with Khartoum, 5000 killed

 July 25 British Cabinet decide to send Relief Expedition

 Aug. 5 £300,000 voted for Expedition 'should it become necessary'

 Sept. 1 Lord Wolseley, G.O.C., left London for Egypt. Loss of steamer *Abbas*. Gordon alone in Khartoum

 Sept. 21 Gordon heard of Relief Expedition, sent three

steamers to wait near Metemmeh. They represented 50 per cent of his defensive power. It was still 'easy' to reach Shendy, 100 miles north of Khartoum

Oct. 5   Wolseley arrived at Wadi Halfa, railhead

Oct. 21   The Mahdi before Khartoum, Islamic New Year 1302. Expedition still at Wadi Halfa, 600 miles, with boats below Second Cataract. Gordon had proof of the loss of the *Abbas*

Nov. 3   Wolseley at Dongola, Adv. H.Q. Kitchener at Debba, 75 miles further south. Kitchener wrote to Gordon in cipher but the key had gone with the *Abbas* and the message could not be read

Dec. 15   Gordon thought he could hold out ten days

Dec. 16   Col. Sir C. Wilson at Korti with vanguard

Dec. 24   Main guard celebrate Christmas in camp

Dec. 30   Wilson started from Korti towards Metemmeh. Last message from Gordon, 'Khartoum all right: 14 Dec.', but verbal report was of starvation, desperation

1885 Jan. 13   vanguard left Jakdul, 1800 men with naval detachment

Jan. 16   battle at Abu Klea

Jan. 20   vanguard arrived at Gubat

Jan. 21
Jan. 22 }   reconnaissance and preparation on making
Jan. 23   contact with the steamers near Metemmeh

Jan. 24   at 0800 hours steamers *Bordein* and *Telawieh* (Col. Wilson, 5 Officers, 20 N.C.O.s, some natives) start south on last lap

Jan. 25   evening, *Bordein* struck a rock, both ships held up

Jan. 26   dawn, Khartoum fell after 317 days of siege, and Gordon died

BIBLIOGRAPHY

ALLEN (B. M.): *Gordon in China*
  Gordon in the Sudan
AMEER (S. A.): *The Life and Teachings of Mohammed*
Anon. (pub. Walter Scott): *Life of General Gordon*
Anon. (by the author of *Our Queen*, etc.): *Life of General Gordon*
BARNES and BROWN: *Charles George Gordon*
BEHMANN: *The Mahdi of Allah*
BERLIOUX (E. F.): *The Slave Trade in Africa, 1872*
BIOVÈS (A.): *Gordon Pacha*
BLAND (J. O. P.): *Li Hung Chang*
BLUNT (W. S.): *Gordon at Khartoum*
BOULGER (D. C.): *General Gordon's Letters from the Danube and Armenia*
  Life of General Gordon
BUCHAN (JOHN): *Gordon at Khartoum*
BULLOCK (J. M.): *The Gay Gordons*
BUTLER (Sir W.): *Charles George Gordon*
CECIL (A.): *Queen Victoria and her Prime Ministers*
CHAILLÉ-LONG: *My Life in Four Continents*
CHESNEY (Sir G.): *Essays in Modern Military Biography*
CHURCHILL (W.): *The River War*
COOPER (J.): *The Lost Continent*
COSTIN (W. C.): *Great Britain and China, 1833–1860*
CRABITÉS (P.): *Gordon, the Sudan and Slavery*
CROMER (LORD): *Modern Egypt*
DÉLÉBECQUE (J.): *Gordon et le drame de Khartoum*
DER LING (Princess): *Old Buddha*
DOUGLAS (R. K.): *Li Hung Chang*
FAWZI (Bey): *The Sudan, Gordon and Kitchener*
FORBES (A.): *Chinese Gordon*
GARRATT (G. T.): *The Two Gladstones*
Gentleman's Magazine, 1886
GORDON (C. G.): *Reflections in Palestine*
GORDON (H. W.): *Events in the Life of Charles George Gordon*
GORDON (M. A.): *Letters of General C. G. Gordon*

GRAHAM (Sir G.): *Last Words with Gordon*
GRANT (Sir H.): *The China War of 1860*
HAKE (A. E.): *The Journals of Gordon of Khartoum*
    The Story of Chinese Gordon
    General Gordon's Last Journey
    Events in the Taiping Rebellion
HANSON (L. and E.): *Gordon*
HARVEY (E. D.): *The Mind of China*
HILL (Dr.): *Colonel Gordon in Central Africa*
    General Gordon in the Sudan
    (ed.) *A Woman's Memories*
HUBRECHT: *Pekin*
Illus. Lond. News
LESSEPS (F. DE): *Recollections of Forty Years*
LE SUEUR (G.): *Cecil Rhodes*
LEWIS (C. S.): *Arthurian Torso*
LI HUNG CHANG: *Memoirs*
LILLEY (W. E.): *Life and Work of Gordon at Gravesend*
LYSTER (T.): *With Gordon in China*
MACDONALD (A.): *Too Late for Gordon*
    Why Gordon Perished
MARGOLIOUTH (D. S.): *On Mahdis and Mahdism*
MORLEY (J.): *Life of Gladstone* (2 vols.)
MOSSMAN (S.): *General Gordon's Private Diary*
MURRAY (T. D.) and WHITE (A. S.): *Samuel Baker*
OHRWALDER: *Ten Years Captivity in the Mahdi's Camp*
POWER (F.): *Letters from Khartoum*
SERGEANT (P. W.): *The Great Empress Dowager of China*
SLATIN (PASHA): *Fire and Sword in the Sudan*
SMALLEY (G. W.): 'Mr. Gladstone' (*Harper's Mag.*, 1898)
SMITH (G. B.): *Heroes of the Nineteenth Century*
STRACHEY (LYTTON): *Eminent Victorians*
WILSON (Sir C.): *From Korti to Khartoum*
WILSON (H.): *The Ever Victorious Army*
WINGATE (F. R.): *Mahdism and the Egyptian Sudan*
WOLF (L.): *Life of Lord Ripon*
WOODHAM-SMITH (C.): *The Reason Why*
WORTHAM (H. E.): *Gordon*

INDEX